Feminism and war

FEMINISM AND WAR
confronting US imperialism

Robin L. Riley, Chandra Talpade Mohanty
and Minnie Bruce Pratt | editors

Zed Books
LONDON | NEW YORK

Feminism and war: confronting US imperialism was first published
in 2008 by Zed Books Ltd, 7 Cynthia Street, London N1 9JF, UK and
Room 400, 175 Fifth Avenue, New York, NY 10010, USA

www.zedbooks.co.uk

Editorial copyright © Robin L. Riley, Chandra Talpade Mohanty
and Minnie Bruce Pratt, 2008
Copyright in this collection © Zed Books, 2008

The rights of Robin L. Riley, Chandra Talpade Mohanty and
Minnie Bruce Pratt to be identified as the editors of this work have
been asserted by them in accordance with the Copyright, Designs
and Patents Act, 1988.

Cover designed by Rogue Four Design
Set in OurType Arnhem and Futura Bold by Ewan Smith, London
Index: ed.emery@thefreeuniversity.net
Printed and bound in the UK by the Charlesworth Group.

Distributed in the USA exclusively by Palgrave Macmillan, a
division of St Martin's Press, LLC, 175 Fifth Avenue, New York, NY
10010.

A catalogue record for this book is available from the British Library.
Library of Congress cataloging in publication data are available.

ISBN 978 1 84813 018 0 hb
ISBN 978 1 84813 019 7 pb

Contents

THREE | Women's struggles and the wars in Iraq and Afghanistan

FOUR | Feminists organizing against imperialism and war

Acknowledgments

This anthology grew out of the 'Feminism and War' conference held 19–21 October 2006, in Syracuse, New York, USA, sponsored by the Women's Studies Program with generous support from the Ray Smith Symposium for the Humanities, and the College of Arts and Sciences of Syracuse University. We gratefully acknowledge the indefatigable work of the members of the Planning and Program Committee who organized the conference: Linda Martín Alcoff, Linda Carty, Elora Chowdhury, Kelly Christian, Susann DeMocker-Shedd, Janet Dodd, Glenda Gross, Nisha Gupta, Chen-I Kuan, Jenna Lloyd, Alice Loomis, Vivian May, Jackie Micielli, Sarah Miraglia, Gwendolyn Pough, Judy Rohrer, Diane Swords.

Special appreciation for assistance with the conference also goes to: Liat Ben-Moshe, Maureen Curtain, Micenis Garrido, the Humanities Council of Syracuse University, Alka Kurian, Leslie Owens-Pelton, Tehmekah MacPherson, Chacine McCoy, Grizelda Rodriguez, Jennifer Wingard, Tom Wolfe, Yuan Zhang, Corri Zoli, and the many student volunteers.

Thanks to Zed Books for their enthusiastic response to this book. And the manuscript would not have been completed for publication without Robin Goettel and her fine editorial work – thank you, Robin!

Chandra Talpade Mohanty is grateful for the sustained and invaluable comradeship of her sister-friends Jacqui Alexander, Zillah Eisenstein, and Beverly Guy-Sheftall. Many thanks to Satya Mohanty, for love, challenge, and three decades of amazing partnership. Chandra also acknowledges her daughter Uma, and Shakti and Zeke (aka the dogs), who always bring joy and wonder into her life.

Minnie Bruce Pratt especially thanks Leslie Feinberg for their political and literary conversations during the continuing adventure of their life together. She is also grateful for her sisters-in-the-struggle in the National Women's Fightback Network.

Robin Riley thanks Margaret Himley for her love, humor, and patience. She is indebted to Linda Carty and Hannah Britton for enduring and buoying friendship that sustains her. She is also grateful to Cynthia Riley for affection beyond biology.

Finally, the editors want to thank each other for the respect and delight that they found in doing this work together, both in organizing the original conference and in the process of editing this book.

Introduction: feminism and US wars – mapping the ground

CHANDRA TALPADE MOHANTY,
MINNIE BRUCE PRATT, ROBIN L. RILEY

'This is the time for feminist revolutions.' (Patricia McFadden)

On a night of torrential rain in October 2006, a thousand people crowded into the Syracuse University chapel, in upstate New York, for the opening of the 'Feminism and War' conference, organized by the university's Women's and Gender Studies Department. Outside, a small group of pro-war protestors held up US flags next to an effigy of Cindy Sheehan, an anti-war organizer and one of the evening speakers. The replica of Sheehan, clad in tie-dyed clothes, was lynched from a stick.

On that night the USA was in the sixth year of war on Afghanistan, and the fourth year of war on Iraq, after twelve previous years of economic sanctions and the first Gulf War of 1991. The nation's military budget was about to increase to over half a trillion dollars a year – a figure reached only three times before, in the wars on Korea, Vietnam, and the military build-up against the USSR in the 1980s (Shanker and Cloud 2006).

US military casualties in Iraq had exceeded three thousand. Civilian casualties in Iraq, estimated by Iraq Body Count, had reached sixty deaths a day from either bombs or gunfire.

As Sheehan and other anti-war activists and feminist theorists opened the conference that night, they were responding directly to the wars launched by the USA against both Afghanistan and Iraq, using the events of 11 September 2001 as a pretext. The administration of President George W. Bush had explicitly argued that US 'intervention' would promote the cause of women's liberation in those countries, thus claiming a 'feminist' motivation for US military aggression.

Since 2001, many feminists have been thinking about women and war, and examining how over these war-filled years women have served as motivation and justification for US war.[1] Feminism, it is popularly assumed, supports women in the military and supports the cause of going to war to ensure women's rights in countries where these rights may be restricted. But there is no monolithic 'feminism' or even a shared set of philosophical, ethical, cultural, or political interests among all women. The relationship between feminism and war is contested and complex. Few feminist theorists continue to accept the claim that women are natural pacifists, yet there is much debate over how to understand what is in women's interests and how to advance those interests. At the 'Feminism and War' conference that generated this volume, speakers and panelists explored the connections between women's lives, gender and sexuality, race and nation, institutions of power, the grinding machinations of capitalism, and the US wars currently being waged. 'War' was examined in the context of world economic globalization and in multiple ways – as direct military intervention and occupation, as the structuring and restructuring of legal and cultural systems, as the creation of economic foreign policy initiatives, and as a tool and technique to expand the reach of imperialism.

Feminism and war: confronting US imperialism builds on the presentations, papers, and dialogue at that conference to reveal and analyze the complicated ways in which those in pursuit and justification of US wars continue to use gender, sexuality, race, class, nationalism, imperialism – and even invoke women's liberation – to legitimize and continue those wars. Given the centrality of US imperial wars in the world today, it is impossible to understand 'feminism and war' on a global scale without understanding the specificities of the racist, heterosexist, and masculinized practices and ideologies mobilized by a USA in pursuit of economic and political hegemony. Feminists critiquing and organizing against war in most places in the world will thus need to contend with the effects of US imperial wars in their own backyards, whatever part of the globe they happen to be living in. The current wars against Iraq and Afghanistan, and the threat of war against Iran, are a continuation of the many US wars of the last fifty years. Since World War II, the USA has waged outright war on China (1945–46, 1950–53), Korea (1950–53), Guatemala (1954, 1967–69), Indonesia (1958), Cuba (1959–60), the Belgian Congo (1964), Peru (1965), Laos (1964–73), Vietnam (1961–73), Cambodia (1969–70), Grenada (1983), Libya (1986), El Salvador (1980s), Nicaragua (1980s), Panama (1989), Iraq (1991–2001), Bosnia (1995), Sudan (1998), Yugoslavia (1999), Afghanistan (2001–), and now, again, Iraq (2003–) (Roy 2002: 128). Global military spending has reached over $1 trillion annually, and the USA spends over half this amount (Stockholm Institute for Peace Research 2007). Meanwhile, US imperialism and global militarism have led to an unprecedented anti-USA resistance in the Global South.

This is the context in which the essays in this volume examine and challenge US imperial wars crafted as rescue missions in the name of democracy and 'civilization.' These wars, with their disproportionate

2

and annihilating effect on the lives of women, with the ensuing traffic in gendered bodies, with the manipulation of racialized discourses of male supremacy and female helplessness as justification, raise profoundly feminist issues, and require a complex, anti-imperialist feminist engagement. In fact, as Angela Davis suggests here, what is required are particular feminist 'habits of perception ... habits of the imagination' that allow us to envision and work toward 'the world without war.' Or, as Mĩcere Gĩthae Mũgo writes in her poem 'In praise of Afrika's children': 'What song/ shall I sing/ in praise of/ our children/ living in/ the mass graves/ of apartheid/ of capitalism/ of imperialism?/ What song/ shall I sing?'

On anti-imperialist feminisms

The anti-imperialist analyses in *Feminism and war: confronting US imperialism* attempt to make visible the ways in which the USA has gendered, racialized, and sexualized its practice of imperialist wars – that is, wars being waged through military and economic policy to advance and consolidate the profit-driven system of capitalism. For a comprehensive look at US practice, these feminist analyses explore the restructuring of both US foreign and domestic policy during the late twentieth and early twenty-first centuries, and how both agendas have been set by military and corporate objectives. The resulting US policies have led to the militarization of daily life for people around the world and within the USA – specifically for immigrants, refugees, and people of color, with a disproportionate number in all these groups being women with their children. This volume is not merely a critique of the war-state as is, but rather is a closer examination of the impact of imperialist war on people within and outside the USA in terms of their daily, lived realities. For feminist analysts, what becomes immediately apparent is that US militarization has meant a new mobilization of historically embedded colonial practices and rhetorics of male superiority and white supremacy; of female vulnerability, inadequacy, and inferiority; and of the subjugation of oppressed masculinities of men of color. In the service of conquest this mobilization deploys gendered roles that embody oppressive power relations. It depends on the manipulation and demonization of complex cultural structures of sexuality, including same-sex and queer sexualities, and on the assumption that a Eurocentric heteronormative heterosexual 'order' is an underpinning for both nation and empire.[2]

This mobilization can be understood through a critique of the racialized and gendered logic of a narrative of 'civilization' that US ruling elites have used for domestic nation-building, and now marshal anew in order to create and re-create empire. Thus, for instance, as Miriam Cooke has

3

suggested, and Shahnaz Kahn argues in this anthology, 'saving brown women' in Afghanistan is used to justify US imperial aggression because this fulfills the rescue mission of a civilizing and civilized nation.

Meanwhile, 'saving the nation' means racist targeting of immigrants and people of color domestically, along with justifying the curtailment of civil liberties and the increased militarization of domestic law enforcement and the policing of US borders in the name of the 'War on Drugs,' and its successor, the 'War on Terrorism' (Mohanty 2006). Jennifer Fluri's careful analysis of US congressional discourse in this volume illustrates the trope of colonial rescue as it is mobilized to justify the US invasion of Afghanistan. Drawing on feminist, post-colonial analyses of civilizational narratives anchored in 'saving brown women,' Fluri illustrates the 'misuse' of feminism by the US war-state.

While the US imperial project calls for 'civilizing' men of color and oppressed nationalities – black, brown, Arab, Central and South Asian – and for 'rescuing' women of color outside US borders, the same state engages in targeting, criminalizing, imprisoning, and killing these very peoples within its own borders in the context of the 'endless wars' required to sustain capitalist expansion. Since the USA launched its wars on Afghanistan and Iraq after 9/11, there has been an increasingly harsh legal regime within the country, accompanied by the militarization of domestic law enforcement. There have been dramatic increases in funding; a growing use of advanced military technology by local municipal, county, and state governments; a sharing of personnel, equipment, and training by the military with domestic law enforcement; a flow of personnel and techniques of torture and degradation between US prisons and the military; and the general promotion of a warlike culture in domestic law enforcement and also in a range of public agencies (welfare, schools, hospitals), which are subjected to an accelerated culture of surveillance and enforcement (Silliman and Bhattacharjee 2002).

The effects of these conjoined economic–military policies of the US imperialist state represent an alarming increase in violence against women, children, and communities bearing the brunt of its military dominance within the USA and around the world. In the USA these policies and practices not only increase domestic and sexual violence against women (Wokusch 2003), but they also increase poverty by diverting spending and by undermining economies that meet people's daily needs. The essays in this volume by Nellie Hester Bailey, Berta Joubert-Ceci, and Zillah Eisenstein address this development in detail. Huibin Amelia Chew's contribution suggests concrete examples of the war's gendered effects in both Iraq and the USA. Launching a direct, persuasive critique of

4

'imperial feminism,' Chew explains how imperialism relies on gendered inequality, showing that after the 2003 US invasion of Iraq, women were the hardest hit by unemployment in both countries. Similarly, her essay and a number of reports show that the wars in Iraq and Afghanistan have led to a rise in sexual violence against women in all three countries (Bjorken et al. 2003; Brown and Romano 2006; Colson 2003).

The inextricable connections between the domestic and international impact of US gendered, sexualized, racialized wars point to important sites for feminist, anti-imperialist critique and organizing. These include scrutiny of the militarized US state at the administrative, legislative, judicial, and military levels; corporate globalization and economics producing unequal power relations of racialized gender and sexuality; questions about discourses of 'freedom' and 'liberation' when raised by an imperial, neoliberal state, by embedded media, and by complicit feminisms; and the lessons of cross-border struggles and the politics of feminist resistance on individual, community, national, and international levels.

By focusing on the above issues, *Feminism and war: confronting US imperialism* develops a collective anti-imperialist feminist project anchored in the power dynamics and relations of rule that constitute the globe and specifically an imperial USA within it. The volume, organized in four broad sections, 'Feminist geopolitics of war,' 'Feminists mobilizing critiques of war,' 'Women's struggles and the wars in Iraq and Afghanistan,' and 'Feminists organizing against imperialism and war,' brings scholarly, creative, and activist feminist voices together under the rubric of a collective anti-imperialist feminist front in the USA.

This is the context for the following broad review of feminist perspectives on current US wars and the policing, manipulation, mobilization, and destruction of gendered and racialized bodies. That review is followed by a brief discussion of the theoretical and organizational claims of the anthology as a whole, particularly highlighting ways of thinking about anti-imperialist feminist projects as practiced in the United States of 2008. We conclude with a call to thought and action, staying with the spirit of an anthology that foregrounds simultaneously the activist implications of scholarly work, and the intellectual anchors of anti-war organizing.

Gendered bodies and US wars

Women of many races, ethnicities, nationalities, and religions around the world – in various geographic spaces, social and cultural contexts; as partners, wives, sisters, daughters, mothers, mourners, and victims – experience war. Their experience of war and their participation in it, either as actors or resisters, victims or perpetrators, cheerleaders or critics, are always influenced by the construction of gender operating in and around their lives. Notions about the proper practice of femininity have a profound impact on how women are regarded in relation to war, what they are expected to do, and the strength of the repercussions suffered for acting outside the accepted boundaries of femininity operating within particular spaces. Ideas about femininity and femaleness are also exploited to determine how women from opposing sides will be treated – often used – as a means of warfare.

While constructions of masculinity and femininity are always circulating in and around militarism and war, women's bodies are sometimes primary considerations for military and state leaders who ask: Are there enough female bodies to fill the ranks of male-decimated militaries? How many female bodies must one side kill, rape, or impregnate in order to demoralize the other? What will the presence of women's bodies inside militaries mean for the practice of maleness and masculinity within such institutions? How will these bodies influence morale? When women take their bodies into the streets to protest against war, what does this mean for societies' ideas about armed conflict, about femininity, about motherhood?

For feminist theorists and activists considering US-propagated wars, there are counter-questions to ask: What are the implications of a US imperial state laying claim to women's liberation? What is the relation between this claim and resulting US foreign policy and military action? Did US intervention and invasion in fact result in liberation for women in Afghanistan and Iraq? What multiple meanings are embedded in the phrase 'women's liberation'? In her essay, Zillah Eisenstein says that US 'imperial democracy mainstreams women's rights discourse into foreign policy and militarizes women for imperial goals.' Shahnaz Khan gives an invaluable history of US intervention in Afghanistan long before the beginning of the 2001 war re-enacting 'colonial rescue,' while Isis Nusair, Elizabeth Philipose, and Patricia McFadden expose the ethnocentrism, racism, and imperialist nationalism embedded in US foreign, judicial, and military policy.

How are the multiple meanings of 'women's liberation' connected to the specifics of religion, culture, history, nation within the current US conflicts? What is the relation between the lives of Afghan and Iraqi women before and after the US invasion, and that of women living in the USA? How do USA-based women who define themselves as feminists take the state's claim into account in current theory and organizing? In her essay LeiLani Dowell asserts the connections between women within and outside US borders: 'We can look to the situation for women in the

Mohanty, Pratt, Riley

6

United States to answer the question of whether or not to believe the US government's claim that it wages war in other countries to liberate women.' Cynthia Enloe and Patricia McFadden caution us about the ideological mobilization of motherhood during wartime. While Enloe warns against US military recruiters appealing to mothers as patriots, McFadden warns women activists that 'motherhood is a slippery slope to conservatism,' and calls for feminists to rethink our analyses of motherhood and militarism. Recalling the description of Cindy Sheehan as an activist mother, McFadden argues: 'An uncritical embrace of the notion of motherhood is not only dangerous for feminist values and achievements, but it can also easily distract us from the less intimate issues of militarism and state impunity, particularly when such practices are deployed against those who are not our kin or social counterparts.'

Other essays – such as that by Jasbir Puar, who argues that, through a process she refers to as exceptionalism, certain queer people and some feminists in the USA are persuaded to do the work of empire by allowing themselves to be held out as superior to Muslim sexuality, and a piece by Berenice Fisher, who writes about family connections between Baghdad and New York – raise important and challenging questions for US feminists who aim to work on 'women's issues' across international borders at the same time as the USA is waging its current wars of aggression.

The contributors to the anthology tackle these and other questions with many layers of complexity. Their work, and the contents of this volume, reflect the intensified scrutiny that sociologists, anthropologists, feminist international relations scholars, women's and gender studies scholars, race, ethnic, and area studies scholars, human rights activists, journalists, anti-war activists, and community organizers are giving to the matter of women's lives in relation to war. In all of this work, the visibility/invisibility/hyper-visibility problem of women in wartime is apparent.[3]

In wartime, sometimes women are visible, sometimes they are not. Sometimes women's bodies are hyper-visual – focused on to be counted, battled over, and controlled. Other times, views of the female body recede so that constructions of femininity are more prominent in obscuring the motivations of militarized masculinity, in providing ongoing means of justification, or in shaming the enemy most egregiously. Whether embodied or constructed as an ideal, women are forced to endure wars in which their actions are constrained, their agency is compromised, and their well-being is constantly threatened. Of course, gendered bodies are also racialized bodies, and 'race' as a concept is profoundly significant in the ways that women's bodies are made visible/invisible. For instance, Berta Joubert-Ceci's argument shows how US economic aggression through pro-capitalist, neoliberal policies like the 1993 NAFTA (North American Free Trade Agreement) has warlike consequences for women in Latin America, who are rendered virtually invisible in those economic policies. Forced to migrate to survive, the women, as immigrant women in the USA, experience the brunt of ramped-up Homeland Security racist policies and surveillance against 'illegal immigrants.' These US manipulations are attempts to justify, strengthen, maintain, and extend imperialism by creating or emphasizing old divisions among people, between states, and within ethnicities.

In fact, ideas about the proper practice of femininity and ways to live as 'woman' have divided and still divide white women from women of color within the USA, and divide US women from Iraqi and Afghan women, and from other women around the world. Isis Nusair, in looking at US government statements and documents, makes visible how orientalized notions of difference and ideas about 'the other' in the US imaginary shape and legitimize the torture committed by soldiers at the US military prison Abu Ghraib, in Baghdad. The struggle to accurately understand the autonomous perspectives and actions of oppressed women, at the same time that US imperialism attempts to manipulate information about and perception of 'women,' is a crucial goal of an emerging anti-imperialist feminist front in the USA to which this volume contributes.

In the Western media, where one story about war gets told, women are portrayed as helpless, and at the same time as essential to the US all-'volunteer' military charged with carrying out the war. Expanding on this idea, Alyson Cole analyzes the evolution of the notion of 'victimhood' in the Bush war machine's justification of war. Cole argues persuasively that ideas of victimhood are used as a motivator for war, to feminize 'terrorist' men, and recuperate US masculinity. Racialized gender and colonial discourses thus lie at the heart of such constructions of victimhood. Certain women are used as icons as if they represent all women of a certain identity, position, or profession. Jessica Lynch is put forward to represent all US women soldiers, and Condoleezza Rice to represent all women of color in the USA. Iraqi microbiologists Dr Rihab Rashid Taha al-Azawi and Dr Huda Salih Mahdi Ammash are vilified as 'Dr Germ' and 'Mrs Anthrax' in the US press and are the most frequently named Iraqi women in US media, blamed for the production of the weapons of mass destruction – weapons that were never found. They are supposed to represent all Iraqi women. Iraqi and Afghan women are put forward as both demons and victims of the Taliban, Al Qaeda, and Saddam Hussein. But the US media rarely shows these women as actual victims or resisters of the US war. Nadine Sinno analyzes a counter-narrative that challenges dominant media representations, arguing that bloggers like Riverbend, a young Iraqi woman making web-blog entries since 2003, have been able to critically access and humanize the war for readers in the USA and Iraq.

As US wars proliferate, increasingly some women volunteer for national military service, join resistance movements and become suicide bombers, or do military intelligence work. Other women duck bombs and dodge landmines, hide from occupying troops, continue to nurture, send supplies, or sell their bodies as recreation for male soldiers. Women's participation as US soldiers in this war has expanded under the economic pressures of the 'poverty draft,' with a disproportionate risk of assault and death falling on women of color, who were over 50 percent of US enlisted women in 2003 (Manning 2005). The conversation between women-of-color veterans Anuradha Kristina Bhagwati and Eli PaintedCrow details the complex experiences of women within the US military and the connections between 'race, militarism, Abu Ghraib, US culture, feminism, and peace.' Yet the reality reflected in their lives has been obscured by a continued emphasis in the US media and public debates that focuses only on women's need for protection or their role as the supporter of male-instigated wars.

Complicity, consequences, and claims

The terrible reality of the impact of war on women is obscured by the language of collateral damage. Contemporary methods of combat result in enormous casualties among civilian populations, and estimates are that 80 percent of the casualties of all contemporary wars are women and children (Nadar 2002). Women, and their children, are deliberately raped, maimed, and killed during war. Even those who do not suffer direct physical harm endure the loss of someone they love or of their homes or their livelihoods, and have their existence utterly changed by proximity to war, as the systems of sex and gender that structure their lives are disrupted.

As women in other countries struggle with the impact of US invasion, war, and imperialism, these wars are changing the lives of women within the USA in dramatic ways. US mothers – long portrayed as the providers of sons and nurturance during the nation's wars – are now sending their daughters off to war as well. They also have become protectors and military suppliers, raising money to send flak vests to their children because the US government has not provided the proper equipment to the soldiers. Cynthia Enloe tells us that military recruiters target women as mothers in order to legitimize the enlistment of their children. She urges us to use feminist lenses to 'see' and take apart these militarized practices that occupy motherhood.

In the US military, there is still a prohibition against women serving in combat roles. Given contemporary means of warfare, however, the notion of 'the front line' is mostly imaginary. And, in the war on Iraq, US military women have been placed in harm's way to a greater degree than ever before without any official acknowledgment of a change in policy. In addition, as LeiLani Dowell points out in her essay, the US military remains a hostile place for women where there is frequent harassment, sexual abuse and even rape perpetrated by fellow soldiers. In the US military in 2004 alone there were 112 complaints of sexual assaults of servicewomen by US men in Iraq, Kuwait and Afghanistan (Riley 2006: 183). The persistent danger to women from their own colleagues is expressed in a quote obtained by journalist Jim Bartlett, who reports that women being oriented to life at Camp Udarai in Kuwait are told that 'no woman was to be anywhere on post unescorted or alone at any time' (Bartlett 2004).

As women suffer and die in countries targeted by the US wars, as well as within the US military, the cost of these wars is mounting for non-military women within the USA, as Pentagon needs result in severe budget cuts to social service safety nets. Nellie Hester Bailey makes connections between the militarization of the USA, the gentrification of its cities, and the impact on women of color. The most dramatic example of the impact of US wars on women inside the country was the devastation wrought by Hurricane Katrina on the poor and working-class black population of New Orleans in 2004; federal money designated for engineering repair and maintenance of the levees that eventually failed had been 'moved to handle homeland security and the war in Iraq' (Grissett 2004). Those unable to escape the hurricane and subsequent flooding were primarily poor women of color and their children.

While normative constructions of femininity mean that women are told that their role in wartime is to be quiet supporters of militarized men, some women in the USA are once again stepping outside of these traditionally determined roles to actively resist governments that wage armed conflict. These women are sometimes characterized as the true essence of femininity, living up to the construction of women as soft, caring, non-aggressive, life-affirming – a characterization even made by some feminists. But this construction of femaleness and femininity is double-edged – it can be used as justification for an increasingly militarized masculinity that can protect these soft, caring, naive women.

As the war toll mounts for women both inside and outside the borders of the USA, women have been active within the country in organizing opposition to the 'endless wars.' Women within the USA participate in various peace and anti-war groups, including CodePink, FIST (Fight Imperialism, Stand Together), Global Women's Strike, Gold Star Families for Peace, the International Action Center, the Raging Grannies, the School of the Americas Watch, the Syracuse Peace Council, United for Peace and Justice, Veterans for Peace, the Women's Fightback Network, and Women in Black. Of course, not all women who resist US war do so as an enactment of their passive, peace-loving assigned social role. Nor are anti-war activists all mothers, or grandmothers, or women reacting against war because of a relationship to a man, as Melanie Kaye/ Kantrowitz makes clear in her essay on anti-war Israeli women.

In fact, there is no unified political position among women who decide that war is not the answer. Instead, they are unified in opposing the consequences of US war as delineated by Cawo Abdi (2007: 183), who notes:

> The gendered consequences of war go beyond the physical and psychological violence to which women are subjected through rape and terror, extending to insidious practices and invented traditions that further consolidate patriarchy and exacerbate women's social subordination.

Women practice many varied approaches to interrupting war. Whatever shapes their anti-war or peace work, these resistant women are a challenge to those in power, as they raise questions about the inevitability of war, the decision-making maneuvers that lead to war, the practice of femininity, and the proper role of women in these processes.

In that tradition of women's resistance, the essays in this anthology collectively foreground four important analytic and political issues: 1) the complicities of some US feminisms and the politics of 'rescue' in US wars; 2) the camouflaging of women's rights by imperial states to provide alibis for war and for torture; 3) the bartering of democracy by naturalizing (and re-presenting) war and militarism; and 4) the mapping of women's agency and resistance onto war-torn spaces and, in the USA, highlighting anti-imperialist and anti-capitalist feminist praxis.

Thus, a number of essays (see especially Fluri, Philipose, Nusair and Puar) discuss the continuities between ideologies of orientalism, colonialism, and the US imperial project, pointing to rhetoric about the 'civilizing mission' of the current US state, and the mobilization of discourses of modernity and tradition, in the creation of a gendered, racialized and sexualized subject peoples who 'cannot govern themselves.' Contributions by Khan, McFadden, Puar, and Chew argue explicitly that the colonialist, racist, and imperialist narratives of complicit US feminisms must be challenged head-on in the effort to build anti-imperialist, feminist coalitions.

Woven into the essays is another theoretically and methodologically innovative strand tracing state and trans-state practices in terms of gender and race essentialism – in US congressional discourse (Fluri), government documents on Abu Ghraib (Nusair), the racial grammar of international law (Philipose), and the rhetoric of 'victimhood' (Cole). Each of these essays develops arguments about governing institutions providing 'alibis' for war and for torture. Similarly, in her analysis of US sexual exceptionalism, Jasbir Puar argues: 'The temporality of exception is one that seeks to conceal itself; the frenzied mode of emergency is an alibi for the quiet certitude of a slowly normativized working paradigm of liberal democratic government, an alibi necessary to disavow its linkages to totalitarian governments.' And Zillah Eisenstein provides an analysis of 'sexual decoys' underlying practices of domination in current US wars.

A third theoretical focus involves discussions of the naturalization and re-presentation of war, militarism, and violence against women and children, which is emphasized especially in the essays by Davis, Enloe, Eisenstein, and Setsu et al. Nellie Hester Bailey's discussion of gentrification, community 'improvement,' and university involvement shows the links between such projects in Harlem – the historic African-American community in New York City – and Pentagon money. Jennifer Hyndman's essay problematizes 'body counts' in terms of representing actual death, while Mĩcere Mũgo's poetry provides a narrative that both reacts to the actual war and creates a new representation of war from the point of view of those 'unrepresented' in the hegemonic worldwide narrative.

Finally, the anthology as a whole makes a strong argument for feminist anti-imperialist and anti-capitalist praxis as central to engaging US wars in the present and the future. Thus, Leslie Cagan's personal narrative is a lesson in how 'feminism' expands in one person's life to a more comprehensive analysis of the world. The conversation of US armed service veterans Anuradha Kristina Bhagwati and Eli PaintedCrow highlights the way war can politicize working-class women forced or propagandized into enlistment as they expand their comprehension of the worldwide connections between themselves and the people 'like them' being killed for the US government. Establishing the links between militarism and broad capitalist goals, LeiLani Dowell discusses young women's anti-recruitment resistance, and Huibin Amelia Chew speaks of the 'economics of patriarchy' and 'the coercion of sexual commodification' within the context of imperialist war. Berta Joubert-Ceci argues that the same economic war generates both Iraq and NAFTA, with similarities, including cross-border immigration. She comments on the acts of immigration by women as not just flight or attempts at refuge from this economic war, but also as forms of resistance. In other looks at women's resistance to imperialist war, Kaye/Kantrowitz discusses feminist resistance to a military draft in Israel while Judy Rohrer analyzes feminist direct action in the USA. Mĩcere Mũgo's final poem represents the underlying strength of mass movement to make change.

While a number of the essays reiterate concerns evident in the growing worldwide literature on gender and war, we believe the intimate interweaving of scholarly and activist voices, and the theoretical directions gestured to above, constitute an important development in feminist anti-imperialist work in the USA.

A call to thought ... and action

In one of the community organizer workshops at the 'Feminism and War' conference, the panelists touched on the connections between US global war and their work on women's issues such as domestic violence, immigration, and refugee flight from wars. The women organizers were asked by participants whether anything had changed in their work for women over the last ten years – had there been any changes in matters related to sex and gender? The community organizers replied that they felt they were seeing progress in attitudes, that there was less sexism, more room for gender and sex equality and complexity.

But, they emphasized, they always hit one limit in what they could do in their work – the economic system. With budget cuts because of the US wars, there was the loss of financial aid to women, children, and families in desperate need of housing, heating, healthcare. There was the loss of scholarships and loans to working-class students. As the military budget swelled and defense spending accelerated in an attempt to boost a faltering US economy, non-military industries ensured profits by sending their factories to countries where they could pay lower wages – so at home there were cutbacks in employment, lowered pay, and often the complete elimination of jobs. All of this meant interruptions and sometimes the ending of their work at building alternative means for women to have safer, stronger, healthier, more autonomous, and happier lives within the USA. Inevitably, as organizers they would 'hit the wall' – of the existing economic system.

Someone raised the need for structural change, the need to fundamentally change the economic system. And one panelist said, 'Well, that means revolution – and that's risky to talk about ...'

Mohanty, Pratt, Riley

But there must be the risk of a discussion about thoroughgoing change – about 'revolution.' This is not a question that comes up in a vacuum, but rather will be answered only through the passionate debate and militant actions of millions of people who are now being assaulted, exploited, and colonized by US imperialism.

What would it mean – what would it take – to fundamentally change the economic structure dominating the world that so devastatingly ties together women and gender and sexually oppressed people, and the imperialist wars being waged – overtly and covertly – through military and diplomatic and economic action – for capitalist profit?

In fact, all over the world people are questioning and mobilizing against globalization – with the leadership of women. The people of the world are engaged in a ferocious struggle against all US wars for profit and domination, and that struggle is inevitably calling into question for them the issue of women's and gendered oppression – and resistance.

Feminism and war: confronting US imperialism continues in the spirit of that struggle by asking and exploring: What is the relation of feminist theorizing and organizing to the struggles under way? In a world where there are intense pressures from the powers that be to close down places for radical and revolutionary thought, the hope is that this book will make some room for thinking and acting anew – through an anti-racist, feminist politics that will put the analysis of imperialist power, and forms of resistance to it, at the front and center of our understanding of, and our action against, the current US wars.

Notes

1 Statements on impending US wars were circulated on the Internet – for instance, 'Transnational feminist practices against war: a statement', by Paola Bacchetta, Tina Campt, Inderpal Grewal, Caren Kaplan, Minoo Moallem, and Jennifer Terry, in October 2001, and 'Women's liberation and the new war', by Minnie Bruce Pratt, in November 2001; as well as statements issued by the Revolutionary Association of the Women of Afghanistan (RAWA). In 2007 *Signs: Journal of Women in Culture and Society* issued a special double issue focusing on war: 33(1). See also Alyson Cole, *The Cult of True Victimhood: From the War on Welfare to the War on Terror* (Stanford, 2006); Cynthia Enloe, *Globalization and Militarism: Feminists Make the Link* (Rowman & Littlefield, 2007); Zillah Eisenstein, *Sexual Decoys: Gender, Race and War in Imperial Democracy* (Zed, 2007) and *Against Empire: Feminisms, Racism and the West* (Zed, 2004); *W Effect: Bush's War on Women*, ed. Laura Flanders (Feminist Press, 2004); *Sites of Violence: Gender and Conflict Zones*, ed. Wenona Giles and Jennifer Hyndman (University of California, 2004); *After Shock: September 11, 2001/Global Feminist Perspectives*, ed. Susan Hawthorne and

14

Bronwyn Winter (Raincoast Books, 2003); Jasbir K. Puar, *Terrorist Assemblages: Homonationalism in Queer Times* (Duke, 2007); *Interrogating Imperialism: Conversations on Gender, Race, and War*, ed. Robin L. Riley and Naeem Inayatullah (Palgrave McMillan, 2006).

2 See Alexander and Mohanty (1997) in the introduction to *Feminist Genealogies, Colonial Legacies, Democratic Futures* for a discussion of the militarized practices of the US state.

3 See Eisenstein, this volume, for a complex discussion of this problem. See also Riley (2008), forthcoming in *Sociology Compass*.

References

Abdi, Cawo Mohamed (2007) 'Convergence of civil war and the religious right: re-imagining Somali women', *Signs: Journal of Women in Culture and Society*, 33(1).

Alexander, Jacqui and Chandra Talpade Mohanty (1997) 'Introduction', in Jacqui Alexander and Chandra Talpade Mohanty (eds), *Feminist Genealogies, Colonial Legacies, Democratic Futures*, London and New York: Routledge.

Bartlett, Jim (2004) 'Females wary as military rapes surface', United Press International, 27 February.

Bjorken, Johanna, Clarisa Bencomo and Jonathan Horowitz (2003) 'Climate of fear: sexual violence and abduction of women and girls in Baghdad', *Human Rights Watch*, 15(8).

Brown, Lucy and David Romano (2006) 'Women in post-Saddam Iraq: one step forward or two steps back?', *NWSA Journal*, 18(3).

Colson, Marie-Laure (2003) 'Iraqi women have lost the post-war: rapes, sequestrations and a return to the veil develop', *La Liberación*, 2 September.

Cooke, Miriam (2002) 'Saving brown women', *Signs*, 28(1).

Eisenstein, Zillah (2004) *Against Empire: Feminisms, Race and the West*, London: Zed Books.

— (2007) *Sexual Decoys: Gender, Race, and War in Imperial Democracy*, London: Zed Books.

Grissett, Sheila (2004) 'Shifting federal budget erodes protection from levees: because of cuts, hurricane risk grows', *New Orleans Times-Picayune*, 8 June.

Manning, Lory (2005) 'Military women', *Women's Review of Books*, 31(5).

Mohanty, Chandra Talpade (2003) *Feminism without Borders*, Durham, NC: Duke University Press.

— (2006) 'US empire and the project of women's studies, stories of complicity and dissent', *Gender, Place, and Culture*, 13(1).

Nadar, Carol (2002) 'Women and children main casualties of war', *The Age*, www.theage.com.au/articles/2002/10/03/1033538723853.html.

Riley, Robin (2006) 'Valiant, vicious, or virtuous: representation and the problem of women warriors', in Robin Riley and Naeem Inayatullah (eds), *Interrogating Imperialism: Conversations on Gender, Race, and War*, New York: Palgrave Macmillan.

— (2008) 'Women and war: militarism, bodies, and the practice of gender', *Sociology Compass*, forthcoming.

Roy, Arundhati (2002) *Power Politics*, Cambridge, MA: South End Press.

— (2003) *War Talk*, Cambridge, MA: South End Press.

Shankar, Thom and David S. Cloud (2006) 'Rumsfeld shift lets army keep larger budget', *New York Times*, 8 October.

Silliman, Jael and Anannya Bhattacharjee (eds) (2002) *Policing the National Body: Race, Gender and Criminalization*, Cambridge, MA: South End Press.

Stockholm Institute for Peace Research (2007) 'Recent trends in military expenditure', www.sipri.org/contents/milap/milex/mex_trends.html.

Wokusch, Heather (2003) 'Bringing the war back home: linking war and domestic violence', *Common Dreams*, 9 February.

ONE | **Feminist geopolitics of war**

1 | A vocabulary for feminist praxis: on war and radical critique

ANGELA Y. DAVIS

I begin by questioning what it means to live in a country that is at war, a country whose president, in announcing a global war on terror, has, in effect, declared war on the rest of the world. This question requires us to consider the unrepresentability of war in the United States, a country that has not experienced war within its own borders since the mid-nineteenth century. Yet we have experienced a comprehensive militarization of this society, and multiple wars are still being waged on many of our communities. Moreover, the war on terror that is unfolding both within and outside US borders has produced a moral panic that urges us to feel and act as if we were living under a state of siege.

Many years ago, when I first traveled to Europe, I was struck by a prevailing popular consciousness of war. It was almost two decades after the conclusion of World War II, although there was still material evidence of the assault of fascism. I was struck by the extent to which war was still palpable, by the contemporaneity of historical memories of war. And I compared these historical memories to what I considered to be an inability of people in the United States to cross the temporal divide that placed war in an inaccessible past.

Later, in 1973, I had the opportunity to meet a young girl who survived the My Lai massacre in Vietnam, and at that moment experienced a disjunction between the ways our movement against the war in Vietnam tended to represent war and the unimaginable suffering the US military was causing the people of Vietnam. Today people refer to the Haditha massacre that took place in November 2005, when US Marines killed fifteen Iraqi civilians in their homes, as the contemporary counterpart to My Lai.

But, despite our flaws in that era, we did respond, we did rise up in massive numbers, and we did take to the streets. As in previous historical periods, women were the key organizers of the anti-war movement, though they were not necessarily the most visible spokespersons and frequently were unable to move past the single-issue syndrome that focused only on 'ending the war.'

I am not saying that today we are afflicted with a collective apathy that prevents us from achieving the heights of activism that were decisive in bringing the Vietnam War to an end. That is not my point. Indeed, it might be possible to argue that popular anti-war consciousness is far more widespread in the USA now in face of the war in Iraq than it was in relation to the war in Vietnam.

Yet I remain concerned about the failure to translate the vast anti-war sentiment within the country into a sustained movement that can effectively counter the imperial belligerence of the USA. If we are to reflect on ways feminism can aid us in contesting the culture of war, I want to pose the question of how feminist approaches can help us decipher the challenges we face today, which are, I believe, far more complicated than the challenges of the Vietnam War era. How can feminism help us to meet these contemporary challenges?

Before attempting to answer this question, I should say that the tradition of feminism with which I have always identified emphasizes not only strategies of criticism and strategies of transformation but also a sustained critique of the tools we use to stage criticism and to enact transformation. This tradition of feminism is linked to all the important social movements – against racism, against imperialism, for labor rights, and so forth. This tradition of feminism emphasizes certain habits of perception, certain habits of imagination. Just as it was once important to imagine a world without slavery, to imagine a world without segregation, to imagine a world in which women were not assumed to be inherently inferior to men, it is now important to imagine a world without xenophobia and the fenced borders designed to make us think of people in and from a southern region outside the USA as the enemy. It is now important to imagine a world in which binary conceptions of gender no longer govern modes of segregation and association, and one in which violence is eradicated from state practices as well as from our intimate lives – from heterosexual and same-sex relationships. And, as in the past, it is important to imagine a world without war. And, of course, this is just the beginning of the list.

But it is not enough simply to imagine a different future. We can walk around with ideal worlds in our heads while everything is crumbling around us. Feminist critical habits involve collective intervention as well. The feminist critical impulse, if we take it seriously, involves a dual commitment: a commitment to use knowledge in a transformative way, and to use knowledge to remake the world so that it is better for its inhabitants – not only for human beings, for all its living inhabitants. This commitment entails an obstinate refusal to attribute a permanency to that which exists in the present, simpy because it exists. This commitment simultaneously drives us to examine the conceptual and organizing tools we use, not to take them for granted.

This is the very core of feminism – at least the feminism with which I identify. Of course, there are many feminisms, including the George and Laura Bush version, which evokes the putative status of women under Islam as a rallying call for state terrorism. In this 'feminism,' Islam – within the Samuel Huntington 'Clash of Civilizations' framework – produces the terrorist enemy of democracy and the victimized woman who has to be saved by US democracy.

But a more thoughtful, a more radical, feminism exists, and with it we can make gains in our efforts to end war, torture, and pervasive militarization. This more radical feminism is a feminism that does not capitulate to possessive individualism, a feminism that does not assume that democracy requires capitalism, a feminism that is bold and willing to take risks, a feminism that fights for women's rights while simultaneously recognizing the pitfalls of the formal 'rights' structure of capitalist democracy.

So, for example, this feminism does not say that we want to fight for the equal right of women to participate in the military, for the equal right of women to torture, or for their equal right to be killed in combat. This feminism rejects, as I have heard Zillah Eisenstein relate, the claims of a US military officer attending the graveside service of a female soldier killed in Iraq – a man who wept at what he spoke of as a palpable expression of women's equality, the dead woman's right to a military funeral.

But even as we are critical of an exclusive insistence on formal rights, we can consider other approaches to struggles for 'equality.' Instead of conceptualizing equality using a standard established by the dominance of men in the military, we can advocate for the equal right of women and men to refuse participation in the military. Moreover, we can extend our anti-military advocacy to include the dismantling of the military machine, even within a struggle for 'equality.'

But the larger issue here is the relationship between individual and collective accomplishments. Victories achieved by individuals do not necessarily count as collective victories. For instance, women of color who manage to reach the highest level of government and who position themselves as architects and defenders of war do not advance the collective struggle of communities historically subjugated on the basis of race and gender. Rather their situation militates against gender and racial equality.

Feminism is concerned with women's equality, it is concerned with gender equality, and it is also concerned with issues of sexuality and race.

But there may be something more important than the particular issues traditionally associated with feminism. It may be far more important to emphasize feminist methodologies than the abstractions that count as the objects of feminism. The importance of this approach is suggested by the history of feminisms in the twentieth century – a history that consisted largely of contestations over who gets to represent the abstraction 'women' and particularly the raced and classed character of those representations.

When I refer to feminist methodologies, I include both scholarship and organizing – in other words, methodologies for interdisciplinary analysis, and also methodologies for building movements. These feminist methodologies impel us to explore connections that are not always apparent. They enable us to inhabit contradictions and to discover what is productive about those contradictions. These are methods of thought and action that urge us to think things together that appear to be entirely separate and to disaggregate things that seem to naturally belong together.

Feminist scholar/activists present at the 2006 'Feminism and War' conference – Zillah Eisenstein, Cynthia Enloe, Chandra Talpade Mohanty, Minnie Bruce Pratt, and Jasbir Puar, for example – have given us conceptual tools that are applicable both to research and to organizing practices. There continues to be a need for the development that was so exciting at the conference – scholars talking to activists, scholar/activists talking to activist intellectuals about a whole host of questions raised by the current state of US wars.

Feminist scholars and feminist activists attempt to peer through the ideological veil. And feminists have always been in the forefront of the peace movement. But as we now know, it is not enough simply to call for peace. And peace cannot be envisioned as the simple cessation of war. Aristophanes' play *Lysistrata* was not only about the women withholding sex from the male warriors in order to compel them to stop making war, it was also about restructuring a gendered society.

Let me return to my earlier reflections on My Lai and Haditha as a way of engaging with the ways in which the circumstances of war are represented, and with the attempts to pierce the ideological veil thrown over it. It cannot be denied that the widespread circulation of photographs of the My Lai massacre, during the Vietnam War era, played a role in crystallizing opposition to the war. But it was certainly not the case that the photographs by themselves mobilized millions of people. The mistaken assumption that the mere existence of visual evidence of war atrocities elicited the anti-war sentiment that ended the Vietnam

War leads people to ask today why a similar response was not generated by the images of the war in Iraq.

It is true that the embeddedness of war journalism has restricted what we see and hear and read about Iraq. Yet we have seen horrendous images of torture. There were the accidental images of torture in the Abu Ghraib prison that were never meant to be publicly released. If photographs by themselves were able to spur people to action, long ago we should have been in the street by the millions twenty-four hours a day. Even though we have not seen the worst images. Even though we have yet to see images of women who were detained and interrogated in Abu Ghraib. Even though we have not seen and have to imagine the conditions of prisoners who have been subject to extraordinary rendition. Even though we have not seen prison cells that are the size of a coffin – six by three in places like Syria, where people labeled by the US government as enemy combatants are being held. Even though we have not seen visual evidence of these atrocities, we have accessed this information in other ways. So we are aware, for instance, of the massacre at Haditha.

But let's return to the question of the images we have actually seen. It seems that we think about them in eighteenth-century terms. We still believe in enlightenment. I am not suggesting that we shouldn't be enlightened and that we shouldn't enlighten others. The problem to which I am referring emanates from the assumption that rational communication and publicity are sufficient – as Immanuel Kant suggested.

We tend to relegate so much power to the image that we assume not only that the meaning of the image is self-evident but we also fetishize the image, thinking that it will spur us to action.

The images of My Lai and other instances of massive violence that did not distinguish between military personnel and civilians are not what organized the anti-war movement. The photographs did not organize the movement – it was organized by committed women and men who were enraged and engaged, not only at the point of mobilization, but in other areas of their lives as well. Their engagement created the context for the reception of those photographs. Their engagement produced the meaning that was attached to the photographs.

The images depicting torture at Abu Ghraib were released into an environment so charged with assumptions about the hegemony of US democracy that the images themselves were overdetermined by the need to explain them in relation to democracy. The concern with the need to rescue US democracy pushed the real meaning of torture, and especially the suffering of prisoners depicted, into the background. People voicing widespread expressions of shock and revulsion in relation to the photographs asked, 'How is this possible?', 'How can this happen?', and asserted, 'This is not supposed to happen' – all within certain assumptions about US democracy. There was disbelief and an impulse toward justification, rather than an engagement with the contemporary meaning of torture and violence seen in the images.

As feminists, we cannot relinquish our own agency to the image. We cannot even assume that the image has a self-evident relation to its object. And we must consider the political economy that constitutes the environment within which images are created and consumed. Feminists adopt critical habits, including a critical stance toward the visual.

And we are also vigilant with respect to the vocabulary we use to conceptualize and implement strategies for change. As I indicated before, we should develop habits that impel us to engage in constant criticism of the things that we wish to change, as well as criticism of the tools that we use to conceptualize what we want to change.

In this context, I want to bring the term 'diversity' into my discussion. The danger of this term consists in the way its use has colonized histories of social justice, so that much of what we were once able to talk about with greater specificity is forced into hiding behind the concept of 'diversity.' The use of the term also promotes a hidden individualization of problems and solutions that ought to be collective. For instance, one hears about the 'diversity' of US military forces – with respect to people of color and increasingly with respect to women – as a model for racial and gender equality in other institutions. As a matter of fact, besides the military, another place you might go if you want to see diversity is in the US prisons.

And – what is immensely important – 'diversity' is a concept that provincializes the relationship of people within the USA to the world. The concept emerges from US ideology that equates racial and gender justice with color blindness and gender blindness. But undocumented immigrants live outside the embrace of official diversity. With the re-tooling of a racism that equates the practice of Islam with terrorism, people of Middle Eastern and South Asian descent live outside the embrace of diversity.

And if we are feminists vigilant with respect to the vocabulary we use in thinking and implementing strategies for change, we must consider that 'democracy' is also a term that requires constant criticism, for wars are being conducted in its name, torture is justified in its name, and democracy has become a watchword for the most abominable violations of human rights. The official deployment of the term 'democracy' by the administration of US President George W. Bush has led to its equation with torture, terror, and a wholesale denial of individual and collective rights. The ideological strategies of the Bush administration involved the invocation of the struggle to preserve and expand democracy as a justification for the rapid erosion of democratic rights. Feminism is committed to a constant criticism of these ideological processes.

We now face a situation in the USA in which torture is not recognized as torture, secret prisons are not revealed, extraordinary rendition amounts to routine torture, and domestically there is fencing off of the Mexican border to prevent people whose lives have been destroyed by the impact of global capitalism from entering this country. And, of course, the number of people in US jails and prisons continues to rise – there are now 2.2 million people behind bars – which means that the United States incarcerates proportionally more people than any other country in the world. Feminist approaches insist on exploring the relationship between militarization and the prisonization of our local and global landscapes.

So when we say that we are dedicated to eliminating violence against women, we cannot stop with the project of addressing individual acts of violence committed either within intimate relationships or by individual strangers. Violence is not only individualized and domestic, and the perpetrators of violence are not only individual men. We therefore place state violence, war, prison violence, torture, capital punishment on a spectrum of violence. And while we cannot simultaneously eliminate the entire spectrum of violence, we can always insist on an awareness of these connections. In other words, feminism is not only about women, nor only about gender. It is a broader methodology that can enable us to better conceptualize and fight for progressive change.

Torture, for example, cannot be treated as an aberration, as a spectacular exception, but rather we try to understand its links to regimes and practices associated with the punishment of imprisonment within the domestic framework as well. Isn't capital punishment a form of torture? What is the link between the torture at Abu Ghraib and the routine, unquestioned torture associated with imprisonment? Why are we so quick to speak out against these spectacular examples of torture – and indeed we should – while ignoring what happens to thousands and millions of domestic prisoners within the USA? Why do we cry out against secret prisons, when only a small fraction of the population has ever bothered to find out what happens behind the walls of US state and federal prisons – that is, if we have not been a prisoner or relative of a prisoner ourselves? Aren't maximum-security prisons secret places? Aren't women's prisons, wherever they might be located, also secret places?

I conclude by evoking the case of a woman who is a former US political prisoner and whose current circumstances reveal connections between militarization and prisonization, between domestic and global terror. I refer to the case of Assata Shakur, who was arrested in the 1970s, but escaped from prison and made her way to the island of Cuba, where she has been living for the last several decades.

Recently, in conjunction with the war on terror and the establishment of the Department of Homeland Security, a one-million-dollar reward has been offered to anyone who captures Assata and brings her back to the USA. The Hands Off Assata Campaign would like to bring her home – but as a free human being. Twenty-five years after she was the target of efforts by the government to criminalize the black liberation struggle, she is now represented as a 'terrorist.' How, then, do we understand the articulations of historical struggles for liberation in relation to contemporary ideologies of terrorism? What does it mean that an African-American woman, residing in the socialist nation of Cuba, is the target of the newly constituted Department of Homeland Security? But, most important of all, how do we defend her, recognizing both her individual humanity and the dangerous symbolism involved in the effort to entrap her in the machinery of the war on terror?

The 2007 birthday celebration that the network Hands Off Assata organized throughout the USA to celebrate Assata's sixtieth birthday was one of many feminist campaigns that incorporate an awareness of the important connections we need to make if we are to build strong communities of resistance against war. This campaign suggests a feminism that can help us to meet the contemporary challenge of continuing US wars – a feminism that does not capitulate to possessive individualism, a feminism that does not assume that democracy requires capitalism, a feminism that is bold and willing to take risks.

My final message is a general plea to you, those listening, those reading: Please get involved. Whatever you decide to do, please try to make a difference. And as you do so, consider the tradition of feminism that emphasizes certain habits of perception, certain habits of imagination – the feminism that emphasizes not only strategies of criticism and strategies of transformation but also a sustained critique of the tools we use to stage criticism and to enact transformation.

2 | Resexing militarism for the globe

ZILLAH EISENSTEIN

Since September 11 2001, there has been a female face to the wars on/of terror, but the meaning of this is not self-evident. Females assist in the orchestration of the US wars of/on terror, and therefore women have more complicity in these wars. Yet there is nothing more undemocratic than war, so it is highly unlikely that women's presence can mean anything good. No one's rights – especially not women's – can be met in war; or by waging war.

Females, although still a minority, are more present in militaries, as government officials, as suicide bombers, as soldiers in Third World countries than in earlier times. There are more women being militarized for and against imperial power. Today there are more women at these sites of power, or what were sites of power, fighting on behalf of the powerful, *and* they are more visible. This visibility is unusual because females are more often than not out of view – made absent, silenced – rather than seen. So the fact that women appear more present needs attention.

US Secretary of State Condoleezza Rice wields power, but not as a woman – whatever this might really mean today – and not for women and their rights – but for an imperial democracy that destroys women's equality and racial justice. Imperial democracy uses racial diversity and gender fluidity to disguise itself – and females and people of color become its decoys. Condi's black skin and female body operate to cloud and obfuscate. Imperial democracy mainstreams women's rights discourse into foreign policy and militarizes women for imperial goals. Imperial democracy creates women combatants both inside and outside the military, and First Lady Laura Bush authorizes this process as civilian-in-chief. My point is not that nothing has changed, or that these changes do not matter, but rather that these changes do not mean what they seem to mean.

War bespeaks exceptional circumstances and is also naturalized as part of the human condition: there will always be war(s). War is then awful and normal; universal and yet unique. Each war is both similar and different to a previous one; it is both changed and static. The Vietnam War is different than the Afghan and Iraq wars, and not. Each war is defined by and defines anew its racialized gender power relations.

And these power relations are defined by early global capitalism and anti-communism toward Vietnam, and US unipolar capitalism and anti-terrorist rhetoric toward Afghanistan and Iraq.

More than a quarter-century of US feminist activism partly initiated by the Vietnam War defines new trajectories today. Sexual politics and the sexual/racial/gender systems of violence have new exposure and visibility because militarism and militarization redefine both masculinism and femininity, alongside a hyper-sexuality and neo-racism that construct new-old racialized gender formations. Although women's bodies that birth have also always been maimed in war, today's wars make this more complex with more females as actors in war. The newest technologies of war, alongside feminist activism and the demands of global capital, de-essentialize and de-naturalize the earth mother.

I am therefore focused on the resexing of gender in the past quarter-century to better understand this stage of highly militarized global capital. Post-1989, with the fall of the Soviet Union and the revolutions in eastern Europe, ushered in this stage of US unipolar power. The start of the Gulf Wars in 1991 solidified the militarist phase of US global power: more surveillance, more privatization, more concentration of power, more military expenditure. September 11 2001 authorized this militarism in its heightened form and began the slide from neoliberal to fascistic democracy. With the rejustification of this militarized frame – be it the growth of prison facilities or the activation of the National Guard and reserve units or declaring Code Orange and red alerts for the civilian population – racialized gendered configurations are being rearticulated in established but revisionist form.

Remilitarizing daily life

A culture of pre-emptive strikes and unilateral power plays out on both the battlefield and everyday life in the USA. An aggressive self-absorption justifies a heightened individualism on the part of most successful people. And our leaders think they do not need to heed international law that defends against torture, or need to sign treaties to help protect the environment. The USA controlled 32 percent of the world trade in weapons in 1987; and in 1997 controlled 43 percent. And, of the 140 nations it gave or sold arms to in 1995, 90 percent did not have democratic elections or were known for human rights abuses (Kolko 1994: 111).

The USA has the most advanced arsenal on the face of the earth and is becoming more and more conditioned by a military style of discipline because of this. The presence of our military – at home and abroad – is too significant to not affect the very culture that surrounds and is

28

surrounded by it. The USA spent more on its military – $329 billion in 2002 – than China, Russia, Japan, Iraq, North Korea, and all other NATO countries combined (Baker 2003: 35–46).

The USA also spends greater amounts on its prisons – much more than it does on its schools. There was an 81 percent increase in the number of prisons from 1990 to 2000. Sociologist C. W. Mills's 'military-industrial complex' is now termed a prison-industrial complex by Angela Davis. She states that there are at present more women in prison in California than there were women in prison in the whole country in the 1970s. In 2003 there were approximately two million prisoners in the USA and about one and a half million people in the military (Davis 2003: 88, 92). Our militarized culture spends 52 percent of the federal budget on the military and 6 percent on health (ibid.: 24, 27).

War is our cultural metaphor. We war on drugs, on AIDS, on cancer, on poverty, on terrorism. But 'war' as metaphor obfuscates. Its language is as deceptive as its end goals. War is a danger to democracy because it justifies and therefore normalizes secrecy, deception, surveillance, and killing. This mentality of war spills out into everyday life. The games our children play naturalize war at home while US troops in Iraq use these games for training and relaxation. The popular video games console PlayStation is a recruiting tool – one thinks one can play with war, be in war and have fun, be warlike and win (Thompson 2004: 33–7). Meanwhile, in 'real' life, Governor Jeb Bush of Florida, brother of President George W. Bush, supports the use of a computer cyber-matrix program that has marked thousands of citizens as potential terrorists (Defede 2004: 24).

US feminist theorist Cynthia Enloe writes of militarization as a process that impacts on and pervades everyday life, from the site of the military. The actual military is only a small, even if central, aspect of this disciplining and regulating of social relations. Hierarchy, surveillance, authoritarianism, and deference become a part of the way people live both inside and outside military barracks (Enloe 2000: 3, 4). US Homeland Security defines civilian psyches in militarist fashion. Its security alerts – Code Orange and Code Red – demand a kind of unconscious consciousness of fear. They authorize the need for a security state; a war of a different sort – the kind you might not see, or feel first hand, but which is there. The 2004 US presidential election was embedded in these militarist frames: calling forth particular memories of the Vietnam War to construct the new heroes and patriots of today.

Enloe worries that militarized culture mystifies its own significance by focusing on the military *as* the location for militarized ways of thinking/living. She argues that by focusing on the military as the site of warlike life we normalize 'the militarized civilian sites.' She insightfully argues that the newest way that militarization is 'camouflaged' is by presenting women's service in the military as though it were connected to women's liberation (ibid.: 45). Instead of liberation, women's entry into the military is better understood as the newest stage of militarizing global capitalism. In this post-1989 era the constructions of racialized patriarchy are being re-formed once again. New-old constructions of the dutiful wife, the black 'mammy,' the welfare mother, the soccer mom, the professional woman, are being refashioned for and with militarization. More women are forced to join the military out of economic necessity; and more non-military women have been disciplined by the demands of a privatized public sphere that restructures gender with its intensified demands.

Women in the military may make the military look more democratic as though women now have the same choices as men, but the choices are not truly the same. So this may be a more modern military, if modern means changed, but it is not more democratic or egalitarian. Actually, it is because there is less democracy, if democracy means choice and opportunity, that more women have joined the military. At present, this stage of patriarchy often requires women to join the army in order to find a paying job or a way to get an education. The military – given this militarist stage of global capital – is a main arena where working- and middle-class women can find paid work, as domestic labor was for black women in the 1950s. Given the structural changes of labor in the global economy, marriage no longer affords most women – no matter their race or class – life without paid labor. These women are looking for ways to get medical and housing benefits, educational resources, career training. These are significant shifts in women's needs and lives, and in the institutions of marriage and family, which cut across racial and class divides.

According to Enloe, whereas women made up only 1 percent of the Soviet army, in post-communist Russia they made up 12 percent of the armed forces. In the USA during the Vietnam War women made up 2 percent of military personnel and by 1997 constituted 13 percent. As of September 2003, 213,059 women made up 15 percent of those serving on US active duty. Eighteen percent of new army enlistees were women, 17 percent of the navy, 7 percent of the marines, and 23 percent of the air force. Almost all say they joined for the education and job training. Over 50 percent of enlisted women are from ethnic minorities: 33.2 percent African-American, 1.8 percent Native American, 4.1 percent Asian-American, and 10.2 percent Hispanic (Manning 2004: 7). The presence of women is also growing in the militaries of Croatia, Mexico, Jordan,

Argentina, Chile, Japan, and South Korea (Enloe 2000: 280, 281). In Iraq, one in seven service members and one in three in the army's military intelligence personnel is female (Burke 2006: 3).

Young women make up a near-critical mass in the Maoist movement in Nepal. This highly militarist movement is defined by male leadership and female combatants. Nearly 30 percent of the Maoist movement are women, and many of them find their military involvement both a problematic and a liberating opportunity. These women are surrounded by domestic and state violence so that the 'People's War' gives them new and different options. These militarized struggles reproduce and unsettle stereotypic gender relations. Women's involvements are thought to be in some sense emancipatory and yet constraining as the patriarchal relations of their country are both in play and subverted by their mobilization (Manchanda 2004: 237, 238, 245).

It is important to note that the militarization of women's lives is complex and disorderly. The military has offered women entry before as a place of survival. Japanese-American women signed up for the military during World War II to prove their loyalty and to further their education. Brenda Moore writes about the Japanese-American women who served during World War II. Many of these women saw military service as an 'avenue of upward mobility,' especially given their minority racial status. Citizenship has been offered to immigrant groups in exchange for military service. Six thousand Nisei – children of Japanese immigrants, born in the USA – trained to serve with the military in the Pacific. 'An estimated 5000 Nisei men were on active duty before the US declared war on Japan.' After declaring war, most of these individuals were 'denied the very rights they were willing to fight and die for' given the injustices of American racism. In the end, over 100,000 people of Japanese descent were 'relocated' – to internment camps; approximately 80,000 of these persons had been born in the USA. Some Nisei women in the end entered the military straight from internment camps. And this was then used as a 'show' of democracy: the US army will open itself to even those of 'enemy extraction.' Nisei women broke the norms of both US culture in general and their more private lives. Their desires were various: to use their particular skills for the war effort, to prove their loyalty as US citizens, to see the world (Moore 2003: 1, 3, 22, 30).

African-American women suffered extreme stigma and discrimination in the US military during World War II. There was a racial quota of 10 percent and a policy of racial segregation was practiced. African-American women were segregated into an all-black platoon and were isolated from their white counterparts. Many of these women were trained professionally but were assigned menial tasks simply because of their race. Given this segregation there were African-American Women Army Corps officers to lead their segregated units, but there were no officers among the Nisei women. All Japanese-American women remained in the enlisted ranks (ibid.: 130–34). These women served their country – both coffee and war.

Traces of patriarchy continue as gender is re-formed and modernized for the new needs of combat. Racial segregation is now illegal and gender hierarchies are nuanced so patriarchal privilege is camouflaged but not less present. And the nuances are embedded in inadequate knowledge about the varied actual lives of women in the military across the globe.

Hundreds of thousands of women fought for Germany, the Soviet Union and Britain during World War II; and many of them engaged in combat. According to D'Ann Campbell, approximately 800,000 women served in the Red Army and over half of them were in front-line units. The Soviets could not afford the luxury of the non-combat/combat classification that preoccupied the Americans, British and the Germans (Campbell 1993: 301–23). A lack of sufficient 'man'-power drew women into combat, not democratic priorities. Women soldiers died in hand-to-hand combat in Okinawa – while necessity drew women to combat roles rather than a feminist quest for 'equality.' Slightly more than 200,000 women serve in the enlisted ranks in the US military at present. Necessity should not be misunderstood here for progress, or democracy, or feminisms.

Women in war-torn countries live this new militarized life sometimes as combatants but more often as refugees and displaced people. Countries like Palestine, Israel, Sudan, Iraq, and Afghanistan do not have neat divides between civilian and military realms. Private life and familial relations take on militarized form as the usual divides of home and battle are smashed. Sexed and gender relations are remixed in war alongside the remix of militarized zones like the USA.

Militarizing gender

First World countries get to make the distinction between militarized life and war more readily than countries elsewhere. War-torn countries live without the luxury of this divide. Gender violence in India and the Sudan is publicized and put in view, as both horrific and ordinary. Gender violence and the gendering of violence appear as one process. Gender violence can be practiced against males and females, which both loosens the grip of traditional meanings of gender, while also reinforcing them. Public rape and publicized gender humiliation are the newest forms of very old practices.

People in the USA were horrified by September 11 2001, because they felt a bit of what war feels like up closer than usual. People in the USA with loved ones in Iraq and Afghanistan also feel a bit of war up close. But most of us do not consciously feel the wars in the sense that we do not walk around with a constant aching and fear. Yet more women in the USA are away at war. As such, women have joined the once-male landscape in greater numbers. These changes alter gendered relations both inside and outside the military. Women are mobilized for and by combat. It remains to be seen exactly what of established gender remains in these newest wars and how war will change with these newly gendered constructions (Katzenstein 1998).

Peace is often identified with females; and war with males. Because war unsettles previously gendered life, space itself is reconstructed. The language of war – home front, battle zone, combatant, civilian – challenges established notions of home, safety, and privacy. Death creates new necessity. So many men lost their lives in the Rwandan massacres that women now lead most of their local councils. In Iraq, so many men have been taken into custody by US forces – more than ten thousand men and boys – that women now do men's work. They till their fields and guard their homes (Gettleman 2004: A1).

Much of war is covert. Yet war itself is an overt and violent form of politics. War is seeable, and in view, even if not knowable. Because the obscene inequities and injustices of global capitalism are more visible today, more crushing systems of power are needed to protect it. The USA protects itself with its fists while democracy is still trotted out as a defense and its women in khaki (Enloe 1983) are used as a decoy. Meanwhile the protection of women along with children – as civilians – is simultaneously used as a justification for war, despite the fact that 95 percent of the casualties of war are civilians and the majority of these are women. These civilians are also militarized as refugees, as wage-laborers, as haulers of wood and water, as mothers.

Women who enter the military enter a masculinist bastion. Military culture seeks to stabilize and punish the dangerous female. At the US Naval Academy a nightly ritual is practiced in which the new plebe says, 'Goodnight, Jane Fonda'; and the entire company responds, 'Goodnight, bitch' (Burke 2004: 14). Domestic violence is found to be three to five times higher in military couples than civilian ones. Men who have been in combat are four times more likely to be physically abusive. In 2002 five military wives were brutally killed by their husbands upon returning from Iraq to Fort Bragg (Lutz 2004: 17). Before the September 11 2001 attacks, the Miles Foundation – a non-profit agency in Connecticut that deals with abuse in the military – received about seventy-five calls a month from military families reporting domestic violence and sexual abuse. After 9/11 it starting receiving 150 calls a week. Eight soldiers after returning from Iraq committed suicide; another drowned his wife in the bathtub (Davey 2004: A1).

War supposedly exposes the evilness that lurks beneath the surface, which gives purpose and trivializes everything else. War is both desired and despised. It is an 'orgy of death,' destruction and violence. As such war seduces. Christopher Hedges describes and authorizes this Hobbesian version of life and death as one of male conquest. Men are driven by *eros*, their flirtation with life, and *thanatos*, death (Hedges 2002: 3, 158, 171). Thomas Hobbes's world was a world of men – women were missing. War does not give me meaning. Nor do I think war gives most people – male or female – meaning. Hobbes was not right about most men or women. Yet the naturalization and normalization of war are maintained by this notion of a mythic human nature, which is also constructed as male.

It is dangerous to think that war is inevitable, and intrinsic to human nature. I do not think genes are simply nature, nor do I think human nature is natural at all. The concept of nature is truly political at the start. It is a construct that reifies the needs of those who need us to fight their wars. In this techno-masculinist world that we inhabit we are shown war as the drama of manhood. Sometimes it is named the 'Oedipal compulsion,' and the 'psychic quest for the father.' Yet over 120,000 dutiful sons who fought the Vietnam War came home to commit suicide, twice the number killed in the war (Boose 1993: 504, 605).

Gender naturalizes war; and war is gendered. Masculinity and femininity are set as normal oppositions. And the sexual body itself is left silenced. The very process of birthing is most often not in view, or is trivialized, or is fantasized (Ruddick 1993: 291). None of these options helps real live women. This process silences and obfuscates the female body and leaves it unreadable. War, in Hobbesian fashion, starts from this mythic place. Women are absent giving birth; men kill. Or, as Klaus Theweleit says, 'War ranks high among the male ways of giving birth' (Theweleit 2003: 284). Women, then, are supposedly peaceful; and men make war. The essentialist argument assigns these categories in nature while masking the artificial gendering of wars.

Women are sexed in particular ways and birth in a world that demands that they nurture as well. If we give up the fixedness of both sex and gender then we are left to examine the changeability of sexing gender and gendering sex. This does not erase sex or gender but rather demands an accounting of their politicized contextual meanings. So some women may look to preserve life rather than smash it, but many females will enter the military. This means that the practices of gender will change even though the authorized essentialized views of femininity and manliness can remain static.

War institutionalizes sexual differentiation while also undermining it. War demands opposition, differentiation, and the othering of peoples. The privileging of masculinity underscores all other processes of differentiation. War is a process by which masculinity is both produced and reproduced. The heroic warrior is the standard (Hooper 2001: 76, 95). Everyone else is a pussy, a wimp, a 'fag.' It is why the defeat of the USA in Vietnam was viewed as emasculating. The defeat required a rearticulation of gender as much as a refocusing of foreign policy. As recently as 2003 the US gay newspaper *The Blade* ran an exposé of the Tiger Forces – the elite unit that 'savaged civilians in Vietnam.' This highly trained unit of paratroopers, in 1967, cut off the ears and scalps of their prisoners and donned them as necklaces of triumph (Sallah and Weiss 2003: 45). It is now well documented that US troops maimed and raped innocents in a series of Vietnamese villages. Yet the Tiger Forces are still fighting US wars, leading some to say that the only difference between the Afghan and Vietnam wars is that Afghanistan is brown, and Vietnam was green (Alexievich 1990). One is left to ponder how the ghoulish war atrocities in Vietnam are a part of the Tiger Forces' strategy in Iraq.

Vietnam continues to be a reminder of the unsettling demasculinization of the USA in defeat. It is why Jane Fonda is still hated for her anti-war activity and remains nothing but 'pussy' to defenders of this war. She sadly continues to apologize for her anti-war activism, but to no avail. Gertrude Stein had it right when she said that patriarchal is supposed to be the same as patriotic and the patriotic woman is supposed to be silent and supportive, not subversive (Higonnet 2003: 205–26).

Post-Vietnam politics turned to remasculinizing the US military for global capitalism. The US defeat in Vietnam was used to justify the downsizing and privatizing of the 'feminized' inept government. A leaner and meaner state is what global capitalists wished for along with Donald Rumsfeld's desire to restructure and privatize the military as well.

My own trajectory back to thinking about the Vietnam War was when I read about the Tiger and Delta Forces, but this time in Iraq. And then the 2004 US presidential election brought Vietnam up once again. Democratic Party nominee John Kerry was a Viet vet and was tainted with it, rather than embraced because of it.

Too much hateful happened there. Millions of tons of bombs were dropped on civilians and soldiers alike. Three and a half million

Vietnamese died; 58,000 US soldiers were killed. Those who returned came home with terrible memories that they could not live with. They tell their stories in the documentary *Winter Soldier* (20/20 Productions 2004). They speak against the war and tell the horror: women and children indiscriminately murdered, mutilated, burned and killed, cut open while still living, prisoners thrown alive from helicopters. They speak of how they were trained to think of the Vietnamese as 'gooks' and 'commies' and not human beings. They say they were totally scared for their own lives and did what they had to to survive.

Recently I watched *Winter Soldier* again. I sat listening and watching and not quite able to do so. The footage of young Vietnamese women screaming and begging for their lives was beyond bearable. I kept thinking that if this is the truth, we should not be allowed to forget. These acts cannot be forgiven because they must not be forgotten. They must be remembered. I am not speaking of the need to punish when I renounce forgiveness. But I am speaking of the need to not forgive the making of war.

The feminizing loss of the Vietnam War was a significant US historical moment that refashioned the historical process of gender renegotiation. The war became a 'vehicle for expansion and specification of altered gender relations' (Jeffords 1989: 5, 168). The oppositional gender relations became more transitory and fluid. Gender would become more supple; but not more equal. The gender divide would still exist but not in simply old formations. War would be shaped less by biological sex – by one's male body, by maleness – and more by masculine discourses that can be adopted by males or females. Discourses shape what gender looks like. There is a move 'away from gendered individuals and toward gendered discourses' (Cohn 1995). This process of gender renegotiation took on particular significance in the Gulf War of 1991. This was the first US post-Vietnam war, and it was the first US war that acknowledged the troops as both male and female.

The Iraq wars from 1991 to 2006 have been an expression of rehabilitating the post-Vietnam US military through a resexing of it. In part femininity has been militarized while the military has not been demasculinized. The story of US army private Jessica Lynch's capture by the fedayeen in Nasiriyah was used to mobilize US male soldiers to action. They would find her and 'protect' her (Bragg 2003: 124). Jessica Lynch, along with her maintenance company fellow soldiers Lori Piestewa and Shoshanna Johnson, represented the shifting sexual and racial make-up of the US military. Of the three, only Lynch was white, while all three were working-class and female. They remained gendered as women while being militarized like men. These young females were in harm's way. Both Lynch and Johnson came home with serious injuries. Piestewa – a single mom – died.

The Iraq war of 2002 was initiated by a Texas 'cowboy' – President George W. Bush – with no military record to speak of, while women at home in the USA face a refeminization – be it liposuction or a remake of *The Stepford Wives* – in their everyday lives. In 2005, the film *Brokeback Mountain*, about a relationship between two actual cowboys, was a hit. Now even cowboys can be gay. The gender confusion is real.

Global capitalism requires a rearticulation and regendering of patriarchy. This involves a use of class differentiation among women to affirm masculinist privilege across class lines. And working-class women, especially women of color, are most often the new masculinist warriors. As class differences exacerbate inequality and injustice globally these class realities are written into the militarization of gendering everyday life.

Rape as gendered war

Rape articulates the violence encoded in gender; in wartime it reinscribes the continuity of gender inscription of woman as victim rather than actor. Yet enemies, male or female, are also feminized in this process. Rape in Bosnia or Darfur sexually violates girls and women while attacking the gendered system of masculinity. Men are demasculinized by the rape of their daughters or wives. Everyone is shamed in this process.

Rape is war in brutal, torturous form, not simply war's effect, or its crime. As such, the female body is the battlefield. Women's bodies are appropriated, conquered and destroyed. War rape smashes all distinction between private and public life. It destroys the ownership and privacy of one's body as individual lives are destroyed as barter in gendered wars. There are no civilians left. It disallows the mapping of a civilian status in war or the confinement of torture to a context that is disconnected from home and family (Youngs 2003: 1209).

The enemy nation is demasculinized while the victor is remasculinized. Systematic rape policy – as a 'murderous misogyny' – often exists as integral to military policy (Allen 1996: 47, 62). There have been different forms of this process: the sexual slavery of Jewish women for Nazi soldiers, the enforced institutionalized rape of 'comfort women' by the Japanese army in World War II, the genocidal Serb rape camps of the Bosnian war, the rape and mutilation of Tutsi women in the Rwandan massacres, sometimes initiated by Hutu females themselves.

Over 500,000 girls and women were raped in the 1994 Rwandan genocide. Tens of thousands of girls and women have been raped in Bosnia,

Resexing militarism for the globe

Sierra Leone, and East Timor. In many of these countries, as in Serbia and Pakistan, a raped woman will be shunned by her community, and suicide is often thought to be her only avenue of escape. Despite this stigma and shaming, in Sierra Leone war rape was so common that rape survivors were allowed back into their communities despite all else (McKay and Mazurana 2004: 45).

If I build on military historian Clausewitz and cultural critic Foucault here, rape can be said to be a form of war in yet another inhumane form – an integral form of war rather than an effect (Stiglmayer 1992; Eisenstein 1996). War and rape are both normalized as though they are inevitable, almost biologically driven, as in the mythic warrior's state of nature. Yet bodily violation destroys established gendered stereotypes. A violated female is no longer a woman that a man wishes to lay claim to. In war rape females are reduced to their patriarchal definition as a body vessel and also denied the status of a privileged womanhood. In war rape the woman is totally occupied, which is the 'ultimate invasion' (Ensler 2005: 28).

Although less acknowledged and less systemic, homosexual rape – man on man – occurs, but is less publicized given the way it collides with established notions of hetero-masculinity. Rape in war – whether hetero- or homosexual in form – structures a regendering of gender. When raped, males become womanlike or like a 'fag'; they become feminized as helpless. In this instance, gender floats from the biological body in horrific form.

According to Yvette Abrams, one in two females has been raped in South Africa owing to the institutionalization of violence, starting with slavery and following with colonial wars. This violent sense of trauma underpins any possibility of viable politics today (Abrams 2005). And the more war-ravaged the globe becomes, the more necessary it is to recognize rape as politics in yet another form. Nevertheless, General Musharraf of Pakistan speaks dismissively of the claims of Pakistani women in fall 2005, saying that many of them make false or exaggerated claims of rape in order to get financial support and visas from foreigners. He likened rape to a 'money-making thing' if you want to go abroad. He does so despite the publicity surrounding Mukhtar Mai, who was raped – as an act of honor revenge – on the orders of a village jurga in 2002; and the threats against Shazia Khalid's life after she went public about her rape (Masood 2004: A3). Pakistani feminists were outraged and demonstrated in the streets to make their counter-statement.

Rape as war in another form also exists much closer to home in the USA. Dozens of servicewomen in the Persian Gulf area have claimed sexual assaults and rape by their fellow troops. During 2002–04 there were over one hundred reports of sexual misconduct in the Central Command area – Iraq, Kuwait, and Afghanistan (Schmitt 2004: A1). These sexual assaults simultaneously construct these females as both the womanly warrior and the womanly victim.

The US military needs female recruits. This means that the military is becoming more female with approximately 14 percent of the army, 17 percent of the air force and 13 percent of the navy now female. But military life still nurtures masculinist sexual predators (Raynor 1997: 24–55). By 2004 at least thirty-seven servicewomen had sought sexual trauma counseling from civilian rape crisis organizations after returning from war duty in Iraq, Afghanistan, and Kuwait. Eighty-eight cases of sexual misconduct were reported by the 60,000 women stationed in these areas (Herdy and Moffeit 2004: 23).

Although the now famous Jessica Lynch has no memory of sexual assault, Rick Bragg writes that she was probably tortured and raped – her medical report cites 'anal sexual assault' (Bragg 2003: 95). The intra- and transnational presence of sexual humiliation and rape defines and constructs enemies, nations and their wars. Women's bodies become the universalized representation of conquest while male bodies are both masculinized in victory and feminized in defeat.

The sexed body – whether whole or maimed, male or female – is usually forgotten in war. Sometimes we are forced to remember. US army aviator Tammy Duckworth returned home as an amputee after losing both her legs to a rocket-propelled grenade. After scouting the Tigris river in Iraq, she came home to run for public office in Illinois. Legs and arms are shattered and blown off, vaginas are violated, people are blinded, psyches are tortured by unforgiving nightmares and little is said of this. This silencing of the racial, sexual and gendered body is vital to the persistence of war.

Patriarchy, suicide bombers, and war

Patriarchal gender continues to morph according to context. Many US women looking for job training and steady-paying work continue to join the military in significant numbers. Over 50 percent of enlisted women are from ethnic minorities (Manning 2004: 7). Similarly positioned women in countries elsewhere also look to the militarized zones of their lives. Palestinian women – living some of the most militarized lives of any women across the globe – find themselves smack up against the daily life of war. As such they are some of the most activist women in the world today – struggling to survive and build their nation. Their lives have little space for what is usually considered private and familial and few of them could claim civilian status in their war-torn circumstances. They suffer and struggle and die in equal numbers to their men.

Women suicide bombers reflect similar gender bending to other militarized arenas. Female suicide bombers do not bespeak the demise of patriarchal relations in these countries – Lebanon, Palestine, Chechnya – but rather the new fluidity of gendered roles performed out by male and female alike. According to Barbara Victor in *Army of Roses*, as early as 1985 Syrian intelligence officers were encouraging young Lebanese women to blow themselves up in attacks on Israeli troops. Palestinian authorities distribute a lifetime stipend of $400 a month to families of male suicide bombers; and to families of *shahida*s – female suicide bombers – like Wafa Idris, $200 per month. Once again the economic needs of these young women play a part. And patriarchy in obvious ways devalues their lives in relation to men's. According to Victor these women who give their lives do so out of a mix of economic necessity and their own personal despair. 'Suicide attacks become the ultimate "smart bombs" of the poor' (Victor 2003: 7, 16, 35).

Several of the women suicide bombers were bright, intelligent, divorced, and mothers. Yet they are also described as irrational and distraught and remain within the masculinist discourses as emotional, unstable, and vulnerable women. They are feminized as such, while occupying the masculinist position of bomber. When the reality of women suicide bombers is discussed, the query is always, why? It is assumed that politics cannot sufficiently describe the actions of women so there must be something else to the story, some other reason for their actions. So their acts are described as ones of 'personal despair' and their reasons are coined in terms of their personal stories of 'moral transgressions' needing redemption through a 'martyr's death.' Whereas male suicide bombers are explained in terms of a 'psychosis of martyrdom' given the 'humiliation of occupation' and the 'hopelessness of deeply stagnant societies,' female bombers are explained in terms of jilted love, and failed marriages (ibid.: 8).

Jacqueline Rose wonders why suicide bombers are seen as more irrational than other soldiers. Or why dying is a greater sin than living when you kill. She thinks that suicide bombing – which kills far fewer people than conventional warfare – is no less sane than killing in general. Rose also thinks that Victor is wrong about the women suicide bombers. Victor envelops them in their gender – they are simply scorned and rejected women, not Palestinians or politically passionate people or martyrs (Rose 2005).

Palestinian women are crucial to the armed resistance/intifada, which needed women to crush the Israeli army just as the Bush administration has needed women to help fill the ranks for the Iraq wars. At the same time patriarchal privilege is protected in these scenarios, especially as suicide bombers are depicted as irrational and pathological. In part this pathology is defined by fear of and aversion to death; but in part the gendered viewings of female irrationality feature significantly in these instances.

The Black Widows are suicide bombers in Chechnya. Some report that in order to make these girls choose death the Chechnyans rape them and videotape the rapes. Then they have nothing left to live for and have a reason to die. This explanation begins and ends with patriarchal gender: women are not viewed as political agents so they must be raped to force them to take such action, *and* rape is used as the narrative for domination. One is left to wonder why else a woman would choose to be a bomber. Rape once again denies women as actors in their own right, as agents of their own selves. But not all Black Widows are described as such. Another female bomber is described as cultured, and 'modern' (Meyers 2003: A6).

In Russia these women are also known as *shakhidki*, the feminine Russian variant for the Arabic word that means holy warriors who give their lives. They are seen as nihilistic and have taken part in at least fifteen different attacks since 1999. Although many were not Black Widows, nineteen of the forty-one captors who took part in the hostage siege of the Moscow Theater in October 2002 were women. A decade of war has created the new woman suicide bomber. And this is as much a part of a deep commitment to Islamic culture as it is to feminist democratic theory (Meyers 2004: A1).

A female suicide bomber was killed in Iraq for the first time in September 2005. She initially dressed as a woman, in traditional robes and veil, and was not searched at the checkpoint. After clearing this hurdle she switched to men's clothes and traveled to where she detonated the bomb, killing eight and injuring fifty-seven. The veils of gender – both as woman and man – are used to enable the making of war. Bodies are clearly not what they seem.

Literary critic Terry Eagleton writes that 'blowing yourself up for political reasons is a complex symbolic act, one that mixes despair and defiance.' It expresses the tension between living a life under occupation that has no self-determination and determining one's death. By becoming invulnerable suicide bombers taste a kind of freedom. Their only power is to die a devastating death that makes life appear 'monstrously unrecognizable' (Eagleton 2005: 5).

Once you are preoccupied with death and dying, martyrdom feels like a real choice. But people are not expected to think this way; especially not women. The female suicide bomber denies traditional gender essentialism; she denies hetero-normative gender in its usual construction.

Women's rights and the military police

The USA claims to free Iraqi and Afghan women in war; meanwhile women in the USA join the military. Many of these young women choose to join the Military Police Corps because its jobs in the field are open to women. Thirty-four of the 171 soldiers in the corps are women. These units often perform the same duties as all-male combat units. Many of the MP gunners are women. The jobs are dangerous. Private Tracie Sanchez, thirty years old, mother of four, had her face hit by fifteen pieces of shrapnel from a rocket-propelled grenade. She is a combat machine gunner in a kill zone. Her children are twelve, ten, seven, and four years old. She had a boring job after high school so she turned to the army. She has bad dreams, not because she froze in combat, but because she did not. She killed people and wishes that she hadn't (Lock 2003: D01). This is the new-old gender geography.

Specialist Danielle Green, a former college basketball star for Notre Dame, also a member of the military police, returned home after losing her left hand. She says she is disappointed in her tour of duty because she didn't do what she thought she would. She said that they did not rebuild neighborhoods or schools, but spent time doing too much of nothing. Given the way things have turned out, she now thinks the USA should not have gone to war: 'I thought we were going for humanitarian reasons' (Berkow 2004: A17). She too is another expression of new-old gender.

On the other hand Iraqi teenage girls find themselves with new restrictions and less freedom. They are not allowed out of their homes by themselves for fear of kidnapping and/or rape. Their lives too have been militarized: they live with little security, and if they are lucky enough to still have a semblance of family life, it is under strict surveillance from parents. One mother says, 'You have to keep your daughters in the house' (Sengupta 2004: A1). There is no easy call to make here. The limited changes in post-Saddam Iraq have not been sufficient to justify the turmoil and sadness.

Women and girls may lose a great deal depending on how the intra-Islamic conflict and imperial democratic forces play out. Imperial democracy does not look too good for women because women will be bartered once again. The USA has never truly stood with women's liberation abroad or at home. A militarized notion of women's rights is a far cry from women and girls' liberation. It is significant that Spain's prime minister, José Luis Rodriguez Zapatero, was elected on the promise that he would withdraw Spanish forces from Iraq. Shortly after his election he spoke out on behalf of women's rights, especially the right to abortion, and women constitute half of his ministers. Whether these females will be gender decoys in another form, or instigators of democracy, has yet to be seen.

Continuing onward

It is impossible to know in advance how sex and gender and their racialized formations will continue to shift and change. Present-day war politics necessitates opening the racialized and gendered configurations of this period to careful scrutiny.

Domestic violence and sexual rape are gendered constellations of a politics of war and terror. So are the new diverse gender expressions of women's lives in all colors. Without naming and seeing these new configurations of racial and sexual inequities, the resexing and gendering of war cannot be uncovered in its newest forms. Until then the bartering of democracy in the name of women's rights and freedom will continue to mask the destruction of democratic possibilities.

This *may* be a critical historical juncture where gender will be truly destabilized with the help of feminisms across the globe; *or* masculinist formulations of gender in defense of imperial democracy may hold sway but in more variegated forms. In just the past year there have been a series of firsts: women have been elected president in Chile, Germany, and Liberia; Cecelia Fire Thunder has been elected leader of the Oglala Sioux tribe; Tzipi Livni serves as the first Israeli foreign minister since Golda Meir; and six women were elected to the newly chosen Hamas parliament. The meanings of each of these happenings are not obvious. Some of these victories reflect enormous political struggle and achievement. Gender remains incredibly complex and confused amid these changes. On the one hand so much is changing ... and on the other it is not clear what exactly is changed.

So sex and gender and race can be used as decoys because their meanings can always be multiple and varied at the same time that they are ossified. Sex and gender, though distinct and multiple, are more often than not conflated as one. The variations of femaleness and femininity, and maleness and masculinity, stand counter to the homogeneity of heteronormative gender. This creates confusing, illegible, and unknowable readings and meanings (Najmabadi 2005). The illegibility and unreadable aspects of sex, gender, and race allow for their deceptive role today as occasional decoys for imperial and fascistic democracy. But gender cannot always or completely be deceiving or it would not work as a decoy. This furthers the difficulty of reading the meanings of sex and gender and race. This complex decoy process – of allure, deception, and entrapment – defines history and also takes on 'new-old' historical meanings.

At this juncture, as more and more females become heads of state, and with Hillary Clinton's ultimately unsuccessful attempt to win the presidency of the United States, much is at stake. Unless the complexities of sex, gender and racial formations are understood for their urgency, females can present a kinder and softer face to militaristic global capitalism. It is more urgent than ever that women's rights, along with their female bodies, are not used to obfuscate the moves toward fascistic democracy. Not in our name.

References

For a fuller accounting of the ideas in this article, please see Eisenstein (2007).

20/20 Productions (2004) *Winter Soldier*, PO Box 198, New Hampshire.

Abrams, Yvette (2005) 'Feminist identities and global struggles', Future of Minority Studies Conference, National Summer Institute, Cornell University, 1 August.

Alexievich, Svetlana (1990) *Zinky Boys, Soviet Voices from the Afghanistan War*, New York: Norton.

Allen, Beverly (1996) *Rape Warfare, the Hidden Genocide in Bosnia-Herzegovina and Croatia*, Minneapolis: University of Minnesota Press.

Baker, Kenn (2003) 'We're in the army now', *Harper's*, 307(1841).

Berkow, Ira (2004) 'A star athlete, a soldier, a challenge', *New York Times*, 3 June.

Boose, Lynda (1993) 'Techno muscularity and the "boy eternal"', in Amy Kaplan and Donald Pease (eds), *Cultures of US Imperialism*, Durham, NC: Duke University Press.

Bragg, Rick (2003) *I Am a Soldier Too, the Jessica Lynch Story*, New York: Knopf.

Burke, Carol (2004) 'Why they love to hate her', *The Nation*, 278(11), 22 March.

— (2006) 'One of the boys', *Women's Review of Books*, 23(2), March/April.

Campbell, D'Ann (1993) 'Women in combat', *Journal of Military History*, 57, April.

Cohn, Carol (1995) 'Wars, wimps and women: talking gender and thinking war', in Miriam Cooke and Angela Woollacott (eds), *Gendering War Talk*, Princeton, NJ: Princeton University Press.

Davey, Monica (2004) 'At Fort Riley soldiers just back from Iraq get basic training in resuming life', *New York Times*, 31 May.

Davis, Angela (2003) *Are Prisons Obsolete?*, New York: Seven Stories Press.

Defede, Jim (2004) 'Mining the matrix', *Mother Jones*, September/October.

Eagleton, Terry (2005) 'A different way of death', *Guardian*, 26 January.

Eisenstein, Zillah (1996) *Hatreds, Racialized and Sexualized Conflicts of the 21st Century*, New York: Routledge.

— (2007) *Sexual Decoys: Gender, Race, and War in Imperial Democracy*, London: Zed Books.

Enloe, Cynthia (1983) *Does Khaki Become You?*, Boston, MA: South End Press.

— (2000) *Maneuvers, the International Politics of Militarizing Women's Lives*, Berkeley: University of California Press.

Ensler, Eve (2005) 'The new paradigm: we hold within', in Media Benjamin and Jodie Evans (eds), *Stop the Next War Now*, San Francisco, CA: Inner Ocean Publishing.

Gettleman, Jeffrey (2004) 'US detains Iraqis, and families plead for news', *New York Times*, 7 March.

Hedges, Christopher (2002) *War Is a Force that Gives Us Meaning*, New York: Public Affairs.

Herdy, Amy and Miles Moffeit (2004) 'Camouflaging criminals, sexual violence against women in the military', *Amnesty International Report*, 30(1), Spring.

Higonnet, Margaret (2003) 'Not so quiet in no-woman's land', in Miriam Cooke and Angela Woollacott, *Gendering War Talk*, Princeton, NJ: Princeton University Press.

Hooper, Charlotte (2001) *Manly States, Masculinities, International Relations and Gender Politics*, New York: Columbia University Press.

Jeffords, Susan (1989) *The Remasculinization of America, Gender and the Vietnam War*, Bloomington: Indiana University Press.

Katzenstein, Mary (1998) *Faithful and Fearless, Moving Feminist Protest inside the Church and the Military*, Princeton, NJ: Princeton University Press.

Kolko, Gabriel (1994) *Century of War*, New York: New Press.

Lock, Vernon (2003) 'Combat heroine', *Washington Post*, 23 November.

Lutz, Catherine (2004) 'Living room terrorists', *Women's Review of Books*, xi(5), February.

McKay, Susan and Dyan Mazurana (2004) *Where Are the Girls?*, Montreal: Rights and Democracy.

Manchanda, Rita (2004) 'Maoist insurgency in Nepal: radicalizing gendered narratives', *Cultural Dynamics*, 16(2/3), October.

Manning, Lory (2004) 'Military women', *Women's Review of Books*, xi(5).

Masood, Salman (2004) 'Pakistani leader's comments on rape stir outrage', *New York Times*, 24 September.

Meyers, Steven (2003) 'Female suicide bombers unnerve Russians', *New York Times*, 24 May.

— (2004) 'From dismal Chechnya, women turn to bombs', *New York Times*, 10 September.

Moore, Brenda (2003) *Serving Our Country*, New Brunswick, NJ: Rutgers University Press.

Najmabadi, Afsaneh (2005) *Women with Mustaches and Men without Beards*, Berkeley: University of California Press.

Raynor, Richard (1997) 'Women in the warrior culture', *New York Times Magazine*, 22 June.

Rose, Jacqueline (2005) 'Deadly embrace', *London Review of Books*, 26.

Resexing militarism for the globe

Ruddick, Sara (1993) 'Notes toward a feminist peace politics', in Miriam Cooke and Angela Woollacott (eds), *Gendering War Talk*, Princeton, NJ: Princeton University Press.

Sallah, Michael and Mitch Weiss (2003), 'Buried secrets, brutal truths', *The Blade*, 12 May.

Schmitt, Eric (2004) 'Military women reporting rapes by US soldiers', *New York Times*, 22 June.

Sengupta, Somini (2004) 'For Iraqi girls, changing land narrows lives', *New York Times*, 27 June.

Stiglmayer, Alexandra (ed.) (1992) 'Mass rape', in *The War against Women in Bosnia-Herzegovina*, Lincoln: University of Nebraska.

Theweleit, Klaus (2003) 'The bombs, wombs and the genders of war', in Miriam Cooke and Angela Woollacott, *Gendering War Talk*, Princeton, NJ: Princeton University Press.

Thompson, Clive (2004) 'The making of a box warrior', *New York Times Magazine*, 23 August.

Victor, Barbara (2003) *Army of Roses, Inside the World of Palestinian Women Suicide Bombers*, New York: St Martin's Press.

Youngs, Gillian (2003) 'Private pain/public peace: women's rights as human rights and the Amnesty International Report on Violence against Women', *Signs*, 28(4), Summer.

3 | Feminists and queers in the service of empire

JASBIR PUAR

One mapping of the folding of homosexuals into the reproductive valorization of living – technologies of life – includes the contemporary emergence of 'sexually exceptional' US citizens, both heterosexual and otherwise, a formation I term 'US sexual exceptionalism.' Exceptionalism paradoxically signals distinction from (to be unlike, dissimilar) as well as excellence (eminence, superiority), suggesting a departure from and mastery of linear teleologies of progress. Exception refers both to particular discourses that repetitively produce the USA as an exceptional nation-state and Giorgio Agamben's theorization of the sanctioned and naturalized disregard of the limits of state juridical and political power through times of state crisis, a 'state of exception' that is used to justify the extreme measures of the state (Agamben 2005). This double play of exception speaks to Muslim and Sikh 'terrorist' corporealities as well as to homosexual patriots. The 'sexual torture scandal' at Abu Ghraib, the US military prison in Baghdad, is an instructive example of the interplay between exception and exceptionalism whereby the deferred death of one population recedes as the securitization and valorization of the life of another population triumphs in its shadow. This double deployment of exception and exceptionalism works to turn the negative valence of torture into the positive register of the valorization of (American) life; that is, torture in the name of the maximization and optimalization of life.

As the US nation-state produces narratives of exception through the war on terror, it must temporarily suspend its hetero-normative imagined community to consolidate national sentiment and consensus through the recognition and incorporation of some – though not all or most – homosexual subjects. The fantasy of the permanence of this suspension is what drives the production of exceptionalism, a narrative that is historically and politically wedded to the formation of the US nation-state. Thus, the exception and the exception*al* work in tandem; the state of exception haunts the proliferation of exceptional national subjects, in a similar vein to the Derridean hauntology in which the ghosts, the absent presences, infuse ontology with a difference (Derrida 1994).

Through the transnational production of terrorist corporealities, homosexual subjects who have limited legal rights within the US civil context gain significant representational currency when situated within the global scene of the war on terror. Taking the position that heterosexuality is a necessary constitutive factor of national identity, the 'outlaw' status of homosexual subjects in relation to the state has been a long-standing theoretical interest of feminist, post-colonial, and queer theorists. The outlaw status is mediated through the rise during the 1980s and 1990s of the gay consumer, pursued by marketers who claimed that childless homosexuals had enormous disposable incomes, as well as through legislative gains in civil rights, such as the widely celebrated 2003 overturning of sodomy laws rendered in the *Lawrence and Garner* v. *Texas* decision. By underscoring circuits of homosexual nationalism, I note that some homosexual subjects are complicit with heterosexual nationalist formations rather than inherently or automatically excluded from or opposed to them. Further, a more pernicious inhabitation of homosexual sexual exceptional/ism occurs through stagings of US nationalism via a praxis of sexual othering, one that exceptionalizes the identities of US homosexualities vis-à-vis orientalist constructions of 'Muslim sexuality.' This discourse functions through transnational displacements that suture spaces of cultural citizenship in the USA for homosexual subjects as they concurrently secure US nationalist interests globally. In some instances these narratives are explicit, as in the aftermath of the release of the 'Abu Ghraib photos,' where the claims to exceptionalism resonated on many planes for US citizen-subjects: morally, sexually, culturally, 'patriotically.' This imbrication of American exceptionalism is increasingly marked through or aided by certain homosexual bodies, a formation I term homonationalism, short for homo-normative nationalism.

What is nascent is not the notion of exceptionalism, nor of a gender exceptionalism that has predominated the history of Western feminist theoretical production and activism. Current forms of exceptionalism work or are furthered by attaching themselves to, or being attached by, non-heterosexual, 'homo-normative' subjects. Exceptionalism is used not to mark a break with historical trajectories or a claim about the emergence of singular newness. Rather, exceptionalism gestures to narratives of excellence, excellent nationalism, a process whereby a national population comes to believe its own superiority and its own singularity, 'stuck,' as Sara Ahmed would say, to various subjects (Ahmed 2004: 117–39). Discourses of American exceptionalism are embedded in the history of US nation-state formation, from early immigration narratives to cold war ideologies to the rise of the age of terrorism. These narratives about the centrality of exceptionalism to the formation of the USA imply that indoctrination à la exceptionalism is part of the disciplining of the American citizen (as it may be in any nationalist foundation). Debates about American exceptionalism have typically mobilized criteria as far-ranging as artistic expression, aesthetic production (literary and cultural), social and political life, immigration history, liberal democracy, and industrialization and patterns of capitalism, among others (Zinn 2005). Discussions of American exceptionalism rarely take up, however, issues of gender and sexuality. While for the last forty years scholars have been interrogating feminist practices and theorizations that explicitly or implicitly foster the consolidation of US nationalism in its wake, a growing cohort is now examining queer practices and theorizations for similar tendencies. Forms of US gender and (hetero)sexual exceptionalism from purportedly progressive spaces have surfaced through feminist constructions of 'other' women, especially via the composite of the 'Third World Woman' (Mohanty 1988: 61–88). Inderpal Grewal (2005: 150), for example, argues against the naturalization of human rights frames by feminists, noting that the USA routinely positions itself 'as the site for authoritative condemnation' of human rights abuses elsewhere, ignoring such abuses within the USA. Grewal alludes to the American exceptionalism that is now requisite 'common sense' for many feminisms within US public cultures: 'moral superiority has become part of emergent global feminism, constructing American women as saviors and rescuers of the "oppressed women."' The recent taking up of the 'case' of Afghani and Iraqi women and 'Muslim women' in general by Western feminists has generated many forms of US gender exceptionalism. Gender exceptionalism works as a missionary discourse to 'rescue' Muslim women from their oppressive male counterparts. It also works to suggest that in contrast to women in the USA, Muslim women are, at the end of the day, unsavable. More insidiously, these discourses of exceptionalism allude to the unsalvageable nature of Muslim women even by their own feminists, positioning the 'American' feminist as the feminist subject par excellence (Manji 2005).

One pertinent example is culled from the interactions of the Revolutionary Association of the Women of Afghanistan (RAWA) with the Feminist Majority Foundation, which ended with an accusation of appropriation and erasure of RAWA's efforts by the Foundation. A letter written on 20 April 2002 condemns the Foundation's representation of its handiwork as having 'a foremost role in "freeing" Afghan women' while failing to mention RAWA's twenty-five-year presence in Afghanistan (indeed, failing to mention RAWA at all), as if they had 'single-handedly freed the women of Afghanistan from an oppression that started and ended with the Taliban' (Miller 2002). Calling the Feminist Majority Foundation 'hegemonic, US-centric, ego driven, corporate feminism,' RAWA notes that it has 'a longer history than the Feminist Majority can claim' and cites multiple instances of its erasure of RAWA's political organizing. RAWA also berates the Feminist Majority for their omission of the abuses toward women undertaken by the Northern Alliance, atrocities that at times were more egregious than those committed by the Taliban, stating that 'the Feminist Majority, in their push for US political and economic power, are being careful not to anger the political powers in the US ...' (ibid.).

In the ranks of 'hegemonic US-centric' feminists concerned with the plight of Afghan women under the Taliban rule, the Feminist Majority Foundation had launched 'Our Campaign to Stop Gender Apartheid in Afghanistan' in 1996 (Smeal 2001: 66). This campaign arguably led to commodity fetishes such as US performance artist Eve Ensler's V-Day benefit with her 'tribute to Afghan women,' a monologue entitled 'Under the burqa' performed by US talk show host and media star Oprah Winfrey, at New York City's largest arena, Madison Square Garden, to a sold-out audience in February 2001 (Ensler 2001). The event also promoted the purchase, in remembrance of Afghan women, of a 'burqa swatch,' meant to be worn on one's lapel as a brooch to demonstrate solidarity with Afghan women through the appropriation of a 'Muslim' garment. While these forms of celebrity feminism might provide us with momentary sardonic amusement, they are an integral part of US feminist public cultures and should not be mistaken as trivial. Their agendas are quite conducive to that of 'serious' liberal feminists in the USA, such as those within the ranks of the Feminist Majority, and in the age of professionalized feminism these purportedly divergent circuits divulge their imbrication through various modes of commodification. These US feminists, having already foregrounded Islamic fundamentalism as the single greatest violent threat to women, were perfectly poised to capitalize on the missionary discourses that reverberated after the events of September 11. Despite their active stance against the invasion of Afghanistan, they were caught in a complicitous narrative of US exceptionalism with regard to the removal of the Taliban (Lerner 2001: 53–5). As Drucilla Cornell notes, the silence of the Feminist Majority Foundation at the replacement of the Taliban by the Northern Alliance 'forces us to question whether the humanitarian-intervention discourse of the US government was not a particularly cynical effort to enlist US feminists in an attempt to circumscribe the definition of what constitutes human rights violations – to turn the Feminist Majority into an ideological prop that delegitimizes the political need for redressing human-rights violations' (Bumiller 2001: 314–15). Cornell basically infers that mainstream US feminists traded RAWA's stance against punitive state laws penalizing women who refuse to wear the burqa (but not a stance against women wearing burqas, an important distinction) for the celebratory media spectacle of unveiling rampant in the US media after the 'successful' invasion of Afghanistan (ibid.: 2). 'Under the burqa,' indeed. But as a final comment, it is worth heeding Gayatri Chakravorty Spivak's observation that 'we will see, every time, the narrative of class mobility.' Complicating any indigenous positioning of RAWA, she writes: 'It is the emergence of [the] middle class that creates the possibility for the kind of feminist struggle that gives us a RAWA. And this middle class, the agent of human rights all over the world, is altogether distanced from the subaltern classes in "their own culture," epistemically' (Spivak 2004: 89). Despite RAWA's feud with the Feminist Majority, invariably they remain complicit with a displacement of other Afghan women's organizations that cannot so easily enter the global feminist stage.

With the USA currently positioning itself as the technologically exceptional global counter-terrorism expert, American exceptionalism feeds off other exceptionalisms, particularly that of Israel, its close ally in the Middle East. The exceptional national security issues of Israel, and the long-term 'existential' threat it faces because of its sense of being 'entangled in a conflict of unparalleled dimensions,' for example, proceeds thusly: 'exceptional vulnerability' results in 'exceptional security needs,' the risks of which are then alleviated and purportedly conquered by 'exceptional counterterrorism technologies' (Merom 1999: 413, 414). In this collusion of American and Israeli state interests, defined through a joint oppositional posture toward Muslims, narratives of victimhood ironically suture rather than deflate, contradict or nullify claims to exceptionalism. In other words, the Israeli nation-state finds itself continuously embroiled in a cycle of perceived exceptional threats of violence that demand exceptional uses of force against the Palestinian population, which is currently mirrored by US governmental officials' public declarations of possible terror risks that are used to compel US citizens to support the war on terror.

Reflecting upon contemporary debates about the USA as empire, Amy Kaplan notes that 'the idea of empire has always paradoxically entailed a sense of spatial and temporal limits, a narrative of rising and falling, which US exceptionalism has long kept at bay' (Kaplan 2004: 3). Later, she states that 'the denial and disavowal of empire has long served as the ideological cornerstone of US imperialism and a key component of

51

American exceptionalism' (ibid.: 3). Thus, for Kaplan, the distancing of exceptionalism from empire achieves somewhat contradictory twofold results: the superior USA is not subject to empire's shortcomings – the apparatus of empire is unstable; ultimately empires fall; and the USA creates the impression that empire is beyond the pale of its own morally upright behavior, such that all violences of the US state are seen, in some moral, cultural, or political fashion, as anything but the violence of empire. US exceptionalism hangs on a narrative of transcendence which places the USA 'above' empire in these two respects, a project that is aided by what Domenico Losurdo (2004) names 'the fundamental tendency to transform the Judeo-Christian tradition into a sort of national religion that consecrates the exceptionalism of American people and the sacred mission with which they are entrusted ("Manifest Destiny").' Kaplan, claiming that current narratives of empire 'take American exceptionalism to new heights,' argues that a concurrent 'paradoxical claim to uniqueness and universality' is coterminous in that 'they share a teleological narrative of inevitability' that posits America as the arbiter of appropriate ethics, human rights, and democratic behavior while exempting itself without hesitation from such universalizing mandates (Kaplan 2004: 5–6).

Whether or not one agrees that American exceptionalism has attained 'new heights,' Kaplan's analysis perfectly illustrates the intractability of state-of-exception discourses from those of exceptionalism. Laying claim to 'uniqueness' (exception = singularity) and 'universality' (exceptional = bequeathing teleological narrative) is not quite as paradoxical as Kaplan insists, for the state of exception is deemed necessary in order to restore, protect and maintain the status quo, the normative ordering that then allows the USA to hail its purported universality. The indispensability of the USA is thus sutured through the naturalized conjunction of singularity and *telos*, the paradox withered away (Agamben 2005: 21). State-of-exception discourses rationalize egregious violence in the name of the preservation of a way of life and those privileged to live it. Giorgio Agamben, noting that biopolitics continually seeks to redefine the boundaries between life and death, writes that 'the state of exception is neither external nor internal to the juridical order, and the problem of defining it concerns precisely a threshold, or a zone of indifference, where inside and outside do not exclude each other but rather blur with each other' (ibid.: 23). The temporality of exception is one that seeks to conceal itself; the frenzied mode of emergency is an alibi for the quiet certitude of a slowly normativized working paradigm of liberal democratic government, an alibi necessary to disavow its linkages to totalitarian governments. The state of exception, thus, works to hide or even deny itself in order to further its expanse, its presence and efficacy, surfacing only momentarily and with enough gumption to further legitimize the occupation of more terrain. Agamben (ibid.: 37) likens the externally internal space of the state of exception to a Möbius strip: at the moment it is cast outside, it becomes the inside. In the state of exception, the exception insidiously becomes the rule, and the exceptional normalized as a regulatory ideal or frame; the exceptional at once embodies the excellence that exceeds the parameters of proper subjecthood and, by doing so, redefines these parameters to then normativize and render invisible (yet transparent) its own excellence or singularity.

Sexual exceptionalism also works by glossing over its own policing of the boundaries of acceptable gender, racial, and class formations. That is, homosexual sexual exceptionalism does not necessarily contradict or undermine heterosexual sexual exceptionalism; in actuality it may support forms of hetero-normativity and the class, racial, and citizenship privileges they require. My book *Terrorist Assemblages: Homonationalism in Queer Times* (Duke 2007) tracks the historical and contemporaneous production of an emergent normativity, homo-normativity, which ties the recognition of homosexual subjects, both legally and representation-ally, to the national and transnational political agendas of US impe-rialism. Homo-normativity can be read as a formation complicit with and invited into the biopolitical valorization of life in its inhabitation and reproduction of hetero-normative norms. One prime mechanism of sexual exceptionalism is mobilized by discourses of sexual 'repression' – a contemporary version of Foucault's repressive hypothesis – that are generative of a bio- and geopolitical global mapping of 'sexual cultural norms.' Unraveling discourses of US sexual exceptionalism is vital both to critiques of US practices of empire (most of which only intermittently take up questions of gender and rarely sexuality) and to the expansion of queerness beyond narrowly conceptualized frames that foreground sexual identity and sexual acts.

Given that our contemporary political climate of US nationalism relies so heavily on homophobic demonization of sexual others, the argument that homosexuality is included within and contributes positively to the optimalization of life is perhaps a seemingly counter-intuitive argument. Nonetheless, it is imperative that we continue to read the racial, gen-der, class and national dimensions of these vilifying mechanisms. So I proceed with two caveats: first, to aver that some/certain homosexual bodies signify homo-normative nationalism – homonationalism – is in no way intended to deny, diminish, or disavow the daily violences of discrimination, physical and sexual assault, familial ostracism, economic disadvantage, and lack of social and legal legitimacy that sexual others must regularly endure: in short, most queers, whether as subjects or populations, still hover amid regimes of deferred or outright death. What I work through are the manifold trajectories of racialization and un-nationalization of sexual others that foster the conditions of possibility for such violent relegation to death. The spectral resistances to gay marriage, gay adoptive and parental rights, the 'Don't Ask Don't Tell' policies of the US military – which requires that any member who discloses her/his 'homosexuality' be discharged from the service – and the privatization of sexuality entail that the protection of life granted through national belonging is a precarious invitation at best. Second, there is no organic unity or cohesion among homonationalisms – these are partial, fragmentary, uneven formations, implicated in the pendular momentum of inclusion and exclusion, some dissipating as quickly as they appear. Thus, the cost of being folded into life might be quite steep, both for the subjects who are interpellated by or aspire to the tight inclusiveness of homo-normativity offered in this moment, and the others who decline or are declined entry owing to the undesirability of their race, ethnicity, religion, class, national origin, age, or bodily ability. It also may be the case, as Barry D. Adams argues, that the USA is exceptional only to the degree to which, globally speaking, it is *un*exceptional, another angle that stresses the contingency of any welcome of queer life (Adam 2003: 259–76). In terms of legal recognition of gay and lesbian relationships, Adam notes the irony that to some extent the USA 'lags' behind most European countries as well as Canada, Brazil, Colombia, New Zealand, Australia, and South Africa, a 'backwardness' that the USA often ascribes to others in comparison to itself (ibid.: 259). We can also say that the USA has investments in being exceptionally hetero-normative even as it claims to be exceptionally 'tolerant' of (homosexual) difference. But Adam's reliance on lag reinscribes a troubling teleology of modernity that, despite situating exceptionalism as a narrative that masks or fuzzes over regional differences, impels like-minded countries in a unilateral itinerary rather than multidirectional flows. Some efforts to determine whether the USA is indeed exceptional – efforts that have dominated various debates in history, American studies, and political science, among other fields – have focused on comparative empirical studies that do little to challenge or even question this *telos* (Kammen 1993: 1–43). With the range of discussion of American exceptionalism in mind, my intent here is not to determine whether the USA is indeed exceptional – exceptionally good or ahead, or exceptionally behind or different – but to illustrate the modes through which such claims to exceptionalism are loaded with unexamined discourses about race, sexuality, gender and class. Furthermore, exceptionalisms rely and depend on the erasure of these very modalities in order to function; these elisions are, in effect, the ammunition with which the exception – necessary to guard the properties of life – becomes the norm, and the exceptional – the subjects upon whom this task is bestowed – becomes the normal.

References

Adam, Barry (2003) 'The Defense of Marriage Act and American exceptionalism', *Journal of the History of Sexuality*, vol. 12, pt II.

Agamben, Giorgio (2005) *The State of Exception*, Chicago, IL: University of Chicago Press.

Ahmed, Sara (2004) 'Affective economies', in *Social Text*, Durham, NC: Duke University Press.

Bumiller, Elizabeth (2001) 'First Lady to speak about Afghan women', *New York Times*, Section B, 16 November.

Derrida, Jacques (1994) *Specters of Marx*, New York: Routledge.

Ensler, Eve (2001) 'Tribute to Afghan women is a sold out success at Madison Square Garden', Feminist Majority Foundation, *Feminist Daily News Wire*, 12 February.

Grewal, Inderpal (2005) *Transnational America*, Durham, NC: Duke University Press.

Kammen, Michael (1993) 'The problem of American exceptionalism', *American Quarterly*, March.

Kaplan, Amy (2004) 'Violent belongings and the question of empire today', *American Quarterly*, 56(1), March.

Lerner, Sharon (2001) 'What women want: feminists agonize over war in Afghanistan', *Village Voice*, 6 November.

Losurdo, Domenico (2004) 'Preemptive war, Americanism, and anti-Americanism', *Metaphilosophy*, 34(3), April.

Manji, Irshad (2005) 'America's Wild West', *Los Angeles Times*, 1 May.

Merom, Gil (1999) 'Israel's national security and the myth of exceptionalism', *Political Science Quarterly*, 114(3).

Miller, Elizabeth (2002) 'An open letter to the editors of *Ms* magazine', Pittsburgh State University, International Studies Program, Middle Eastern Affairs Conference, 20 April.

Mohanty, Chandra (1988) 'Under Western eyes', *Feminist Review*.

Smeal, Eleanor (2001) 'Special message from the Feminist Majority on the Taliban, Osama bin Laden and Afghan women', Feminist Majority Foundation, *Feminist Daily News*, 18 September.

— (2002) 'Feminist Majority Foundation', *Ms*, 12(2), Spring.

Spivak, Gayatri C. (2004) 'Globalicities: terror and its consequences', *New Centennial Review*, 4.

Zinn, Howard (2005) 'The power and the glory', *Boston Review*, Summer.

4 | Interrogating Americana: an African feminist critique

PATRICIA MCFADDEN

It has never been a secret in the feminist community anywhere that war is the most powerful instinct of patriarchal state and individual power. Men everywhere have ruled through the deployment of impunity and the glorification of plunder in the public spheres of life as well as in the intimate and private domains of the heterosexual family/home. The excessive accumulation of wealth and its flouting to express privilege and strength have gone hand in hand with the now familiar and well-understood practices of violation and supremacy.

This is a fundamental assertion that I do not think any feminist, anywhere, would deny. What is more open to scrutiny and contestation, however, are the ways in which feminists approach the phenomenon of war and its effects and implications for a particular space – such as the USA – and/or for the wider human community. Where and when war enters (Giddings 1985) into our discourses and lives determines the manner in which we understand its functions within the state, and how we represent, interact with or 'overlook' those who are othered in our societies during such times.

For me as an African feminist temporarily located in the United States, the glaring absence of a discussion of war as it is waged by the US state within the imperial arena – that is, beyond expressions of a national anxiety about how the world now perceives or receives US citizens – as well as the inevitability of deaths among armed US citizens in other people's countries – is of particular interest and concern. Related to this global issue is a more parochial interest in the ways in which a particular brand of bourgeois democracy and consumer privilege are experienced in the United States of America, and how this affects and contours the idea and experience of citizenship and personal identity for all who embrace the identity of being 'American.' These very peculiar features of US society are historically and intimately woven into the plunder of Southern societies, and of Africa in particular, and thus pose an unavoidable challenge to all feminists, but particularly to feminists of color in the so-called South, whose communities are at greater risk of devastation by US jingoism. The history of US state military and ideological rampancy across the societies of Asia, Latin America, the Pacific and, not least of all, Africa screams at us from every corner of our lives.

Having thus prefaced my intervention let me hasten to add that this is not an accusatory text. It could not be, given the commonalities that feminists share as women struggling for justice and dignity. I have given myself license to pose several questions, however, and to make certain observations, which I have no doubt will be received in the spirit of a feminist solidarity in which they are offered. These are particularly trying times for all progressives in US society, and for feminists this moment presents largely still unimagined opportunities and uncertain risks. I hope that my intervention will help to strengthen feminist solidarity and facilitate new and more transformative ways of understanding and contesting the state.

Feminist critique and the US imperial state

Let me begin by saying that I am particularly uneasy about what I have perceived to be an uncritical acceptance of the claim that because the USA has been in the making as an imperial power over the past fifty years (since the end of the Second Imperialist War in 1945) this moment of unbridled US jingoism therefore represents the culmination of this desired global status. This is a claim that is directly and indirectly made by the neoconservative right wing within the US academy as well as in the mass media. From the pantheon of *New York Times* editorials and op-ed pieces over the past four years (at a stretch one could even shift these claims back to the end of the 1980s when the Soviet Union was finally brought down through mainly US machinations), to what is sometimes merely a glimmer of conformity that can be sensed beneath the premises of most feminist analysis about the globalization of militarism and war, the assumption that the US state has become an imperial state is reiterated by the kinds of analyses that position issues of war as if imperial hegemony has become a given in the reality of the world (Schell 2006; Younge 2007; Boron 2005; Amin 2006).

Of greater concern, however, is that this kind of presumption accepts US hegemony as a fact that overwhelms the resistance and agency of peoples beyond the borders of US society, and which, maybe inadvertently, reaffirms notions and experiences of Americana that are founded on a bellicosity and belligerence that is in complete contradiction to the values and dynamics of feminism as an ideology and identity of resistance and transformation. The acceptance of such claims at their face value can lead one to a crediting of this state with an imperial identity that is still in the making, in my opinion, but also such claims reinforce a subjectivity about the state which is reflective of the conflation of individual and social identities into the current character of a state. The spouting of a jingoistic rhetoric of imperial hegemony and prancing about on the global stage as a unilateral power are different from actually being in control of territories and peoples outside your borders in a manner that is concomitant with, let alone equivalent to, imperial power.

Most significantly, such attitudes that reify the state easily translate into the construction and representation of those whom a state is brutalizing and attempting to occupy as passive and 'victim' – waiting to be rescued and redeemed. The politics of rescue lies at the heart of imperial intention and has facilitated the occupation and subjugation of peoples of the South, in particular, for hundreds of years (Narayan 1997). While critical analyses in this regard have emerged through the work of radical political economists like Samir Amin, Atilio Boron, and Jonathan Schell, we nonetheless need to pay closer attention to the manner in which national identity blunts the edge of our critical perspectives, leaving us unable to avoid the slippery slopes and pitfalls of a viscerally embedded experience of nationalism and devoted loyalty (Hedges 2003). In this vein, within the feminist academy, the work of scholars like Zillah Eisenstein, Cynthia Enloe and Angela Davis has led the way in alerting us to the inextricably intimate ties between militarism (as an ideology and a practice of plunder and oppression) and the hegemonic assertion of patriarchal power over the lives of women and their communities/societies globally (Eisenstein and Enloe 2004; Davis 1993).

An analysis that does not begin by establishing a distance between the scholar/activist and the state and hegemonic notions of who the citizen is invariably falls into the trap of conflating the individual into the identity of the state. I am referring to the 'we' that US citizens of various social and ethnic backgrounds so casually use in reference to the prosecution of war (in Iraq and Afghanistan at the present time) and the embrace of a sanctimonious ideal that accompanies the US foreign policy practice of 'regime change' – which aims at supposedly re-establishing the values of humanism and 'democracy' in societies that are being systematically destroyed by this fascistic state.

Establishing the conceptual distance creates the necessary consciousness to resist warmongering without interpolating oneself into the identity and machinations of the state. It is a difficult but necessary shift that needs to happen among feminists who are faced with states that skillfully use the rhetoric of liberal democracy to blunt the edge of a critical consciousness among individuals and communities in the North.

Therefore, I would like to sound a word of caution about the general presumption that the US state and US society are now an imperial political and military formation, and to suggest that US feminists consider the theoretical and activist implication of such a stance. From my privileged purview as an *'outsider'* it is obvious that this assumption has already begun to color (or delete) the existence of communities outside the world of the North.

When *making war* is approached as if it were a strange and peculiar aberration on the part of a state, particularly a state that has long desired to become imperial – having been left behind, so to speak, when the rest of the white world ventured forth and became *'civilized'* through military plunder and nefarious escapades of primitive accumulation in what is today called the South – it is easy to miss the fact that warmongering by present-day Western states was and remains fundamentally bolstered by the discourses and practices of enslavement, racism, classism, and gendered supremacy regarding societies that are 'not white' and/or are located predominantly in the Southern hemisphere (Ahmad 2000).

Such warmongering and jingoistic discourses are usually dressed in the garb of 'international relations and diplomacy,' until the moment when it becomes obvious that the USA or other Western nations are encountering resistance to their presumed hegemony as the guardians and purveyors of 'democracy,' liberalism, 'Westernism' and so-called European modernity. Then the overt recourse to guns and bombs is 'triggered' – almost as a knee-jerk reaction to the perceived insubordination and ungratefulness of 'the natives.' The collusion with Saddam Hussein and his manipulation by the USA and European states against Iran in the 1970–80s, culminating in his later abandonment and execution by the present-day Iraqi 'war courts,' speaks volumes about the practice of international relations as simply a pretext for war and plunder when the moment of convenience presents itself to the regimes of the 'civilized' West.

This anxiety about war as aberrant and discordant with a set of values that have become the national markers of a people, values and claims of decency and humanism that are central to the notion of 'Americana,' resonates with the emphasis that scholars and activists put on themes and concerns that are essentially insular and deeply problematical. For feminism, this translates into several deeply problematical gaps at the theoretical and activist levels.

The critical imperative remains therefore one of ensuring that radical sites are established and sustained, with debates and reflection concerning the inherently destructive character of war as the engine of patriarchal, capitalist state power and repression in all our societies. Each community of feminists should endeavor to bring to such discursive moments the

59

particular political insights and agencies that shape and motivate resistance to patriarchy, especially as it is performed through war and impunity.
Raising the alarm about the tendency toward parochialism and exclusion
of 'the other' in US feminist analyses of war is my personal contribution
to the crafting of a more radical understanding of this phenomenon
and its implications and consequences for women everywhere. This is
particularly the case in those societies that have been the 'backbone' of
US economic and social privilege.

One of the distinctive features of feminism as a political stance is
its ability to be inclusive and transformational, and war as a 'normative
expression of capitalist globalization' requires that we draw upon the
particular strengths of feminist analysis to avoid exclusionary and partial
representations of the people whose lives are devastated by imperial terror. For US feminisms, the ability to see the world beyond the parochial,
white nationalistic anxieties that inform daily life with such persistence
and repetition, pushing the boundaries of our understanding of war is
crucial in the crafting of an alternative ideology – so as to change the
ways in which US communities exist in relation to the rest of the world,
today and into the future.

Over several hundred years, the US and European societies have crafted
a rhetorical and ideological discourse that is vital to the very nature of
these societies as white-dominated, relatively privileged socio-political
spaces. At the heart of their success is the deployment of militarism and
the practice of war, a strategy that involves all classes and ethnicities
in collusion with the state and its key institutions. For the Europeans,
colonialism would not have been possible without the involvement of
religious institutions and the articulation of redemptive ideas through
Christianity. The working classes of Europe were convinced of the idea
and practice of colonialism and imperial domination of Africans, Indians,
and the indigenous peoples of South America, the Pacific, etc., and were
actively recruited into (and often volunteered for) the service of the ruling
classes on these continents, via the promise of the material and social
benefits that colonialism bestowed, albeit differentially based upon social
class and proximity to the colonial state. And while there were certain
groups and individuals that demonstrated and argued against colonization late into the colonial period, the bulk of Europeans understood
that a new and privileged identity was emerging for them in relation to
the rest of the world, and that it was directly linked to the successful
execution of colonial suppression and the extraction of wealth from the
societies of the South (Said 1994).

Therefore, the mobilization and application of war as a tool of repression and colonial rule are distinctive features of all capitalist states, and are really universal phenomena that must be carefully understood in a historical and material context. In the current context, war is no longer only an exercise in bloodletting between large numbers of militarized individuals (soldiers) whose loyalties have been institutionalized on behalf of a national cause that must be 'defended.' No doubt the ruthless massacring of civilians and the creation of mayhem and chaos in societies of *'the other'* remains a distinctive feature of this practice of 'politics by other means.' War has also become, however, a more sophisticated, rapidly mutating, profit-maximizing opportunity – a highly corporatized, globalizing enterprise, controlled by a small group of fanatically driven, fundamentalist right-wing white males, based mainly in the societies of the West, and the soldier is being systematically replaced by mercenaries whose only loyalty is to big capital represented quintessentially by the 'mighty dollar' (Scahill 2007; Bryce 2007; Parenti 2007).

The history of US society reflects these historical and current trends most dramatically. War has always been the motive force of this society's history and identity. War against the indigenous peoples who inhabited this land; war against African communities and against the individual (through enslavement) which persists to this day; war against 'the other' as an expression of the ideal of a racist notion and practice of *'Pax Americana'*; and more recently war as imperial desire and destiny. In fact, this society can truly be described as having been founded on the most brutal expressions of impunity and supremacy ever imagined. The genocide of the indigenous people who had inhabited this subcontinent for thousands of years before the arrival of the primitive European 'settler,' and the wanton enslavement of tens of millions of African people over several centuries, leave me convinced that there is nothing 'abnormal' about the rampancy of US imperial intention at the present time.

US society has remained a fundamentally violent and intolerant social formation, whose rulers clearly understand the significance of imperial practice for the maintenance of white supremacist privilege and power. And too many American citizens have bought into the justification that war is necessary for the maintenance of their social order, even if their access to the glory of Americana is limited simply to the claim that they are 'Americans.' The power of national identity, especially when it is associated with perceived or real expressions of privilege, is in my opinion something that feminists in the USA (and Europe) will have to contend with in order to shift the discourse on war and imperialism.

I do not think that it is possible to 'overlook' the historical and current linkages between what people have come to consider 'a way of life'

– however that is experienced by different groups of people in Northern societies – and the powerful illusion that one can express solidarity and concern with people who are murdered and brutalized by a supremacist state, and still be an American above and beyond whatever else the state does, particularly outside the borders of that society. Something will have to give, and here I would like to turn briefly to what I see as a deficiency in the current analysis of war by US feminists and the unproblematical acceptance of the identity of being American (Salime 2007).

Africa, the politics of 'rescue,' and US feminisms

Invariably, I turn to Africa, as an African feminist. Generally, in the US and European academies, Africans are treated in ways that reproduce the colonial, racist representations of a people who are helpless and inept; victims of brutal and corrupt states whose leaders are constructed as either 'well behaved' or demonic. Those of us who study Africa and the numerous societies of the South know that such representations reflect the othering of people whose societies have been systematically plundered and repressed through well-entrenched systems of economic exploitation, political manipulation and racist media practices that go hand in hand with the unscrupulous, predatory activities of global corporate enterprises that are protected by Western states, through military intervention and/or through so-called diplomatic intervention. Ruling classes have the same interests and engage in the same repressive practices everywhere.

What is of particular interest to me, however, as a feminist who is engaged in the analysis of 'war as statecraft,' is the fact that the US state has been especially vicious in its operations within Africa since the period of nationalist independence in the 1960s. Central to the US strategy of warmongering in Africa has been the strategy of creating and using 'proxy armies' – bandits who rampage across the landscapes of our worlds, specifically countries considered 'essential to US or European strategic interests'; thugs who are trained, funded and protected by the USA in particular, within the global arena. In this regard, US presidents Ronald Reagan and Bill Clinton were kindred spirits in the furtherance of an imperial project that exposed the myth of 'difference' between them and their respective political parties, and the claim that this society engages in a diverse and pluralistic politics (Martin 2001).

Across the African continent, the USA has systematically installed brutally repressive regimes, paying scant attention to the consequences of such fascistic intervention, and in many instances has laid the ground for the proliferation of wars in numerous countries which have resulted in the deaths of tens of millions of Africans, mainly women, older people and children. Countries like the Democratic Republic of the Congo (DRC), Angola, Chad, Sudan, Sierra Leone, Liberia, and Mozambique represent the most vicious expressions of US imperial impunity, and their people have been subjected to and continue to suffer unimaginable atrocities and deprivations. Angola and the DRC (formerly Zaire) are both countries with exceptional wealth in mineral and oil resources, biodiversity and other forms of natural wealth. Yet they feature at the bottom of the list of the poorest countries in the world. Three decades of carnage and imperialistic machination, carried out through the brutal acts of bandits and mercenaries, have achieved the goals of US corporations and the US state in terms of destroying and destabilizing these and many other societies, leaving their wealth readily accessible to the elites of the USA and Europe, while the Africans are vilified as 'hopeless, corrupt and barbaric' (Elich 2006).

For the DRC, it all began when, in 1961, the CIA installed Mobutu, a low-level military official, after it had engineered a coup, and assassinated and incinerated the body of the democratically elected leader of Zaire – Patrice Lumumba. Mobutu was a well-behaved native – he opened up the country's resources to US, Belgian and Canadian multinationals, which proceeded to engage in the most astounding acts of plunder of that country's wealth for over forty years. By the time he had become useless to the West in the 1990s, the country was a wreck and the people had been remobilized under sectarian ethnic identities, devastated and torn apart by war (Nzongola-Ntalaja 2002; Baregu 1999; DeWitte 2001; Hochschild 1999; Mandaza 1999).

Bandits under the patronage of various European states have been waging a war of attrition and incalculable destruction on the working people of that country until very recently, and millions of Congolese women, children, elderly and youth have been traumatized, brutalized, raped and murdered. According to Cecile Pouilly (2007), writing in the UNHCR magazine *REFUGEES*, 'The statistics are numbing: over 12,000 reported rapes in eastern DRC alone in the six months up to October 2006; as many as 3.4 million internally displaced people (IDPs) at the peak in 2003; around 4 million deaths attributed directly or indirectly to the 1998–2003 war, and one in five children dead before the age of five.'

At the core of this so-called civil war (a crucial point that none of the UN or US media actually ever spells out) is the question of which state/corporation will continue to control and exploit the immense resources of the DRC. The eastern DRC is an especially critical area for the extraction of the rare minerals that the US and European armies (and societies) need for their sophisticated military industries, and for the provision of what have become considered essential accessories of a modern lifestyle in the West. The cellphone is one such item – dependent upon the mining of coltan, a rare mineral found only in the Democratic Republic of the Congo and controlled by a handful of European mining companies, whose compounds are guarded mainly by white former South African military elements, now mercenaries (also in Iraq and in various other war zones). Side by side with the extraction of rare minerals are the mobilization and fomentation of internecine wars, which have claimed the lives of over five million Africans – mostly women and children – across the heart of the continent.

When I listen even to the supposedly progressive US radio stations like National Public Radio, however, let alone the mainstream media, I hardly if ever hear an analysis of US involvement in the destruction of governments that were on the side of the working people of Africa. What one gets, which has permeated even to certain schools of feminist analysis of violation and war in Africa, is a repetition of the same old stupid racist stereotypes, the lies and the persistent representation of African women in particular as victims of state and male violence. Apparently, it is easier to present African women as helpless and in need of rescue. It takes more courage to actually step back from the normalized racism about Africans, and imagine an even greater sense of solidarity and self-introspection – so as to contextualize the African state as a politico-military and economic collusionary relationship between African and Western ruling classes that share many common interests.

US feminists have to look for information about the politics and practices of the state in Africa and integrate that knowledge into the ongoing analysis of war and imperial pursuit. Referring to Rwanda and Sierra Leone anecdotally or proclaiming the election of a woman in Liberia as a great achievement are only perfunctory exercises. The recontextualization of US feminism in relation to the jingoism and destruction of societies outside US borders will be more useful to the global feminist movement as well, and it will stimulate the emergence of a different kind of feminist analysis; one that breaks with the demands made upon individual feminists and progressive communities that they not question the essentials of what makes US society 'American.'

Such a stance will also stimulate a more critical assessment and consideration of the ways in which militarization has seeped into the consciousness of US citizens (not only in the blatant ways in which it socially and economically coerces Africans and Latino/a Americans to rely upon that institution for access to the most basic elements of a middle-class lifestyle), at a cost vastly disproportionate to the benefits that accrue to them, particularly for the young people in these communities at the present time. The insidious replication of militarization as fashion, worn and performed by young women and men in US society, and transformed into an everyday event, into an uncritical item of daily living, requires a deeper and more considered scrutiny than has been forthcoming thus far. The reshaping of social consciousness in ways that are deeply embedded in practices and habits that feed and give license to impunity and supremacy must be a cause of widespread theoretical and activist attention, leading to resistance among all feminists, everywhere.

I would like to conclude by referring to the dangers and seductiveness of motherhood as a construct and as an identity of refuge in these terrible times of death and uncertainty. As Zakia Salime's article on Morocco (2007) so insightfully shows, motherhood is a slippery slope to conservatism whether women activists admit it or not. In all our societies and all our movements across the world, we have seen how the execution of war and its persistence are not only nurturing the re-emergence of extreme right-wing elements and narratives around privilege and civilization, but are also allowing for the resurgence of a notion of motherhood that is poorly conceptualized and still treated very cautiously by most feminists, because, I suspect, it so easily elicits right-wing accusation about our humanity and woman-ness as females. This taboo status of critical analysis and debate around motherhood and militarism has been compounded by the general neglect of this subject over the past half-century of feminist theoretical progress, leaving the discursive space largely untheorized (and basically conservative) within feminist scholarship.

The bottom line is, as we all know, that when our lives feel threatened, and when the world feels as if it is in turmoil around us, the tendency is to seek out those familiars that seem to have some kind of solidity and consistency. Women have been mothers in all sorts of ways for as long as our human memory extends, and this, together with the intimacy between womanhood and motherhood in all societies dominated by hetero-normative discourses and practices of social existence, enables such a notion to re-emerge as a 'safe harbor' of sorts for those who are trying to explain the conundrums of the day.

War – even when it seems to be happening far away – lives and thrives under our skins as women, and the tendency to close ranks around those things that are most common to women as defined by patriarchal ideology is something that we must be alert to and vigilantly watch with careful attention. The pain of loss, especially of a child who is loved and wanted, can so easily become a dangerous rallying point for incipiently conservative emotions and alliances. In the USA and across the world, women whose children have been lost to war, whether as aggressors in occupied societies or as defenders of a perceived national sovereignty, can be easily mobilized around emotional bonds that belie right-wing interpretations of security, safety, and peace. Therefore, I think that it is crucial for feminists globally to be vigilant to the implications of reviving our movement (in intellectual and activist terms) on the groundings of motherhood and loss, even as we give due respect to the sorrow that accompanies the loss of our loved ones, especially through the brutality of war.

An uncritical embrace of the notion of motherhood is not only danger-ous for feminist values and achievements, but it can also easily distract us from the less intimate issues of militarism and state impunity, particularly when such practices are deployed against those who are not our kin or social counterparts.

In so many profoundly challenging ways, this moment of intensifying war, seemingly new and yet as ancient as patriarchy itself, represents a unique opportunity for feminist visioning and transformation everywhere. This is the time for a radical politics that goes beyond class, race, gender and otherness. This is the time for feminist revolutions.

References

Ahmad, Eqbal (2000) *Confronting Empire*, Boston, MA: South End Press.

Amin, Samir (2006) *Beyond US Hegemony: Assessing the Prospects for a Multipolar World*, London: Zed Books.

Baregu, Mwesiga (ed.) (1999) *Crisis in the Democratic Republic of the Congo*, Harare: SAPES Books.

Boron, Atilio (2005) *Empire and Imperialism: A Critical Reading of Michael Hardt and Antonio Negri*, London: Zed Books.

Bryce, Robert (2007) 'Any flag will do', *Counter Punch*, 14(5), March.

Crocker, Charles (1992) *Highnoon in Southern Africa: Making Peace in a Rough Neighborhood*, New York: Norton.

Davis, Angela (1993) *Maneuvers: The International Politics of Militarizing Women's Lives*, Berkeley: University of California Press.

DeWitte, Ludo (2001) *The Assas-sination of Lumumba*, New York/London: Verso.

Eisenstein, Zillah and Cynthia Enloe (2004) *The Curious Feminist*, Berkeley: University of California Press.

Elich, Gregory (2006) *Strange Libera-tors: Militarism, Mayhem and the Pursuit of Profit*, Florida: Llumina Press.

Giddings, Paula (1985) *When and Where I Enter: The Impact of Black Women on Race and Sex in America*, New York: Bantam.

Hedges, Chris (2003) *War Is a Force that Gives Us Meaning*, New York: Anchor Books.

Hochschild, Adam (1999) *King Leopold's Ghost: A Story of Greed, Terror and Heroism in*

Colonial Africa, Boston/New York: Houghton Mifflin.

Mandaza, Ibbo (ed.) (1999) *Reflections on the Crisis in the Democratic Republic of Congo*, Harare: SAPES Books.

Martin, William (2001) 'Privatizing prisons from the USA to SA: controlling dangerous Africans across the Atlantic', *ACAS Bulletin*, 59, Winter.

Narayan, Uma (1997) *Dislocation Cultures: Identities, Traditions and Third World Feminism*, New York/London: Routledge.

Nzongola-Ntalaja, Georges (2002) *The Congo from Leopold to Kabila: A People's History*, London: Zed Books.

Parenti, Christian (2007) 'Who will get the oil', *The Nation*, 19 March.

Pouilly, Cecile (2007) 'Huge country, huge problems, huge potential: can DR Congo turn the page?', *REFUGEES – UNHCR Newsletter*, 145(1).

Said, Edward (1994) *Culture and Imperialism*, New York: Vintage.

Salime, Zakia (2007) 'The war on terrorism: appropriation and subversion by Moroccan women', *Signs*, 33(1), Autumn.

Scahill, Jeremy (2007), *Blackwater: The Rise of the World's Most Powerful Mercenary Army*, New York: Nation Books.

Schell, Jonathan (2006) 'Too late for empire: the origins of the crisis of the republic', *The Nation*, 14–21 August.

Younge, Gary (2007) 'The illogic of Empire', *The Nation*, 5 February.

In praise of Afrika's children[1]

MĨCERE GĨTHAE MŨGO

*For the children of Mozambique and all Afrikana children who have
been orphaned biologically, socially, politically, economically.*

Refrain
I want to sing
I want to sing
          a love song
A song exploding
          with feeling
A song blossoming
          with beauty
like the flowering bud
unfolding wide
to embrace the rays
of the inviting sun.

Refrain
I want to sing
          a love song
A song for
          my little
          tender ones
A song in praise of
          my loved ones
from the Cape to Cairo
from sunrise
to sunset
A love song
          for my babies
          cremated
          and buried
          before their birth

Refrain
I want to sing

                    a love song
A song for
                    my little
                    tender ones
A song in praise of
                    my loved ones
scattered by imperialist
                    history
across the Americas
across the Caribbean
Piled up in
                    global mass graves
                    etched shallow
                    under ocean depths
across the length
and breadth
of Western history's
                    murderous face
from Goree to Martinique
from São Tomé to Brazil
from Takoradi to Carolina.

Refrain
Melodies of love
                    well within me
Rivers of love
                    flow through
                    my heart
Torrents of passion
                    flood my veins
I am full to overflowing.
But what song
shall I sing?

Refrain
What song
shall I sing
                    without mocking
                    what I would praise?
What poem
shall I compose

Mũgo

in praise of

> skeleton shapes
> that desperately tug
> my dangling breast
> long drained
> of the last
> drop
> of milk?

What song
shall I sing?

Refrain
What words
shall I utter
in praise of

> ghostly shadows
> that populate
> the wasteland
> that mother Afrika is

in its Somalias
in its Mozambiques?
What song
shall I sing?

Refrain
What language
shall I fashion
in praise of

> half beings
> garbage-piled
> sausage style
> in sprawling ghettoes

from Harlem to Soweto
from Lagos to Brighton
from Mathare Valley to Rio
from Kinshasa to Marseille?
What language
shall I fashion?
Oh, what song
shall I sing?

Refrain
What poem
shall I compose
in praise of
>   decomposing human remains
>   mutilated human corpses
>   walking human skeletons
>   haunting our Mozambiques?

Caricatures of
human form
violated beings
exhibiting
>   pruned ears
>   dug-out eyes
>   butchered noses
>   chopped-off hands
>   sawed-off legs?

What poem
shall I compose?
What song
shall I sing?

Refrain
What poem
shall I compose
in praise of
>   human remains
>   crippled lives
>   walking corpses

Afrika's children
turned
>   into living horrors

Afrika's children
crushed
>   into shapelessness

mashed
>   into formlessness

by Apartheid-Renamo machetes
America's anti-communist dollars?
What poem
shall I compose?

Oh, what song
shall I sing?

Refrain
What dance
shall I dance
in celebration of
> chunks and stumps
> that once held arms
> suspended trunks
> that once carried legs
> gaping holes
> that once encased eyes
> jeering teeth
> that once knew lips
> shattered hearts
> that once pulsated
> with life?

What dance
shall I dance?
Oh, what song
shall I sing?

Refrain
What song
shall I sing
in praise of
> our children

living in
the mass graves
> of apartheid
> of capitalism
> of imperialism?

What song
shall I sing?

Refrain
I will sing
> a war song

My words
will be
> angry bullets

from the
                    volcanic barrel
                    of the well-aimed
                    AK rifle
                    of my poem
Each furious shot
                    the staccato thunder
                    of the well-measured
                    machine gun
                    of my actions
Each telling victory
                    the raised salute
                    of the never-dying
                    people's will
                    people's vision
detonating
                    racism
                    apartheid
                    imperialism
                    and their warlords.
And then
I will sing

Refrain
I will sing
                    a love song
A song
                    exploding with feeling
A song
                    bursting with laughter
A song
                    flowering with beauty
A song
                    caressing with tenderness
A song
                    embalmed with sweetness
A song
                    soothing with comfort
A song
                    for my innocent
                    tender ones

73

A song

        in praise
        of my loved ones

A song

        in ululation
        of my brave ones

from the Cape to Cairo
from Mombasa to Takoradi
from New York to San Francisco
from Trinidad to Belize
from Nova Scotia to Vancouver
from Brazil to Grenada

Refrain
Oh, I will sing
a song
I will sing
a love song

        a love song
        for my children
        a love song
        for my loved ones
        a love song
        for my babies

reborn

        through thunder

reborn

        through pain

reborn

        through death

reborn

        through vision

reborn

        through love.

Refrain – twice over.

Note

1 From *My Mother's Poem and Other Songs* (1994) Nairobi: East African Educational Publishers, pp. 4–11.

5 | What's left? After 'imperial feminist' hijackings

HUIBIN AMELIA CHEW

The relation between imperialism and gender is not just a matter of macho talk. It is about economic sexism and sexual exploitation; it is about who dies. It is not just ideological, but material, institutional, psychological.

Imperialism both perpetuates and relies upon gendered inequalities, both at home and abroad. Yet the pretext of 'liberating women' has served as a justification for the US occupations of Afghanistan and Iraq. This 'imperial feminism' creates quandaries for feminist politics in the USA, by clouding our ability to see systemic patriarchy. What is at stake, and how might we, in the belly of the beast, help build an alternative?

Whose lives are we looking at? Whose lives are we valuing?

The US anti-war movement has primarily fixated on the deaths of our own troops. So much so that describing war as 'sexist' returns blank stares – aren't men most of the people who die in battle? In the twentieth century, 90 percent of all war deaths have been non-combatants – mostly women and children (Sivard 1996). The weapons of modern war – 'shock and awe,' white phosphorus, depleted uranium – are as likely to kill and maim women and girls as males. Using long-distance weapons that help preserve our troops' lives by maximizing 'collateral damage' is a deliberate strategy. And prolonged engagement between our military forces and civilians has resulted in war crimes, like the checkpoint slaughter of entire families.

Our disregard for 'enemy' lives has been reinforced by both racist and sexist ideologies – can we call our boys anything less than heroic? Do we see these other deaths as mere deviations from the supposedly mainstay targets of male 'terrorist insurgents' (Eisler 2007)?

The economics of patriarchy

Women are disproportionately affected by the economic harms of war, as well. Globally, women make up 70 percent of those starving or on the verge of starvation. Imperialism helps intensify the gender gap in poverty, a situation reflected in indicators from health to literacy. Female literacy in Iraq plummeted disproportionately during the sanctions period as girls were pulled from school.

After the 2003 US invasion of Iraq, women there were the hardest hit by unemployment, since men are preferred for the few available jobs. Formerly 72 percent of salaried Iraqi women were public employees, and many lost their jobs when government ministries were dismantled (Zangana 2004). The destruction of basic infrastructure like food rationing impacts on the indigent most – including poor women, many of them widows or single heads of households. Iraq's economic woes will stretch far into the future, under the regime of SAPs (Structural Adjustment Programs) that industrialized nations plan to impose on the country, under the aegis of the International Monetary Fund, because of Iraq's sovereign debt. Feminist scholars have documented how SAPs disproportionately harm Third World *women* across the globe in terms of health, education, and overwork.

Likewise, in the USA, most families in poverty are headed by single mothers, and poor women bear the brunt of public service cuts. In Massachusetts, for example, most Medicaid recipients, graduates of state and community colleges, welfare and subsidized childcare recipients are women – and all these programs have had their budgets slashed (Na'im and Wagman 2004). The majority of public and subsidized housing recipients are female-headed households, but in recent years Section 8 (the common name for government housing subsidy) has continued atrophying; President George W. Bush proposes more cuts for 2008 (Wright 2005).

In addition to wage labor, we must consider the economics of women's *unpaid* work, performed in their traditional gender roles. As hospitals are destroyed or become unavailable, it's women in both Iraq and the USA who disproportionately shoulder responsibility for their families' healthcare. Childcare, healthcare, and homemaking all weigh more heavily upon women without public sector aid – whether due to economic collapse in occupied lands, or budget austerity in the aggressor nation. Mass incarceration increases the burden on women from poor, black, and immigrant communities of color, who manage households alone – even while workfare-welfare programs keep a mostly female underclass from decent jobs. Military wives and mothers are saddled with double duty, to enable soldiers' extended tours.

The coercion of sexual commodification

Economic hardship and oppressive gender relations combine to fuel sexual commodification. Following a pattern observed across different conflict regions by feminist scholars, Iraqi women have faced increasing pressures to earn their subsistence from men by bartering their sexuality. In Baghdad, prostitution became widespread between the fall of the Hussein administration in April 2003 and November 2003, as women disproportionately suffered growing poverty. By 2005, reports surfaced of Iraqi teens working in Syrian brothels, after being displaced from Fallujah, where US forces had launched brutal offensives and chemical weapons attacks on civilians (e.g. Phillips 2005).

US bases foment a sex trade around the globe which often draws in poor rural girls and women. Military leaders play a role in informally managing this industry to motivate their largely male workforce, exploiting global wealth disparities. Recently, reports have surfaced of contractors shipping in Filipinas to work as prostitutes at US bases in Iraq – for $200 per month (Enrile 2007). Women have returned home pregnant, unable to track down the fathers. GABRIELA, a mass women's organization in the Philippines, has decried how the country now has the largest number of prostituted women and children in Southeast Asia – a direct legacy of its use as a US 'rest and recreation' base for GIs during the Vietnam War.

We can also understand sex work in the USA within a structural context. Police and advocates report a growing number of younger teens arrested for prostitution. Most are non-white. If media commentators look beyond the teen herself, they typically hold her parents, first and foremost her mother, to blame. But what structural factors shape girls' intense desire for approval, or male peers' behavior, which makes abusive relationships seem the only recourse? Furthermore, patriarchy cannot be separated from policies of racist economic disinvestment, and 'law enforcement' as the priority method of responding to social problems, in certain communities – in a sense, racialized occupation within the USA.

Sexual violence, domestic violence, violence against women

In Iraq in March 2006, fourteen-year-old Abeer Qassim was gang-raped and murdered by US soldiers; her family and seven-year-old sister were executed in the next room. Soon after, several other women publicly came forward, reporting gang rapes by US-trained Iraqi police. Sadly, it took over three years of occupation to break the media silence on atrocities that are truly the tip of the iceberg (Harding 2004; Shumway 2004).

Imperialism enables foreign and indigenous patriarchies to *collude* in aggravating women's oppression. Sexual violence, as well as the trafficking of Iraqi women and girls, rose horrifically after the US invasion, and continues unabated to this day. While the initial rapes and abductions were perpetrated largely by Iraqi men, the occupation force's disruption of security and disregard provided them with the occasion – its priority, after all, was to secure the oil. Moreover, since at least 2005 the Pentagon has armed, supported, and trained 'death squad'-style militias in Iraq, known to use sexual violence and targeted femicide as tactics for consolidating their power. As the occupation persists, and contact between military forces and civilians grows, sexual brutality directly at the hands of both US troops and Iraqi police under occupation authority has proliferated.

US readers may be surprised to learn that the Abu Ghraib debacle, at the US prison in Baghdad, included the torture of *female* detainees, as well – a fact that went almost unreported in the US media. The first evidence of abuse was a letter from a female prisoner reporting gang rape (ibid.). Congress perused the photos documenting such atrocities, but the only images widely disseminated involved male victims. The Pentagon and government officials collaborated to prevent the other pictures' public release, which should lead us to question what the invisibility of women *purchases*. The sexual abuse of female detainees is widespread throughout Iraq, and well known among Iraqis – yet we were treated primarily to the spectacle of Lynddie England, a female US soldier, participating in the Abu Ghraib tortures. The only pictures of US soldiers assaulting Iraqi women to circulate were hard-core pornography images, later discredited as frauds. Thus, the rape of women abounds in our consciousness, yet has no 'real' existence.

The total number of detained women in Iraq is unknown; in 2005, Iman Khamas of the International Occupation Watch Center reported 625 females in Al-Rusafah prison and 750 in Al-Kadhmiya alone, ranging from age twelve to sixty (Susskind 2007). Women are subject to torture and degrading humiliation; they are dragged by their hair, burned with electricity, forced to eat from dirty toilets, and urinated on. According to Iraqi MP Mohamed al-Dainey, there were sixty-five *documented* cases of women's rape in occupation detention centers during 2006 (Zangana 2007).

A May 2004 Red Cross report disclosed that 70 to 90 percent of 43,000 Iraqis detained in the last year were arrested by mistake. Today, US forces continue to routinely imprison the female relatives and alleged lovers of male suspects for use as hostages and bargaining chips – a form of collective punishment. Over the last year, detentions by multinational forces have increased drastically, by 40 percent (Zangana 2007); detention centers number over 450, according to the US State Department. Women are physically and sexually abused at checkpoints and during house searches.

After brutalizing Iraqis, soldiers bring rape and domestic violence home. Phoebe Jones of Global Women's Strike has traced a prison-military complex of abuse: torture in Abu Ghraib was outsourced to personnel from US prison companies, while former soldiers return to become abusive guards. The connection extends to both sides of the bars: in 1997, the number-one reason for veterans being in jail was for sexual assault (Mackey 2004).

A full exploration of the effects of militarism on gendered violence in the USA is beyond the scope of this essay – but we must consider how state repression, economic violence, and racism all exacerbate violence against women, including on the 'interpersonal' level. Women on welfare suffer high rates of domestic and sexual abuse – both because they lack the resources to leave their abusers and because the law does not protect their right to safe housing (Schram 2002). After Hurricanes Katrina and Rita hit the Gulf Coast of the USA in 2005, poor women forced to live in homeless shelters experienced rape and physical violence from partners they could not escape (LCADV 2005). While the mainstream media laced reports of chaos after the storms with racist undertones, progressives displayed a disheartening lack of concern for connecting gendered experiences of violence to government policy.

Hetero-patriarchy and military effectiveness

Even after the grisly murders of Abeer and her family came to light, coverage in the US press repeatedly insulted and devalued the victims' humanity; headlines primarily directed attention toward the US attackers' 'tears' (Hopkins 2007). Anti-war organizers cannot allow these acts to be treated as mere aberrations. Only when we are willing to recognize a pattern of atrocities can we unmask the *systemic* causes behind them. We must oppose the hierarchy of lives that glorifies rapists and murderers in US uniform – and confront the forces producing these behaviors.

Women and queer people may serve as soldiers, but the US military is a misogynist, homophobic institution that relies on hetero-patriarchal ideologies and relations to function – with far-reaching effects within US society as well as occupied lands. The US military conditions men to devalue, objectify and demean traits traditionally associated with femininity, molding soldiers to adopt a role of 'violent masculinity' that glorifies domination. One soldier reported his training in boot camp:

'Who are you?'

'Killers!'

'What do you do?'

'We kill! We kill! We kill!'

Those viewed as 'feminine' or 'civilian' are at best trophies to be

79

protected, rather than equals to be accountable to. Furthermore, soldiers are purposefully taught to *eroticize* violence – from a heterosexual, male-aggressor perspective. During the first US Gulf War on Iraq in 1991, air force pilots watched pornographic movies before bombing missions to psyche themselves up (Rogin 1993). Internalizing a misogynist, violent sexuality becomes embedded in soldiers' training to function psychologically as killers. The widespread sexual abuse of female soldiers by male colleagues, with overwhelming impunity, is a symptom of this institution's modus operandi. We must interrogate the use of sexual violence as a tool of war and genocide – as well as labor and domestic exploitation – and how such sadistic acts become customary.

Reproductive injustice

War curtails reproductive healthcare – an issue of women's equality, affecting our control over our labor, bodies, and futures. Over 340 tons of depleted uranium were dropped on Iraq during the first Gulf War; the radioactive agent is linked to birth defects, pregnancy complications, and maternal mortality (Al-Ali 2007). Just months after the 2003 invasion, increased back-alley abortions were reported in Baghdad as women lost access to healthcare and contraception (McElroy 2003). In the USA, budget stringency, justified by war priorities, means that universal reproductive healthcare will remain a distant possibility.

The Christian conservative movement has reframed debates on morality in the USA around abortion and gay marriage – stressing policies to control individuals' behavior, rather than to restructure societal wealth to meet human needs. In our historical context, limiting women's control over their reproduction and enforcing a patriarchal family are ideological and economic cornerstones of the US imperial project (Smith 2006). The current attacks on women's reproductive control are located within an agenda to promote a sex-segregated division of labor, where motherhood is woman's glorified role, even as economic imperatives force her to work at least a double shift. Poor or non-white women are criminalized as promiscuously deviant – which in turn facilitates their exploitation as low-wage labor, unfit for motherhood, through policies such as workfare. As Andrea Smith has observed, emphasizing women's place in the private family and, particularly, a racialized cult of motherhood becomes an excuse for disinvestment from public support systems.

Occupation is not women's liberation

The US occupation is not capable of bringing democracy or liberation to Iraqis. Its bottom line is maintaining the political and military power necessary to guarantee the economic interests of the US elite. Toward that end, occupying authorities have, time and again, proved perfectly willing to barter away women's rights. They have played on both sides of the fence, appearing to respond to women's needs – only to roll back their status when convenient. After all, an agenda based on despotic military brutality and the plunder of a nation is best carried out by public relations stunts, rather than actual accountability. And it is waged by perpetuating hierarchy – that is, by offering perks to certain segments of the occupied population because they help subjugate the rest.

Wagering which factions would allow them to retain dominance, US authorities threw their lot in with theocratic parties during the redrafting of Iraq's constitution, removing protections formerly granted to women in Iraq's family civil code. The Pentagon backed Shiite militia groups known for restrictions and atrocities against women, such as the notorious Badr Brigade, because in the words of former marine officer and counter-insurgency expert Thomas X. Hammes, 'Our policy is to equip those who are the most effective fighters.' US interests need some Iraqis to carry out our dirty war by proxy. In the process, our government has inflamed sectarian and gender-based violence, which are interrelated Susskind 2007). US fomentation of armed violence is a historical process that pre-dates this particular occupation. The USA spent the cold war supporting theocratic parties and militias in the Middle East, in opposition to socialist, secular, and democratic movements; this set the stage for their political ascendancy.

The conflict in Iraq has restricted women's public access there, shaping the trajectory of their political participation and resistance. But besides constraints on physical space, the imperialist agenda creates another significant hurdle for both Iraqi and US women who wish to politicize gendered oppression – simply battling the dominant assumption that imperialism is good for women.

Feminism in the belly of the beast

After years of being treated as virtual prisoners in their homes by the Taliban, the women of Afghanistan are going back to work ... the little girls in Afghanistan are now in school. [Applause.] ... wasn't it wonderful to watch the Olympics and see that beautiful Afghan sprinter race in long pants and a t-shirt, exercising her new freedom while respecting the traditions of her country. (Laura Bush at the 2004 Republican National Convention)

Jason Jones: Is America ready for a FLILF [First Lady I'd Like to Fuck]? Ms Kucinich: For a what? (*The Daily Show*, October 2007)

Which of the above – a mouthpiece for the Bush administration, or the mock interviewer on a TV comedy show beloved by many progressives – is an ally for 'feminists'?

We in the US would do well to first recognize that the 'greatest purveyor' of violence is often US military and economic policies; as such, feminist solidarity is impossible without concentrating on our role to oppose these. It is essential that, if we are US residents, we predicate any political solidarity regarding Iraqi women's worsening conditions on demanding an immediate end to occupation – military, economic, and political.

The occupiers' pretensions of 'feminism' and posturing at defending women's interests reinforce a fraught terrain for those in Iraq and the USA concerned with gendered violence. Those protesting women's status in Iraq or Afghanistan may find themselves used as pawns to justify war. Iraqi women's groups risk attack for any foreign ties, or evidence of being agents of occupation. Indeed, these groups are being targeted by Republican organizations and pro-occupation interests for co-optation. We must 'cynically' understand that our support for Iraqi women's groups may help discredit them or lead to their opportunistic attack – both by those who would construe that support as imperialist, and those who would use Iraqi women's predicament to promote military aggression.

An 'imperial feminist' standpoint, exemplified by the quote from Laura Bush, is influential in the self-perceptions of many US women today. Such a view professes a concern for global South, non-white women without acknowledging the role of racism, colonialism, and economic exploitation in shaping their conditions. It tends to impose a 'feminist' vision determined by powerful elite actors, rather than letting local women address the problems most relevant to them. Not simply Republicans but even liberal feminists have supported US occupation and military action to 'liberate' women in Afghanistan and Iraq.

We must face the dominant US ideology: that our culture represents the epitome of women's liberation. Gendered oppression is largely considered irrelevant to women in the USA – a blight instead reserved for people in other countries. Those very qualities that culturally distinguish 'Americans' from the global South 'other' become vaunted as symbols of our superiority – whether 'democracy,' capitalist consumerism, multicultural pluralism, or specifically regarding women's status, a mode of commodified sexual expression. Burqas and veils have come to embody the ultimate in gendered persecution. Bikinis equal freedom; sex is emancipation.

In this way, imperial feminist attitudes help to render our own patriarchy invisible. But US leftists who neglect and fail to grapple with gender are partly responsible, and must be part of the remedy.

Jon Stewart's *Daily Show*, a satiric US television program, provides an example of blind spots and double standards. Female sexuality is repeatedly the punchline, and butt, of jokes – usually through clichés around the female body's desirability, and male expressions of desire. The eroticized male body as object of desire is strikingly absent. Women's sexuality is both salaciously, deliciously enjoyed – and the convenient scapegoat for boys-will-be-boys antics. Hence, in the above 'FLILF' episode – and FLILF does not refer to US Senator Hillary Clinton, wife of ex-President Bill Clinton – the young wives of male candidates are lampooned as potential troublemakers who would tempt hot-headed men to bungle diplomacy. The analysis stops right there: implicating the FLILF. Ironically, she is posited as an edgy transgression, a leap forward for women who not only can be First Ladies, but sexy First Ladies. (In a post-feminist society, what could be more 'progressive' than flaunting it?) How she *is made* to fill the traditional gender role of presidential helpmate, and official proof of his heterosexuality, is no subject for comic critique. The show repeatedly chooses to blame females rather than contest economic or patriarchal pressures creating the premium on standardized looks.

Mainstream US debates on sexual politics – indeed, the pro-sex/anti-sex dichotomy – typically pit a hyper-commodified, patriarchal sexual expression against abstinence-only 'family values.' Progressives especially may view the former as the solution to the latter's harms. In reality, misogyny and male privilege undergird both – ensuring these supposedly opposing dynamics work hand in hand, so males can both enjoy 'sluts,' and then blame them for any social ills. Patriarchy requires *both* of these parts: the sexual availability of women for male-centered enjoyment, and the sexually exclusive motherly ideal. It's not sexual repression we suffer from, but the combination of patriarchal commodified sexuality and a misogynist veneer of 'virginal' values, which ensures that youths' sex education comes directly from the porn industry.

US peace-minded progressives also cede much to right-wing ground when the main critique of sexuality they can garner is that it is distracting. A recent US anti-war Moveon.org action alert charged that the Fox television network 'uses sex to sell right-wing news' (Green 2007). The anti-Fox message merely focused on the network's 'hypocrisy,' asserting that such coverage, aired under the guise of allowing commentators to decry 'immorality,' actually served as an excuse to replace real news with 'smut.'

Here, only sexual explicitness, not its content, is supposedly at fault.

What about the racist misogyny of beauty standards and patriarchal gender roles? The exploitative and unaccountable nature of media geared primarily toward a heterosexual male viewer? Sexualization differs from objectification – the latter implies unequal sexual agency, and possibly power imbalance.

But sexuality *itself* isn't worth serious politicization. To be safe, it must remain fluff, or a joke.

The cost of sexist bias in progressive organizing

I have been told by many an activist that if it were not for the preceding Vietnam anti-war or civil rights movements in the USA, women's liberation organizing in the country could not have blossomed. Such comments may seem only to report a historical sequence of developments. But they also gloss over a story of painful splintering and agency, as women began to refuse sexist practices and coffee-making roles within activist groups. Perhaps the rawness of that rift leaves a legacy of weakness in our movements today. Yet it can only be repaired by addressing injustice rather than denying it in the name of unity – as 'unity without equality is like peace without justice.'

Moreover, a chauvinistic focus *only* on how other movements enabled US women's organizing erases and renders invisible the influences of those who have politicized gender – ignoring women's contributions. Such attitudes imply that gender is a 'secondary issue' other movements need not address: someone else will inevitably take it up later, no matter the cost of the divisions. And this rationale has been used as an argument for why women, or those concerned with a feminist agenda, need not bother organizing with each other – first things first, later things later. But in aspiring to learn from our feminist predecessors, we in the USA need to see what we are losing when we don't have the spaces to support each other in looking at gendered violence.

I direct my discussion to relationship abuse only to highlight both the personal and political costs of sexist inequality. Those engaged in social change work are not exempt – *and* at the very least we should strive to find a collective voice for these harms. Isolated, women in unhealthy relationships with men often seek to reconcile the contradiction between their values and situation, by battling, largely alone, to 'change' their male partners' chauvinism. As individuals, their 'effectiveness' is truly limited, and at a tremendous cost in time, energy, and pain. Choosing to engage in this fight already means conceding to a deep inequality in the very terms of the relationship. The confidence to voice dissent in a relationship must not be confused with 'power'; contemplating a role reversal can bring into focus assumptions about 'fairness,' illustrating the unreturned skills and effort put into relationships.

When we get used to the invisibility of gender, we don't apply the same standards to it as to other systemic forms of oppression. An example is the question of when 'violence' can be considered 'resistance.' Thousands rallied for the Jena 6, a group of young black men in Louisiana given draconian sentences for a schoolyard fight with racist white fellow students. A group of young black lesbians called the New Jersey 4 were sentenced to between three and eleven years in prison, with little public outcry. They were arrested and convicted for defending themselves against a male provocateur who first harassed them with homophobic threats, then physically attacked and choked them (Henry 2007). Within systemic oppression, sexist abuse is a titillating and repeated oddity that seems to catch us by surprise each time – rather than being politicized critically as systemic exploitation. So-called 'intimate violence' – really, any violence involving a woman and someone she knows as more than a stranger – continues to be fetishized as a special case with its own rules of give and take, outside of political context.

The personal is systemic: putting the politics back into anti-violence work

I am reminded of Paulo Freire's words: 'With the establishment of a relationship of oppression, violence has already begun. Never in history has violence been initiated by the oppressed' (1968). Yet 'abuse' is used to describe both a batterer's assault and a woman hitting back, repeated sexist slurs and angry outbursts in response – stripped of a context or pattern of unequal harm. Particularly in our relationships with men, women have internalized a false standard of 'mutuality.' Women are so equal, we must constantly be 'equally' accountable for our every action, 'equally' empathetic, 'equally' apologetic and gentle of others' feelings; whether others give us the same consideration is irrelevant to our response. To 'demand independence' – rather, to reject a patriarchal bind – is to lose any hope of emotional support. When progressives say blacks *cannot* be 'racist' against whites, they have claimed that language for a reason – because more than specific interactions, 'racism' is the systemic, unequal power relations that exacerbate an action's consequences. The language of intimate partner 'abuse' contains no such discernment, however.

In the USA current 'anti-violence' activities too often are simply directed at the most egregious examples of interpersonal abuse, without challenging sexism more broadly. Education for males based on an anti-violence paradigm, instead of an anti-sexist one, teaches that not hitting

85

her is about 'being a real man.' Asking for consent becomes another tool to literally 'add to his playbook' – otherwise preserving the same self-interested, coercive goals and assumptions of 'the game.' Specific behaviors change; perhaps not misogyny.

What's more, by focusing on altering how *individual* males perform violent masculinity in limited circumstances, such work misses the overwhelming structural inequalities that remain in place to prop up abuse. We need to ask, what privileges of economics, politics, social support, or citizenship status allow some people to prey on others in interpersonal relationships? How can community organizing and political mobilization actually challenge the larger societal structures fueling this violence – rather than simply accommodating its existence by providing services like shelters, hotlines, and minimal 'batterer re-education'?

Our struggles must inform each other

To get to the roots of patriarchy, we must link a women's liberation agenda back to the principles behind racial, economic, and other justice struggles. For instance, US legislation now protects the legal status of immigrant women who seek to escape abusive marriages – but we have yet to address the conditions pushing women into 'mail order bride' status in the first place. The latter would require us to implicate the causes of women's economic dislocation and indigence, including the role of US military domination and rampant gender inequality under economic globalization. These same global processes, which render women's bodies into consumable products through sexual and domestic services, shape the billion-dollar Internet pornography industry and our misogyny-filled mass media.

The US movement against workplace discrimination failed to achieve economic equality for women, in part because capitalist and racist exploitation remain unchecked. Women gained access to jobs, but poverty and unpaid labor remain feminized. Global South women continue to be imported by those who can afford it to take care of the kids; this domestic labor and its slave-like conditions are a vital component of corporate globalization. Gains in legal protections against discrimination have not compensated for other significant erosions in workers' status caused by union-busting or public benefits cuts. Welfare proved a low priority for both the male-centered workers' movements and white-dominated women's lobby groups; but its collapse pulled the wage floor down for everyone. We need to set our long-term gaze on institutional causes that require change throughout sectors of society in the USA.

Community-based organizing

We must strengthen community-based organizing approaches, which go deeper than mobilization or lobbying. The power for meaningful change comes not from advocates or well-poised individuals, but the collective assertion of grassroots power. Ideally, community-based organizing seeks to ensure that the concerns of those at the grass roots, rather than elites or a 'vanguard,' play an active role in creating the movement's direction and agenda. To avoid perpetuating hierarchy requires creating spaces where those involved can truly listen to each other, and respect the feelings of those struggling to be heard.

Currently in the USA an overwhelming focus on service provision, which developed with the proliferation of the non-profit system, treats women as clients rather than potential organizers, and seeks individual remedies rather than collective change. We need added energy to rebuild our movements. The ownership of those directly affected by exploitation is essential for movements' momentum and transformative power. Seeds of radical change are planted when those typically controlled by others have the space, and take the power, to decide their participation and shape strategy. The goal of liberation can be reached only when the exploited exercise the power to actively create it. Problems of exploitation within the movement must be addressed not with a naivety that falsely places individuals on a par with institutionalized oppression – rather, only collective accountability and making real a cost can create a meaningful power shift.

When community-based approaches involve those on a low income, the unemployed or informally employed, people of color, and other marginalized groups, this organizing cannot ignore the immediate needs of those involved. Our challenge is to find *cooperative* strategies to meet people's needs, while resisting the political and economic structures causing inequality, by involving those directly affected in building with each other more long-term solutions against exploitation. This project is as much about generating communities, with critical values and new networks for mutual support, as about dismantling the political and economic structures causing oppression.

Conclusion

Mainstream feminism today within the USA has been co-opted and cheapened into the narrow struggle to fill men's shoes – while preserving the capitalist, racist, imperialist, and even patriarchal inequalities that make up the very fabric of those shoes. 'Feminism' is bombing Afghanistan to liberate women. 'Feminism' is breaking gender roles by

87

posing for bikini shots and joining the military. 'Feminism' is becoming a power-CEO or Secretary of State Condoleezza Rice.

This shallow vision of gender justice has so permeated even progressive circles that our very definition of sexism is circumscribed. Too often, sexism is merely seen as a set of cultural behaviors or personal biases; challenging sexism is simply seen as breaking these gender expectations. But sexism is an institutionalized *system*, with historical, political, and economic dimensions.

Just as the USA was built on white supremacy and capitalism, the country was also built on patriarchy – on the sexual subjugation of women whether in war or 'peace,' slavery or conquest; on the abuse of our reproductive capacity; the exploitation of both our paid and unpaid labor. Truly taking on an anti-sexist agenda means uprooting *institutional* patriarchy. Reducing the fight against sexism to transgressing people's assumptions about what a woman can do only obscures the power inequalities that continue to hold patriarchy up. Worse, it relegates a task that can be achieved only through collective action or organizing to the realm of individual exploits.

A deep analysis of how patriarchy operates is typically absent across progressive organizing in the USA – whether for affordable housing, demilitarization, immigrant rights, or workers' rights. In all of these interrelated struggles, women are heavily affected, and, moreover, affected disproportionately in ways particular to gender. Yet too often, organizers working on these issues do not recognize how they are gendered. In the process, they prioritize men's experiences, and perpetuate sexism. Gender is ghettoized, a token appended to the main concerns of other movements, rather than fully integrated into radical struggles. It is at best engaged on a single-issue, not systemic, basis. Women and girls swept up in the dragnet of the US border patrols or immigration raids are increasingly visible, but their gendered harms receive little attention if there is not also mobilization around these issues as they affect males.

The result is that US conservatives (and free-market, warmongering liberals) have a field day claiming to stand for women's interests, while denying the experiences of most women in the USA and around the globe. More importantly, those on the left miss opportunities to treat many instances of gendered exploitation as political, and organize collectively around them. We allow people to face the instances they experience every day as individuals without a united community supporting them. These experiences become silenced and 'forgotten' – even while gender is wielded as a wedge issue against us.

Organizing that centers on gendered experience, which is consciously anti-sexist while remaining connected to other progressive movements, can push an alternative to the fore. We lack the power today to tackle the system comprehensively, because grassroots women's organizing to advance these priorities in concert largely doesn't exist in the USA. We have been divided against each other by our allegiances to other struggles, pegged into single-issue (and often short-term) battles when it comes to gender, according to other movements' priorities. On a basic level, we have to start truly investing in each other – politically and socially, publicly and privately.

Individually, we can choose to wear makeup, or not. To go along with the program, or not. To demand fair treatment at home and work, or not. Certainly, risks are worth taking as individuals to defend a higher cause. But individually, we will suffer the consequences of *either* choice – unless we work collectively to change the structure of incentives we're trapped within. We are in each other's hands.

References

Al-Ali, Nadje (2007) 'Academia vs. weapons of mass destruction: why am I here?', Paper presented at the Academics' Trident Seminar Blockade, Faslane 365, Faslane Naval Base, 7 January, available at: www.faslane365.org/files/Why%20I%20am%20here%20Nadje%20Al%20Ali.doc, accessed 1 March 2007.

Eisler, Riane (2007) 'The Feminine Face of Poverty,' *AlterNet* [internet] 19 April, available at: www.alternet.org/rights/50727/, accessed 1 May 2007.

Enrile, Annalisa (2007) 'Macapagal-Arroyo Declares Open Season On Women of the Philippines,' GABRIELA Network Statement, 2 January.

Freire, Paulo (1968) *Pedagogy of the Oppressed*, 30th anniversary edn, trans. Myra Bergman Ramos, London: Continuum.

Green, Adam (2007) 'Fox attacks decency ... with Bill O'Reilly leading the way', *MoveOn*, 28 November.

Harding, Luke (2004) 'The other prisoners', *Guardian* online, 20 May, available at: www.guardian. co.uk/g2/story/0,3604,1220509,00. html, accessed 21 May 2004.

Henry, Imani (2007) 'Lesbians sentenced for self-defense', *Workers World* online, 21 June, available at: www.workers. org/2007/us/nj4-0628/, accessed 1 July 2007.

Hopkins, Andrea (2007) 'Tearful soldier tells court of Iraq rape-murder', Reuters, 21 February.

LCADV (Louisiana Coalition Against Domestic Violence) (2005) 'Beaten, Sexually Assaulted, and Living in a Hurricane Evacuation Shelter or a Makeshift Tent City ... Katrina Victims of Domestic and Sexual Violence Still Need Your Help,' press release, 13 September.

McElroy, Damien (2003) 'Home Abortions Soar in Iraq as Unwanted Pregnancies Rise,' *Telegraph* [internet] 26 October, available at: www.telegraph.co.uk/news/main.

jhtml?xml=/news/2003/10/26/ wirq26.xml, accessed 1 November 2003.

Mackey, Dorothy (2004) 'US Government and Pentagon Sanctioning of Abuses' [online] 11 May, available at: www.womenagainst rape. net/Latest%20News/Mackey Paper. htm, accessed 30 May, 2004.

Na'im, Alyssa and Nancy Wagman (2004) 'Real cuts, real people, real pain: the effects of the fiscal crisis on women and girls in Massachusetts', Massachusetts Budget and Policy Institute, Boston, December.

Phillips, Joshua (2005) 'Unveiling Iraqís Teenage Prostitutes: Fleeing their war-torn homes, Iraqi girls are selling their bodies in Syria to support their families,' *Salon.com* [internet] 24 June, available at: dir.salon.com/ story/news/feature/2005/06/24/ prostitutes/index.html, accessed 5 September 2005.

Rogin, Michael (1993) 'Make my day! Spectacle as amnesia in imperial politics', in Amy Kaplan and Donald Pease (eds), *Cultures of United States Imperialism*, Durham, NC: Duke University Press.

Schram, Tom (2002) 'Ruling on Housing Law a blow to battered women', *Women's Enews* online, 31 March, available at: www.

womensenews.org/article.cfm/ dyn/aid/863/, accessed 1 January 2008.

Shumway, Chris (2004) 'Pattern Emerges of Sexual Assault Against Women Held by U.S. Forces,' *The NewStandard News*, 6 June.

Sivard, Ruth (1996) *World Military and Social Expenditures*, Washington, DC: World Priorities.

Smith, Andrea (2006) 'Indigenous Feminism Without Apology,' *New Socialist*, No. 58, September–October.

Susskind, Yifat (2007) *Promising Democracy, Imposing Theocracy: Gender-Based Violence and the U.S. War on Iraq*, MADRE, New York City.

Wright, David (2005) *Section 8 Cuts Cause Pain*, Housing Opportunities Made Equal, available at: www.homeny.org/Insight%20 Articles/spring2005/section8cuts. htm, accessed 1 January 2008.

Zangana, Haifa (2004) 'Why Iraqi Women Arenít Complaining,' *Guardian* [internet] 19 February, available at: www.guardian.co.uk/ comment/story/0,,1151087,00. html, accessed 1 March 2004.

— (2007) 'The Iraqi Resistance Only Exists to End the Occupation,' *Guardian* [internet] 12 April, available at: www.guardian.co.uk/ comment/story/0,,2054881,00. html, accessed 14 April 2007.

TWO | **Feminists mobilizing critiques of war**

6 | Women-of-color veterans on war, militarism, and feminism

SETSU SHIGEMATSU WITH ANURADHA KRISTINA
BHAGWATI AND ELI PAINTEDCROW

Women currently constitute 15 percent of US military forces, numbering approximately 200,000 active-duty female personnel (US Department
of Defense 2006). Across all branches of the military, women of color
are over-represented. By 2004, women of color comprised 51 percent of
the total number of enlisted service women and 31.7 percent of female
military officers (Manning 2005: 14). Although there has been a growing
body of literature that examines the militarization of women, there are
few works that specifically examine how different women of color experience the US military (Moore 1995: 15–23). In response to this lacuna,
this dialogue attempts to address the dearth of critical discourse on and
by women of color in the US military through an engagement with the
perspectives of women-of-color veterans.

The dialogue between Anuradha Bhagwati, a former marine officer,
Eli PaintedCrow, a career enlisted soldier in the US army, and Setsu
Shigematsu, a scholar-activist, developed from discussions that began
at the 'Feminism and War' conference in Syracuse, New York, in 2006.
It draws on a longer interview that was recorded on 16 June 2007, in
Corona, California. The experiences of Bhagwati and PaintedCrow illu-
minate the differentiated experiences of this composite category, 'women
of color,' and how various women decide to enter this male-dominated
institution.

This chapter invites a dialogue between feminists and women-of-
color veterans who possess intimate knowledge of the military as a
means to complexify our understanding of how women of color are
being incorporated as part of a hegemonic multicultural state agenda.
The respective backgrounds of Bhagwati and PaintedCrow demonstrate
how vastly different socio-economic conditions shape and structure the
choices available to women of color who enter the military. In the dialogue that follows, PaintedCrow and Bhagwati share their views on the
relationship between race, militarism, Abu Ghraib, US culture, feminism
and peace.

Assimilation and (not) belonging

Setsu Shigematsu (SS): Eli, how did your background as a Native American woman relate to your participation in the military?

Eli PaintedCrow (EPC): As a Native person, there are certain things that come with joining the military. One is opportunity, because for us it is often the only opportunity available. For many of us school is often not an option, especially when you or your parents don't have money. Our work was about meeting everyday needs. By the time I was twenty, I was a single parent with two children. I lived in a one-bedroom cockroach-infested apartment with my two children and I didn't have any support. I was desperate to do something different with my life. In order to join, I had to be married, so I went out and found my ex-husband and got remarried. I was on welfare at the time and I really didn't like that. But I really didn't have any other skills because I didn't go to high school. I got my GE [general education] certificate when I was fourteen. I joined the US military and I gained some skills. I came back and felt a big load off my back, because I said to myself that I would never have to be on welfare again. So I spent twenty-two years serving in the military believing in this idea of patriotism.

As a Native person it was a great honor to be in the military because becoming a soldier is the closest thing to becoming a warrior and we come from a warrior society, but we don't have that anymore. My brothers were in the military and I pushed my sons to be in the military. I became a drill sergeant. I was moving up the ladder as a woman of color. But in hindsight I realize that I was a token for the system. I was the only woman of color in the drill sergeant academy. I ended up leaving, because they gave me some authority until things started moving in a direction they didn't like. So what I quickly learned was that this authority they give you as an officer or as an NCO [non-commissioned officer] is also an illusion. Because they'll give it to you as long as they need you, and then they'll remove you. And if you're a female, it is easy, and if you are a woman of color, then you really don't matter.

Most Americans don't know their history, and if you don't know your history, then it gets defined for you by the government. When I was younger, I had that past missing from my life. I didn't even know about being Native. My parents had a lot of fear and assimilated as best they could. They didn't talk about their heritage or history. My mother never talked about her Apache side of the family. My father never talked about our being Native, our being Yaqui. That fear was embedded in my parents and caused them to say, 'We are American.' And if you are from the rez [the reservation], that can bring a whole other kind of woundedness. Just because you are Native, people expect you to be a certain way, but we sit on different places in the world and in our hearts about being Native so there are many ways that Native persons understand themselves.

SS: Eli, your reasons for enlisting point to how an ostensibly 'All Volunteer Force' is reproduced through systemic design, which involves a structured lack of opportunity alongside recruitment efforts that provide economic and ideological incentives. Your background contrasts significantly with that of Anuradha, who decided to join the marines after graduating from Yale University. As a daughter of two Columbia University professors, and having been raised in a highly educated and liberal environment, your joining the marines was surely an unexpected choice.

Anuradha Bhagwati (AB): At that point in time, I was enrolled in graduate school. I saw my life closely mirroring my parents. I felt constrained and controlled, which was in part a result of my Indian upbringing, and the pressures to conform to my parents' professional expectations. They basically tried to convince me that the more advanced degrees you have, the more valuable a person you are in the world. The marines were a slap in the face to my parents' privileged world and to the world of higher education in general, I thought. I learned more about human behavior and the various dimensions of American society from the marines than I did from years of schooling.

After five years in the marines and leaving as a captain, I came out with the conclusion that not all the women or people of color in the world could alter the vices within the organization, because the organization fundamentally transforms a person's essence into something terribly destructive and self-destructive, regardless of who that person once was. Marine boot camp is so infamous because it succeeds in making killers out of the most timid human beings, and not just killers, but killers who love just how tough and badass they've become. There's a huge difference in a fighting organization that learns to fight because it has no other choice, and one that trains people to love killing, regardless of the context, time, place, or cause. Loving, being obsessed with and turned on by violence, to the point that you are a borderline sociopath, does not make you a warrior, or an empowered person, or a good public servant. I really had no idea how much the institution would fundamentally alter my personality.

I met a lot of children of immigrants in the marines. I think, regardless of the primary reason we joined, we shared a common desire to prove ourselves to be just as American as the average white guy with a crew cut. The insecurity people of color have about not quite belonging to the

American way of life, however large or small it is, is really magnified in a white male institution like the marines. They have racial or identifying terms for many of us, some of which are institutionalized through language. Marines who are black are called 'dark green' [green refers to the old jungle-green camouflage uniform], while marines who are women are called 'WMs,' or women marines. This practice of differentiating 'real marines,' meaning white males, from the rest of us reinforces that no matter how much they tell you your service matters just as much as the next guy's, you are constantly reminded that you do not quite belong, or are not wanted.

The strange thing for me was witnessing the presence of young marines with roots in Southeast Asia, Vietnam, Korea, and also, after 2003, a handful from South Asia and the Middle East. There is an understandable sense among some immigrant children that they owe something to the country that they now call their own. But what about the total disconnect with US history and current events? The United States laid waste, even genocide, upon Southeast Asia, but still, children of survivors of those wars still feel they have something to prove about their American-ness. People will do surprising and sometimes awful things to feel worthy or respected in this country. Sometimes we'd rather erase every ounce of cruel history and pretend we've always belonged to white American culture, than painfully admit maybe our roots lie elsewhere.

Some of the 'finest marines' I knew were people of color and women of color. And therefore I don't think that you can assume that because a person is of a particular race or background that they are necessarily going to come out of the marines thinking a certain way. After 9/11, the issue of race became much more obvious to me. The term 'raghead' became common, like 'gook' was during Vietnam. The military has a real knack for nurturing racial epithets for the enemy, and for summoning the worst filth out of soldiers. Immediately after 9/11, I witnessed numerous conversations about people wanting to kill Arabs and Muslims. I remember an old Hispanic marine saying, 'Let's bomb them all to hell – all Afghan men, women and children.' It wasn't uncommon. Vengeance just fueled our natural inclination to be violent and perverse.

SS: In terms of how you experienced racial difference at work in the marines, you have underscored the ways in which being a person of color doesn't predetermine how a person is going to respond to, negotiate, deny or resist how racism is at work within the military. One's own racial and cultural difference can fuel the drive to do violence to other racialized subjects.

Abu Ghraib and US culture

SS: From your experience in the military, how do you think the US military torture of Iraqi prisoners at Abu Ghraib relates to the rest of American society?

AB: Abu Ghraib is the quintessential milestone in US history. You have acts of torture that are considered 'shocking' only to people who are unfamiliar with racism in the United States or the current US practices of local and federal law enforcement. Abu Ghraib was framed as shocking because that perpetuates the myth that, under normal circumstances, US culture, government, its police force, and beloved military are civilized, and righteous, and ethically superior to all the rest. Abu Ghraib became a very misleading media story because most people analyzed it as an aberration. You have key players in the government, military, and the law enforcement world denying responsibility for the making and indoctrination of those particular soldiers, saying, 'We don't do this, we don't do this, these soldiers do not represent us.' But that kind of pathological violence is not uncommon in the military or in US society.

The kind of twisted sadistic sexual violence that the Abu Ghraib photos depicted is an extremely familiar thing in the marines. I remember the week the photos came out, I was sitting with a bunch of marines, and it seemed like we were more shocked that those soldiers got publicly exposed rather than with what they actually did. The public has a very naive and patronizing view about American soldiers, as if they embark around the world to be boy scouts or diplomats. This kind of idealism is epitomized by this Iraq war generation's 'support the troops' activists, whether the support for the troops comes from the right or the left. Many activists are out of touch with the mind-altering that occurs when a young person is systemically indoctrinated in violence, and taught to wreak havoc upon other human beings who they are told are the bad guys. The overwhelming ideology that anything soft or effeminate is something that should be destroyed is so central to that indoctrination. Hardcore pornography, animal abuse, sexual humiliation, domestic abuse, and good old-fashioned misogyny – these things inform the culture of American soldiers. I wish mothers in this country would snap out of their naive soldier-boy obsessions. Marines love to pull triggers, see things go boom, scream at the top their lungs, make someone else hurt and pay for not being like 'us.'

When did Americans become so blind to how ugly this stuff really is? This stuff happens every day, behind prison gates, behind closed doors, and in every element of our children's entertainment supply. Savage violence is as much a part of the American way of life as shopping malls

97

and SUVs. Within our own borders, we are experts at torture and imprisonment. We are the most experienced prison guards on the planet. No
other country in the world has as many prisons or incarcerated human
beings as we do. It's a great tragedy, an embarrassment, and we don't talk
enough about it. Why is it such a shock that the techniques employed
by US prison guards would be employed by US soldiers? We are born
and bred in the same country, inside the same system that preaches the
notion of empowerment and respect through the use of violence.

EPC: Abu Ghraib provided this opportunity for people to say, 'Oh
my God, we are so innocent.' As if we didn't know that the US was
founded on shit like that. As if we don't remember. Our history is based
on that stuff. So why are we so appalled? They tortured Native peoples.
They scalped them alive. They raped them. What happened to us is not
recognized as an atrocity. Are we not considered human? Can we really
say that was the past and today it is different? I for one certainly can't.
It looks the same to me.

AB: I really only processed after I left the marines the extent to which I
had been programmed, the extent to which I was infatuated with violence.
One summer during graduate school I ended up working in Palestine
with a community-based NGO that specialized in non-violence training,
much of it for teenagers that had grown up traumatized by the violence
of military occupation. I looked Palestinian and much of the time Israeli
soldiers assumed I was Arab. The experience of being at the other end
of a live muzzle at military checkpoints was the most overwhelming
experience I'd ever had. I couldn't do a goddam thing one way or the
other. Like all the local people, I was just a target. I had spent years
training American marines to do the same thing, and here I was at the
other end of it, watching young Israeli kids, who were just like my own
marines, in slow motion, day after day, hollering and waving muzzles
at skulls, strutting around with such ego and contempt. It was surreal
and horrifying. It completely changed me. Those soldiers were me, as
clueless and desensitized and cruel and arrogant, with as giant a chip
on their shoulders. It was the first time I really felt the shame of who
I'd become – in fact, who I had chosen to become.

American kids are immersed in a ruthless culture of violence through
entertainment and television, but unless they've grown up terrorized by
gangs or poverty, they have no idea what war feels like, how it affects
every aspect of your life and psyche. They have no idea what kind of harm
this 'cowboy' culture perpetrates against human beings around the world,
let alone in their own towns and cities. War is the natural extension of
American popular culture and values. Look at the camouflage clothing

parents are drowning their children in. This military clothing is at once a symbol of sex appeal and naive, rebellion without context. And it's shamelessly flaunted while people are being slaughtered in the Middle East as a result of American aggression. We are objects of indoctrination and recruitment the moment we're born. It's the numbness throughout civilian US society that feeds and sustains our current level of warfare.

SS: Your experience in Palestine and being seen as the enemy points to how people of color have to, in a sense, work at denying how replaceable and disposable they are in the eyes of the military and how they too can become the enemy.

Feminism and militarism

SS: Eli, in March 2007 you had a public dialogue with Cynthia Enloe. In her latest books, *The Curious Feminist* (2004) and *Globalization and Militarism* (2007), she encourages a feminist curiosity to take seriously all the complex reasons women end up in the military. By ignoring the condition and perspectives of women in the military, we fail to see the many parallels and connections that exist between the military and the education system and how certain feminist discourses supplement the militarization of women. Through my conversations with you both, my understanding of these parallels has been illuminated. The compartmentalized approach taken by many feminists and civilians is that they believe themselves to be *outside* and *above* the military system; and therefore don't interrogate enough the complementary function of these institutions, and how the education system and the military work together.

Universities are an integral part of the military-industrial complex, funded to develop weapons and military technology; universities reproduce the workforce of engineers and designers who work for private military corporations. Both the academy and the military have been historically patriarchal and sexist, and demand adherence to the established standards of a Eurocentric male-defined rationality and productivity. Both institutions function as essential state apparatuses that maintain and reproduce social hierarchies.

Now we have a select category of women in the US who have risen into the ranks of powerful white men, whether that is in the military, government, corporations, or the academy. The way in which women in the US become 'empowered' often involves a process of assimilation, incorporation and domestication by the values and practices of established institutions.

AB: I'm tired of fighting just to prove a point and get to the top. I think we need to wrestle more with what empowerment should really mean. I believe it's critical to have women in the institutions you just mentioned, as they serve as important reminders that all members of society should be represented in decision-making bodies. But just because you've entered an institution doesn't mean your presence alters its condition, or improves the well-being for others it professes to serve.

SS: The mainstreaming of liberal feminist discourse which promotes women's equality with white men has become part of US popular culture. It has also bled into the cultural production of the genre of superwomen. The transgressive allure of sexy women with guns is a staple across mainstream culture in films, TV and video games.

AB: A large part of me was drawn to these superwomen icons, and shaped my desire to fight the man within whatever institution I was in. If it weren't for Demi Moore playing the role of GI Jane, I might never have joined the military. One of the horrible results of the Hollywood version of the genre of the sexy woman killer is that the causes and effects of violence are rarely explored. Killing is basically a livelihood for these fantasy women. They rarely have to deal with the warping of their soul or psyche.

SS: These popular representations of women's empowerment through their ability to compete with and outdo men – through acts of physical prowess and militarized violence – have become one of the ways in which representations of token and fantasy women not only misrepresent women's experiences in the military, but operate to normativize the use of mass industrialized violence and obscure the gravity of our socioeconomic crises that the cycle of warfare will only exacerbate.

You've both talked about the disconnect between academic feminist analysis and the experience of women in the US military. Part of this disconnect may be a result of the fact that many feminists don't think that the military is a reformable institution. Many feminists who identify themselves as anti-military and anti-war may not pay heed to how the militarization of women may in fact constitute a deep crisis for US feminism.

EPC: Anti-military feminists need to see how people chose their path as a means to get out of their oppressive conditions. If they are anti-militaristic, what are feminists doing to provide viable alternatives for people who enter the military? Are they going to the rez to help? To the barrio or South Central LA?

There is all this judgment without looking at the systematic robotic conditions which young minds are forced to adjust to and accept if they are to be looked upon as successful students and scholars. The education system is like the military in that it has its rank and positions of authority. In both institutions, value is placed on your credentials and your ability to conform to the system.

US feminism has become too much about criticism, breaking down, analyzing, and in doing so, it has become disconnected from the bigger picture, from a broader understanding of ourselves, and this world, and how everything is interconnected. We have forgotten why this all started in the first place and how the idea came about that women should have rights, which was inspired by white women learning from Native communities. We need to remember the roots of the US and how it was settled.

The cycle of genocide

EPC: My tour in Iraq was a real eye-opener for me. When I was in Iraq, my biggest enemy was my own company. I would hear officers who gave briefings referring to enemy territory as Indian country. I found that shocking and I wondered what side I should be on if this is Indian country. I began to realize that perhaps I was on the wrong side.

I got to meet Iraqi people and what I came to understand is that they are very much like Native peoples. They have the drum, they have clans, they have ceremony, and they have an understanding of family in a very different way than Americans. They have their history that is now being erased, like ours was erased. My history isn't told to this day, as if I don't exist. And now I have participated to create genocide in another country against a people who are very much like me. I'm really struggling to look for my past that has been erased and I feel so guilty coming back because now I have been a participant of this genocide that everyone refuses to name. It is not a war, it is an invasion, we are committing a genocide over there, to children, to mothers, to brothers, and nobody wants to use the 'G' word, because if you do it means that you also have to look at what happened here at home in America.

Healing starts at home with the refugee camps here called reservations. It starts with healing our own hearts and admitting our own fears.

We don't need to be pointing fingers at the military or at George W. Bush. That is too easy. Let's stop pointing fingers and fighting for a power outside ourselves. Instead let's look inside ourselves and seek to understand how this US president mirrors this country and what we stand for as a nation. If we don't like it, then it's up to us to change it, that's all.

We are so busy going to work and paying our bills that we have no time to participate in the world to transform things. We say let our government take care of it. We are addicted to our possessions instead of loving our lives and participating in the world to make it a better place for our children. We are too comfortable and too lazy to care about anything that does not affect us directly, that is not directly in our face. The majority of the people in the US who have the power to make change don't because they are afraid of change, and are afraid of facing the truth about us Americans. We are all responsible for the acts our nation has committed against another people for the sake of greed.

This country does not know peace. I've been invited to be part of many peace movements around the United States, but from what I've observed among these movements, I am always disturbed at how much fighting takes place within these peace movements. You can't fight a fight with a fight and call it peace. You can't be anti and call it peace. We cannot give away something we do not have for ourselves. You cannot get peace; you have to be it, nurture it and give it away so that others may be touched by acts of peace and perhaps want it in their own lives.

References

Enloe, Cynthia (2000) *Maneuvers: The International Politics of Militarizing Women's Lives*, Berkeley: University of California Press.

— (2004) *The Curious Feminist: Searching for Women in a New Age of Empire*, Berkeley: University of California Press.

— (2007) *Globalization and Militarism: Feminists Make the Link*, New York: Rowman & Littlefield.

Feinman, Ilene Rose (2000) *Citizenship Rites: Feminist Soldiers and Feminist AntiMilitarists*, New York: New York University Press.

Hall, Gwendolyn M. (1999) 'Intersectionality: a necessary consideration for women of color in the military?', in Mary Katzenstein and Judith Reppy (eds), *Beyond Zero Tolerance: Discrimination in Military Culture*, Boston, MA: Rowman & Littlefield.

Manning, Lory (2005) *Women in the Military: Where They Stand*, 5th edn, Washington, DC: Women's Research and Education Institute.

Moore, Brenda (1995) 'Changing laws and women of color in the US military', *Minerva: Quarterly Report on Women and the Military*, 13.

US Department of Defense (2006) Unpublished data, Defense Manpower Data Center, September, compiled by the Women Research and Education Institute, January 2007.

7 | Decolonizing the racial grammar of international law

ELIZABETH PHILIPOSE

The appeal of international law to legal positivists and feminists alike, in providing compensation for violence endured, derives from the claim that international legal mechanisms are a counter to the otherwise ubiquitous power politics of sovereign states. There are, however, many ways in which international law fails to mitigate the damaging consequences of states' pursuit of power through the use of violence. From the lack of enforcement mechanisms to its simultaneous valorization and condemnation of the use of violence, international law has not been the moderating force to bring about more peaceful relations between states and peoples. In fact, there is a long-standing relationship between law and violence which justifies and legitimizes violence when it is in the service of power, and more specifically when it is in the service of imperial, racialized and masculinist power (Gregory 2007; Orford 2002).

At the same time, the appeal of law and legal legitimacy remains strong. Appeals to international law to stop the torture, rendition (detention) and indefinite incarceration of Muslims, or people perceived to be Muslims, in the 'global war against terror' (GWAT) resound today. In each set of appeals is a sense that international law is and ought to be universally binding and applicable, meaning that every person who is violated by international violence has the right of the protective cloak of international law.

There are synchronous impulses within international law and the use of torture, derived from Euro-colonial history, and iterated today in contemporary debates about the use of torture and the role of international law in mitigating 'terrorist' violence. International law, as it has come to be constituted, derives from European nation-building needs, in a time of Euro-colonial expansion. Though outlawed by European states in the 1800s, torture was retained as a useful and covert method of containing and suppressing non-citizen, 'enemy,' or 'insurgent' populations. Whereas international law has been overtly employed to justify interventions, annexations and occupations of colonized territory and peoples, torture has been the accompanying stealth mechanism designed to facilitate intervention and occupation.

Both international law and torture are employed for the purpose of incorporating the 'backward' and 'uncivilized' into modernity; each is the alibi of the other. These modalities of regulation and governance come together in the US Military Commissions Act 2006, legislation that is said to be contravening international law by sanctioning the use of 'coercive interrogation techniques.' In fact, international law and the use of torture are combined here for the same purpose. No longer 'hidden in plain sight' (Parry 2005), torture emerges as the mechanism through which racial imperial rule will be enacted, and law is put into the service of facilitating that form of rule. The current use of torture in the GWAT follows a long history of sanctioned violence for the purpose of securing European and, later, US domination over neocolonial/post-colonial populations. The use of torture is not a departure from international law, and thus we see the revision of international law to accommodate the use of torture as an overt mechanism reserved for the preservation of US empire. For feminists and advocates of social justice, it is crucial to interrogate the colonial foundations of current legal systems and the intersection of gender, race, sexuality and nation which shapes the nature of global politics today. Without taking on our 'history of the present,' we misunderstand the impulses and intentions of the GWAT and ultimately we cannot make feminist sense of current US foreign policy or international law.

The alibi function of international law

Antony Anghie traces the creation of international law-making and demonstrates that from the sixteenth century CE until today, international law has relied upon the distinction between civilized and uncivilized to construct its proper subjects and objects. Particularly under nineteenth-century European imperial rule, international law developed in tandem with imperial needs to justify colonization, slavery, occupation and decision-making authority over the lands and peoples of non-European extraction. As Anghie states: international law is 'the grand project that has justified colonialism as a means of redeeming the backward, aberrant, violent, oppressed, undeveloped people of the non-European world by incorporating them into the universal civilization of Europe' (Anghie 2005: 3).

Further, within the universe of colonial logic, measuring backwardness is predicated on gendered concepts of what it means to be human and to be self-determining/sovereign. If we consider the colonial configuration of modern Western versions of gender, it is the case that masculinity is a raced, classed and sexualized category, encompassing the attributes of the idea of human as white, Euro-derived, propertied, heterosexual and male. In this sense, to be male and called undeveloped is to be feminized as an unfit male, terms that signal both the abject and object and the assumptions of deviant sexuality, impotency and pollution. To be female and called backward in its colonial connotations conjures a passive, victimized-by-culture object of rescue and civilization (Orford 2002; Narayan 1997). Both gendered configurations signal inferior alien species, non-humans who lack personality, agency or individual uniqueness. Heterosexuality too, in its colonial connotations, is a precious commodity of the ideal human and in need of continuously being proven, protected and coded as unambiguous. Establishing the masculinity, whiteness and heterosexuality of colonial agents demands the production of themselves as the ideal human through the gendered and racialized oppositional terms of self and other (Philipose 2007b; Orford 2002).

Of course, non-Europeans could not ultimately be redeemed; they were not incorporated into 'civilization' as equals, and neither were they civilized, i.e. Europeanized, by their incorporation. Instead, the civilizing project of international law aimed to sustain the ongoing dichotomy between the civilized and the backward. Incorporation into international law meant that the uncivilized were under correct and appropriate tutelage and protectorship so that they could be managed more effectively. This management was seen to be beneficial for all parties: the Europeans could fulfill their universalist mandates of taming the world, and subject peoples would benefit from the guidance of their masters, a need they would never outgrow given the Euro-racist assumptions of the eternal immaturity and hereditary backwardness of subject peoples. As Anghie states:

> [nineteenth-century international law] posits an essentialist dichotomy between the non-European and the European; it characterizes relations between these entities to be inherently antagonistic; it establishes a hierarchy between these entities, suggesting that one is advanced, just and authoritative while the other is backward, violent and barbaric; it asserts that the only history which may be written of the backward is in terms of its progress towards the advanced; it silences the backward and denies it any subjectivity or autonomy; it assumes and promotes the centrality of the civilized; and it contemplates no other approaches to the problems of society than those which have been formulated by the civilized. (Anghie 2005: 112)

Focusing on the basis of international law – the category of sovereignty – Anghie demonstrates that two types of sovereignty were created: one is the sovereignty granted to European powers that was thought to reflect their essential civilized nature; and the other is the sovereignty granted to non-European states, after decolonization and the decline of the European imperial order. Sovereignty is the basic condition of legitimacy for international actors. It grants self-determination and authority over a territorially bounded region and specified populations; it enshrines the principle of non-interference between states; and it establishes the legitimate monopoly over the use of violence within states (police, judiciary, emergency measures), and the right to have standing armies and to engage in armed conflict with external actors for defensive purposes.

The Treaty of Westphalia (1648) enshrined sovereignty as the principle of maintaining peaceful relationships between European states, as a guarantee of their freedom, diversity, self-determination and self-governance. These concepts were developed, however, in a world where non-Europeans were not considered to be sovereign, and as such the principles were not developed to establish equality between all peoples on earth. Sovereignty was not accorded to non-European peoples under European colonization, and as Anghie demonstrates, the entire concept of sovereignty itself depended upon the *exclusion* of non-Europeans from self-determination, and the *inclusion* of them as subject peoples.

As European empires declined and more non-European peoples became independent, sovereignty came to be defined as the ability of non-Europeans to best approximate European civilization. Their sovereignty is not the right of self-determination; rather, it is the surrender of freedom to be self-governing and self-determining, and a surrender of their uniqueness and identity to become more like Europeans. This includes the suppression of traditional practices and indigenous knowledges; establishing centralized government; promoting secular nationalism; retaining the monopoly over the use of violence within the state; enshrining private property rights; and establishing the gendered household division of labour, masculine rule and the public regulation of sexuality (Stoler 1997; Goldberg 1993; Fanon 1967; McClintock 1995; Said 1979; Loomba 1998).

This move in the development of the concept of sovereignty, of splitting between European and non-European versions, is an insight that offers much to understanding current debates about the use of international law in the GWAT. Anghie rewrites the conventional wisdom that suggests that Europeans forged sovereignty rights which were then universalized to non-Europeans in the decolonization period. Instead, he shows that the sovereignty of the non-European is contingent upon acquiring European traits, and dependent upon non-European states' alliance with Europe, and now with the USA. This is an insight that counters a core idea in the field of international relations, for instance, which retains the mythology that sovereignty is the guarantee of equality between states. It is an insight that answers the question of why it is that some states appear to be more sovereign than others. Finally, it answers the question of why international legal sanctions are rarely applied against imperial states.

Sovereign impulses of international law

Sovereignty is foundationalized as the grounds of legitimacy for the use of violence, where sovereignty is inextricably and historically derived from the imperial need to distinguish between legitimate uses of violence – militarism – and the illegitimate uses of violence – terrorism. The application of international laws of war, through tribunals or UN Security Council resolutions or new US legislation, is constitutive of the prevailing conception of militarism and sovereignty. This is not necessarily a permanent feature of the international law system, but it is a relatively enduring feature that has yet to be unraveled from its colonial and imperial precepts, and the commitment to ensuring that European and European-derived states remain the only legitimate purveyors of violence. As such, sovereignty is a feature of whiteness and the central concept in the racial grammar of international law.

The laws of war are notable at least as much for what they sanction and legitimize and make possible as they are for what violences they prohibit (Philipose 1996). The laws of war are attempts to establish a legitimate monopoly on the use of violence by soldiers acting at the behest of sovereign legitimate actors. This is done in tandem with identifying and punishing those who wield, or who intend to wield, non-authoritative violence. The dichotomy of legitimate and illegitimate uses of violence is paralleled by the colonial dichotomy of the civilized and the backward, and both formulations rest upon the construction of sovereignty as the marker of the legitimate monopoly over the use of violence (Philipose 2002). In turn, the constitution of sovereignty in the history of international law-making is inextricably linked to European imperial needs, modernity and the racial grammars of European empire. In fact, the racial grammar of international law structures claims of sovereignty and the legitimate right to use violence against those who are deemed to be non-sovereign, illegitimate, barbarous and subhuman. Further, the racial grammar of international law codes legitimacy as the claim of white, Euro-derived or Euro-allied, masculine, heterosexual, chivalrous agents to defend the honour and dignity of women and to rescue them from the forces of tyranny and barbarism (Orford 1999, 2002; Kapur 2002). The laws of war are part of the larger civilizing mission of international law, designed to incorporate and assimilate the barbarous misogynist other into the imperial order of modernity, chivalry and lawfulness.

The alibi function of torture

The gradual elimination of the public use of torture during the period of the European Enlightenment is attributed to the growing sense that inflicting inhuman pain and suffering dehumanized those who tortured and reflected the practices of less civilized peoples. The official use of torture came to be associated with pre-modern and barbarous methods of treating suspects and criminals. Arguments cast in terms of the standards of civilization and justice were advanced to minimize the infliction of physical suffering on those held in police custody, and modern states increasingly relied on incarceration to punish criminals (Foucault 1995). The concern was not for the suffering of those who were being tortured, but for the humanity of those who tortured, and the desire to incorporate the subject population into Euro-versions of humanity. As Talal Asad states:

> ... in the attempt to outlaw customs the European rulers considered cruel, it was not concern with indigenous suffering that dominated the Europeans' thinking, but rather the desire to impose what they considered civilized standards of justice and humanity on a subject population – ie, the desire to create new human subjects. (Asad 1997: 293)

Asad demonstrates that philosophers acknowledged that the process of civilizing subject peoples sometimes involved inflicting suffering upon them, and there were times and places where the use of torture was necessary and useful. In particular, torture was given the special role of drawing subject peoples into modernity. If torture was simply for the infliction of pain, it was seen to be gratuitous and thus barbarous and uncivilized. For instance, in the case of interrogation, Voltaire considered the use of torture to be gratuitous because it was unlikely to yield verifiable information.

Thus, pain was quantified and slotted into categories of utility and waste. As liberal democracies sought to consolidate their sovereign authority, the use of torture was reserved for non-citizens. Asad demonstrates that the consolidation of these liberal democratic regimes generated new rationales for the legitimate use of torture. Torture was justifiable if it was useful to incorporate subjects into civilization. 'Pain endured in the movement toward becoming "fully human" ... was seen as necessary because social or moral reasons justified why it must be suffered' (ibid.: 295). These uses of torture remained hidden in plain sight, meaning that at the same time that torture was employed, it was simultaneously denied. Awareness of the uses of torture was relegated to the margins of public discourse, shielded both by a moral rationale and by covert practices. Retained as a useful tool for the promotion of civilizing state interests, torture was nonetheless conducted in secrecy (Parry 2005; Asad 1997).

The use of torture parallels and abets the international legal impulse of subsuming subject peoples into becoming human, as defined by Euro-colonial concepts. As Anghie states about sovereignty:

> Sovereignty represents, then, at the most basic level, an assertion of power and authority, a means by which a people may preserve and assert their distinctive culture. For the non-European world, sovereignty was the complete negation of power, authority and authenticity. This was not only because European sovereignty was used as a mechanism of suppression and management, but because the acquisition of sovereignty was the acquisition of European civilization. In effect, then, for the non-European society, personhood was achieved precisely at that point of time when it ceased to have an independent existence; when it was absorbed into European Empires or when it profoundly altered its own cultural practices and political organizations. (Anghie 2005: 104)

International law and the use of torture share a racial grammar that divides peoples into those who are human and those who are not. Each is the alibi of the other, and each supports the efforts of the other to suppress and contain subject peoples.

The colonial occupation of Iraq

Responding to the images from Abu Ghraib, US president George W. Bush's administration denied that the practices depicted were widespread, attributing them to a few officers who made bad judgments. Several soldiers involved were charged and tried for prisoner abuse, including Charles Graner and Lynndie England. The commanding officer, Brigadier General Janis Karpinski, was relieved of her position and demoted. Yet at the same time that the practices at Abu Ghraib were being exceptionalized, the legitimacy of coercive methods was defended by the US Attorney General's office, which offered a redefinition of torture at great remove from that acknowledged in the Geneva Conventions (Levinson 2004) protecting prisoners of war. Prominent ethics and human rights scholars in the United States advanced various arguments defending the use of torture in the GWAT (Ignatieff 2004; Elshtain 2004; Dershowitz

2004). Preserving both prongs of the Enlightenment ideal, government officials and eminent scholars have argued that torture is necessary to civilize people, and in the current case necessary to civilize terrorists/ Muslims.

Consider the Military Commissions Act 2006, which establishes the parameters of US-constructed courts in trying suspected terrorists in the GWAT. The Act is not linked with standing international legal tribunals or mechanisms such as the International Criminal Court or the wider body of humanitarian law. Instead, the authority for the Act is derived from presidential powers applying in time of war: 'the President's authority to convene military commissions arises from the Constitution's vesting in the President of the executive power and the power of Commander in Chief of the Armed Forces' (Military Commissions Act 2006: para. 3).

The Act establishes the possibility of ad hoc commissions that bypass a number of US and international human rights protections, including the right of habeas corpus, and creates unusual rules of evidence which allow hearsay to be admitted. It streamlines the legal process to ensure speedy trials. It eliminates the applicability of Common Article 3 of the Geneva Conventions, the provision in international law that protects prisoners of war from torture and cruel, inhuman and degrading treatment. Instead, the much less prohibitive US Treatment of Detainees Act 2005 is referenced. The Military Commissions Act 2006 establishes its own necessity with reference to the exceptional circumstances of the GWAT, the exceptional elusiveness of suspected terrorists, and the possible magnitude of future terrorist acts against the USA. Paragraph 6 outlines these reasons:

> The use of military commissions is particularly important in this context because other alternatives, such as the use of courts-martial, generally are impracticable. The terrorists with whom the United States is engaged in armed conflict have demonstrated a commitment to the destruction of the United States and its people, to the violation of the law of war, and to the abuse of American legal processes. In a time of ongoing armed conflict, it generally is neither practicable nor appropriate for combatants like al Qaeda terrorists to be tried before tribunals that include all of the procedures associated with courts-martial. (Military Commissions Act 2006: para. 6)

Perhaps the most significant aspect of the Military Commissions Act 2006 is that it is drafted with the purpose of legitimizing the continued use of 'tools to save American lives,' namely to empower CIA officials to continue a program of 'coercive interrogation' to gain 'vital intelligence' from suspected terrorists without fear of sanction or prosecution (White House 2006). In this way, the Act enshrines Enlightenment principles that suggest torture is justifiable and necessary, especially in cases where the combatants are beyond the rehabilitation promised by international law.

The offenses triable by military commissions when committed within a context of military combat include well-documented war crimes such as murder of protected persons, attacking civilians, pillaging, attacking protected property and using protected persons as shields. The Act considers rape an offense, defined as the 'wrongful invasion of body, penetrating however slight of genitalia, anus, with foreign object or otherwise,' a departure from the International Criminal Tribunal for Yugoslavia and Rwanda definitions which refer specifically to violence against women (UN 1993). It also enumerates prohibitions against the use of torture 'following the standard definition, except when used in lawful circumstances,' and considers terrorism as an offense, defined as: 'Any person subject to this chapter who intentionally kills or inflicts great bodily harm on one or more persons, or intentionally engages in an act that evinces a wanton disregard for human life, in a manner calculated to influence or affect the conduct of government or civilian population by intimidation or coercion, or to retaliate against government conduct.' The definition of terrorism in the Act follows the protocol of international laws of war, outlining the deployment of violence that, in the context of a just war, would be acceptable through appeals to military necessity. The irony of the Act is that it prohibits the use of torture by enemy combatants, while securing the right of the USA to continue its use of CIA interrogations, all of which have been well documented as constituting physical and psychological torture methods (McCoy 2004; Parry 2005; Physicians for Human Rights 2005; Philipose 2007a). Beyond irony, this is the function of the colonialist basis of international law, and the racial grammar that ensures that dominant states, the USA in this instance, maintain their monopoly over the legitimate uses of violence.

The regulation and governance of sexuality

An aspect of being 'civilized' in the eyes of international law revolves around sexuality and the self-regulating capacity to be 'sexually appropriate.' Sexuality, in its modern conceptualizations, is a Euro-colonial construct that is central to national and racial preoccupations about lineage, inheritance, and blood (Foucault 1990; Stoler 1997). International law deems those who are sexually inappropriate *justiciable* – that is, subject to incorporation into modernity and civilization through legal prosecution. For instance, international law is increasingly preoccupied with the prosecution of rape and sexual assault in war, a move that has been welcomed by feminist advocates around the world. At the same time, however, the opportunity to construct a war zone as a place of sexual deviance reflects a colonial impulse that mobilizes international law to justify armed intervention, foreign occupation, incarceration, criminal trials and the use of torture against those who come to be understood as 'sexual deviants' ('mass' or 'genocidal' rapists) (Chossudovsky 1996, 1999; Buss 1998). The attention paid to sexual violence against women in war is part of a civilizing impulse of international law, one that aims to incorporate the barbarous, violent, nationalist 'other' into the presumably civilized, genteel and chivalrous modern (Buss 1998; Orford 1999). The application of the laws of war to prosecute violence against women, and in fact to prosecute the violence of war itself, occurs only when the war-makers are 'others' and are constructed as racial others, and when lawmakers have an interest in subsuming the region for self-interested reasons. The application of law itself is productive of the racialized others, predicated on the fact that they rape women in wartime. The fact that soldiers violate women in the course of war-making serves to construct them as deviant masculinities, sexually depraved and perverse, vicious in their violation of a 'woman's honour and dignity,' and in need of assimilation and education at the hands of the superior enlightened lawmakers. Women's bodies in these instances of international law perform a recurring function in colonial systems – they are the justification for intervention, occupation, prosecution and colonialism. This is not to suggest that rape and sexual assault against women ought not to be prosecuted; rather, it is to draw attention to the form that prosecution might take, and the functions of international law given its colonial intent and foundations.

The use of torture is similarly preoccupied with the governance and regulation of masculine enemies on the basis of their sexuality, and militarized masculinities depend upon the depiction of the enemy as sexually deviant and perverse to contrast with the appropriately masculine and heterosexual. Thus we see, as Jasbir Puar and Amrit Rai highlight, the repetition of the sexual perversity of the terrorist in popular depictions of the GWAT. We see posters with Osama bin Laden being anally penetrated by the Empire State Building, websites that depict the torture of bin Laden with sodomy, and exhortations to force bin Laden to have a sex-change operation and live in Afghanistan. As they state: 'American retaliation promises to emasculate bin Laden and turn him into a fag' (Puar and Rai 2002: 126). Further, Muslims and Muslim states are held as the example par excellence of misogyny in the Western imagination, an imagination that provokes the colonialist narrative that white men, in their enlightened masculinity, have the duty to save brown women from brown men (Puar 2005; Kapur 2002).

In many ways, the Abu Ghraib photos of the torture and sexual humiliation of Muslim detainees express the desire to turn the detainees into 'fags,' thereby undermining their potency and power to hurt women and to harm Americans. Puar (2005) argues that the photos express the intricate relations between orientalist knowledge production and the peculiar sexual and bodily shame attributed to Muslims and/or Arabs. Informed by Raphael Patai's *The Arab Mind*, which purports to explain the deep psyches of Arabs, US officials deploy their orientalist sexual fantasies in the torture of Muslim detainees.

Mission accomplished: an agenda for transnational feminism

US public debate about the war in Iraq (the occupation of Afghanistan is rarely discussed) revolves around establishing the appropriate benchmarks and conditions for declaring the war over and the USA as victorious. At the same time, in what was a hypermasculinized and absurd visual display, President George W. Bush declared on 1 May 2003 the 'mission accomplished' aboard the USS *Abraham Lincoln*. If we recast the GWAT as a colonial bid to occupy Iraq, to extract its resources for the benefit of the USA and its allies, and to contain and suppress Iraqis through the use of torture, the mission *is* accomplished. Despite the widespread violence, the absence of basic needs and services, and the approximately one million dead and over four million displaced Iraqis that marked Iraq in 2007, the USA and its corporate and state allies are in business. There is no question that the Iraq war is already 'won'; as long as there is an occupation, the USA is winning. From the perspective of the US administration, the 'success' of the war is not judged in terms of turning power over to the Iraqi people, bringing the troops home, or seeing a sovereign Iraq restored. The purpose of the GWAT as deployed in Iraq is occupation, the framework is colonial, and it has been accomplished. Further, it is unlikely that anything but a second-tier sovereignty is intended for Iraq, one that installs a malleable regime and ensures that the USA continues to control the country and, thereby, extend and maintain its imperial reach.

Without an active decolonizing of the foundational assumptions of international law, its implementation reproduces the colonial efforts to civilize those who are deemed backward and incorporate them into a culturally specific version of modernity, albeit as lesser beings. Without recognizing the colonial function of the use of torture, we miss the point that structurally the GWAT is a war against racialized peoples for the retention of 'First World' domination. The governance and regulation of sexuality are clues to the embedded racial grammar, as is the move to legitimize the use of torture, written on the surface of domestic and international law. At stake is the need to understand the political culture of humanitarian law, and the context and assumptions that support its legitimacy. Between placing wholesale faith in international law to counter violence, and rejecting international law as hopelessly colonialist, I am suggesting that decolonizing international law ought to be as significant to our work as ensuring its gender sensitivity and its universality.

To avoid inadvertently doing the work of empire, we need to understand that, through and through, international legal systems are imperial and racialized and supremacist. To not take on the task of decolonizing these systems that govern and regulate international behaviour is to reproduce and re-enact the violence of racism and racial supremacy against those whom we aim to protect. It is not a question of working within the parameters of existing systems, but of revolutionizing those systems through our advocacy and activism, and creating analytics that refuse to be complicit in recolonizing the world.

References

Anghie, Antony (2005) *Imperialism, Sovereignty and the Making of International Law*, Cambridge: Cambridge University Press.

Asad, Talal (1997) 'On torture, or cruel, inhuman and degrading treatment', in A. Kleinman, V. Das and M. Lock (eds), *Social Suffering*, Berkeley: University of California Press.

Buss, Doris (1998) 'Women at the borders: rape and nationalism in international law', *Feminist Legal Studies*, 6(2).

Campbell, David (1996) 'Violent performances: identity, sovereignty, responsibility', in Yosef Lapid and Friedrich Kratochwil (eds), *The Return of Culture and Identity in International Relations Theory*, Boulder, CO: Lynne Rienner Publishers.

Chossudovsky, Michel (1996) 'Dismantling former Yugoslavia, recolonising Bosnia', www.nadir.org/nadir/initiativ/agp/free/chossudovsky/dismanteling.htm.

— (1999) 'NATO's war of aggression against Yugoslavia: an overview', www.nadir.org/nadir/initiativ/agp/free/chossudovsky/overview.htm>.

Dershowitz, Alan (2004) 'Tortured reasoning', in S. Levinson (ed.), *Torture: A Collection*, Oxford: Oxford University Press.

Elshtain, Jean B. (2004) 'Reflection on the problem of "dirty hands"', in S. Levinson (ed.), *Torture: A Collection*, Oxford: Oxford University Press.

Fanon, Frantz (1967) *Black Skin, White Masks*, trans. Charles Lam Markham, New York: Grove.

Foucault, Michel (1990) *History of*

Sexuality: An Introduction, 2nd edn, New York: Vintage.

— (1995) *Discipline and Punish: The Birth of the Prison*, 2nd edn, New York: Vintage.

Goldberg, David T. (1993) *Racist Culture: Philosophy and the Politics of Meaning*, Oxford: Blackwell.

Gregory, Derek (2007) 'Vanishing points', in D. Gregory and A. Pred (eds), *Violent Geographies: Fear, Terror, and Political Violence*, New York: Routledge.

Ignatieff, Michael (2004) 'Evil under interrogation: is torture ever permissible?', *Financial Times*, 15 May, available at www.ksg.harvard.edu/news/opeds/2004/ignatieff_torture_ft_051504.htm.

Kapur, Ratna (2002) 'The tragedy of victimization rhetoric: resurrecting the "native" subject in international/post-colonial feminist legal politics', *Harvard Human Rights Journal*, 5.

Levinson, Stanford (2004) 'Contemplating torture: an introduction', in S. Levinson (ed.), *Torture: A Collection*, Oxford: Oxford University Press.

Loomba, Ania (1998) *Colonialism/Postcolonialism*, New York: Routledge.

McClintock, Anne (1995) *Imperial Leather: Race, Gender and Sexuality in the Colonial Context*, New York: Routledge.

McCoy, Alfred W. (2004) 'Torture at Abu Ghraib followed CIA's manual', *Boston Globe*, 14 May.

Narayan, Uma (1997) *Dislocating Cultures: Identities, Traditions, and Third World Feminism*, New York: Routledge.

Orford, Anne (1999) 'Muscular humanitarianism: reading the narratives of the new interventionism', *European Journal of International Law*, 10(4).

— (2002) 'Feminism, imperialism and the mission of international law', *Nordic Journal of International Law*, 71.

Parry, John T. (2005) 'The shape of modern torture: extraordinary rendition and ghost detainees', *Melbourne Journal of International Law*, 6(2), mjil.law.unimelb.edu.au/issues/archive/2005(2)/11Parry.pdf.

Philipose, Elizabeth (1996) 'The laws of war and women's human rights', *Hypatia*, 11(4), Fall.

— (2002) 'Prosecuting violence, performing sovereignty: the trial of Dusko Tadic', *International Journal for the Semiotics of Law*, 15.

— (2007a) 'The politics of pain and the uses of torture', *Signs: Journal of Women and Culture*, 32(4), Summer.

— (2007b) 'The politics of pain and the end of empire', *International Feminist Journal of Politics*, 9(1), March.

Physicians for Human Rights (2005) *Break Them Down: Systematic Use of Psychological Torture by US Forces*, retrieved from www.phrusa.org.

Puar, Jasbir K. (2005) 'On torture: Abu Ghraib', *Radical History Review*, 93, Fall.

Puar, Jasbir K. and A. S. Rai (2002) 'Monster, terrorist, fag: the war on terrorism and the production of docile patriots', *Social Text*, 20(3).

Said, Edward (1979) *Orientalism*, New York: Vintage.

Stoler, Ann L. (1997) *Race and the Education of Desire*, Durham, NC: Duke University Press.

UN (United Nations) (1993) Statute of the International Tribunal

(Security Council Resolution 827, 25 May), *The Laws of War: A Comprehensive Collection of Primary Documents on International Laws Governing Armed Conflict*, ed. W. M. Reisman and C. T. Antoniou, New York: Random House.

United States Congress (2006) *A Bill: The Military Commissions Act of 2006*, 109th Congress, 2nd Session.

White House (2006) *The Military Commissions Act of 2006*, Fact sheet, www.whitehouse.gov/ news/releases/2006/10/20061017. html.

8 | The other v-word: the politics of victimhood fueling George W. Bush's war machine

ALYSON M. COLE

Feminist scholars have skillfully deconstructed the retrograde gender politics fueling US president George W. Bush's 'war on terror.' They have exposed how his administration appropriated feminist language and the banner of oppressed women to justify the invasions of Afghanistan and Iraq, installed 'gender decoys' in the press and female ventriloquists as official spokespersons, resurrected patriarchy and entrenched inequality (e.g. Eisenstein 2005; Hawkesworth 2005; Young 2003). In this essay, I seek to supplement this work by exploring an aspect of Bush's ideology that has gone largely unnoticed. I will suggest that at the foundation of the president's war on terror is a particular notion of victimhood; and further, that we cannot fully grasp the logic of either his rhetoric or his policies until we comprehend the radical transformation our conception of victims and victimization has undergone over the last fifteen years.

Since the early 1990s, the victim idiom has been pivotal to battles in the USA over the welfare state and civil and criminal justice reform, as well as the so-called culture wars. Conservative critics bemoaning the alleged proliferation and excess of victim claims – especially those advanced by feminists and other political progressives – employed a new, decidedly pejorative, use, coining expressions such as 'victimism,' and 'victim politics.' Without much precedent, 'victim' became a term of derision, deployed to dismiss, ridicule, and condemn. This anti-victim campaign associates victimization with weakness, passivity, dependency, and effeminacy. Conversely, it also portrays victims as manipulative, aggressive, and even criminal – as actual or potential victimizers – a danger to themselves and society. Discussions of social obligations, compensations, and remedial or restorative procedures have become instead criticism of the alleged propensity of self-anointed victims to engage in objectionable conduct. By investing victimhood with new meanings and rendering it a badge of shame, anti-victimism has made it extremely difficult to address pervasive forms of injustice that advantage some by subordinating others; instructing us that if we each were self-determining, then no one need be a victim. At the same time, anti-victimists depict a world in which a dominating victim politics victimizes society. This incongruous view of victimization

– ridiculing victims while exalting victim status – is at the core of what I term 'the Cult of True Victimhood' (Cole 2006).

Two aspects of anti-victimism are especially important to our discussion. First, both the victimized and the victimizer are gendered female. Second, while the attack on victims relies on a distinction between bogus victimists and real victims, the line quickly dissolves. Anti-victimism taints all forms of victimization. Being a victim is no longer a matter of injuries or injustices endured – a verifiable condition – but instead a stigmatizing judgment of individual character. Those who claim victim status are cast as shamefully passive or cynically manipulative. The good victim – in other words the only victim who merits our attention and sympathy – is the victim who refuses to be a victim.

We might assume that the tragedy of 9/11, which brought forth in the US new groups of victims and gave definitive form to the idea of the nation-state as a victim, would curb anti-victimism. On the contrary, efforts to embrace and commemorate those who perished during the attacks, to assess national and individual responsibility, and to validate warmongering abroad, all relied on anti-victim discourse. Even as President Bush and his supporters promote the notion of the United States as an innocent victim of a radical evil force, they remain uneasy with victimhood to the point of obscuring, evading, and often simply denying victimization.

As we shall see, anti-victimism generates two seemingly contending responses. One is more recognizable: We allowed ourselves to become weak, vulnerable, and, ultimately, victims. We redeem ourselves, therefore, through a process of remasculinization in which we reclaim our damaged manhood by feminizing our victimizers. The other response begins in reverse, by depicting the terrorists as feminine victimists: our enemies' dangerous indulgence in victimhood constitutes the real threat we must fight. In the following pages I examine anti-victimism in US public debates after 9/11 by focusing on three themes: the conception of victimization, the identity of the victimizer, and the reasoning behind Bush's policies.

Victim is a woman and women are victims

Consider the range of feminine, feminized, and unmasculine tropes that populate post-9/11 discourse. Some characterized 9/11 as 'America's Holocaust.' For many others, it was the crime of rape – often at great remove from actual violated bodies – which served as the central paradigm for framing events. In the aftermath of attack, public reflections metaphorically dressed the nation in a skirt. 'Gendered images and narratives migrated from embodied subjects to discursive constructions of the nation,' Mary Hawkesworth (2005: 132) observes. 'The US was stripped of its sense of invulnerability. The impregnable fortress was breached.' America's poet laureate, Billy Collins, unambiguously represents the incident as the day the United States 'lost our virginity' (Gross 2001). This language of sexual violation genders the victim as less than a man – wounded, exposed, weak, dominated, invaded; in a word, penetrable. According to this view, victimization emasculates or feminizes the victim by constituting a loss that indicates a prior lack.

William Bennett also contends that on September 11 we paid dearly for the feminization of America. In *Why We Fight: Moral Clarity and the War on Terrorism* (2001/03), he describes glaring evidence of pervasive national weakness – a country unprepared morally and intellectually, immersed in uncertainty and relativism. Who is responsible for the laxity that rendered America soft and left her vulnerable to evildoers? The usual suspects: academic post-structuralists, self-indulgent pacifists, busybody feminists – those he calls 'the victimology-mongers.' These groups diluted the country's military resolve, depleted its arsenal, undermined Americans' freedom (to carry guns), and invaded private homes to interfere with the manner in which parents raise their children (boys in particular). Fortunately, we now have 'George W. Bush, a "cowboy" president like Ronald Reagan, to revive the language of good and evil' (ibid.: 54).

Discussions about victimization drifted from metaphoric rape to actual women's bodies and psyches, as Bush's war machine ramped up. The administration repackaged the war in Afghanistan (and to a lesser degree the subsequent war in Iraq) as a momentous struggle for the emancipation of women. Suddenly, conservatives of all stripes were versed in the entire feminist vocabulary – reproving 'misogyny,' 'gender apartheid,' and even 'the feminization of poverty.' In another historic first, Laura Bush, the First Lady, substituted for her husband during the president's Saturday morning radio address to christen the new crusade on behalf of Third World women (17 November 2001). The president soon signed the 'Afghan Women and Children Relief Act' (AWCRA), a gesture that helped redefine America's mission as less to protect itself than to wage battle for its values and mores. Laura Bush's appeal harked back to a late-nineteenth-century discourse that championed colonialism as a tool for introducing progress to underdeveloped societies, whose ill treatment of their womenfolk evidenced their backwardness. As importantly, the contemporary outpouring of official empathy for the oppressed women of the world gave credence to Washington's peddling of its new Middle East mission as a 'war for freedom.' America could displace her victimization and assume instead the role of masculine liberator.

The administration's account of Middle Eastern women as victims abides by the rationale of the Cult of True Victimhood, whereby only the incontrovertibly pure and innocent merit recognition as deserving victims. Cynthia Enloe (2000) offers the neologism 'womenandchildren' to denote the condensed singularity of this view of victimhood as entirely powerless and desperately needing rescue. This archetype supports a triangulated gendered logic in which two masculine types – the dominator and the savior – act upon the feminized victim. While a more benign form of power, masculine protectionism is simply the flipside of masculine domination; as Iris Young (2003: 13) theorizes, both sustain relations of subordination: '[T]his relationship carries an implicit deal: forgo freedom, due process, and the right to hold leaders accountable, and in return we will make sure that you are safe.'

Feminists recognize how such representations of women's suffering have displaced arguments for all women's empowerment with campaigns for particular women's rescue, and in doing so have upheld inequality (whether patriarchal or colonial). Often the attention solicited for the cruelties veiled women abroad endure seemed primarily to veil the realities of Bush's anti-feminism or anti-womanism at home. Less than a year after Bush's self-congratulatory announcement about the AWCRA, for instance, he refused to sign the 1979 UN international treaty prohibiting the oppression of women, the Convention on the Elimination of All Forms of Discrimination Against Women.

The victimizer is a victimist

It is deplorably commonplace to associate victimhood with weakness and passivity and therefore code it feminine. The 9/11 perpetrators, however, have also been gendered female, both unmanly and treacherous. Though brutal and terrifying, our enemies, we are told, are not real men, but cowards (Egan 2002). In American public discourse, the individuals who stood behind the attack came to symbolize an ideology (the ephemeral 'terrorism'), immorality, and also a pathology. America's nemesis is variously described as sick – maniacal, murderous, deviant, even homosexual (cf. Robin 2001; Puar and Rai 2002). 'Their grievance is rooted in psychology,' Thomas Friedman (2002) elucidates, 'not politics.' Probing deeper, terrorist expert Jerrold Post (1984) diagnoses 'negative childhood experiences' and 'low self esteem.' Of course, such observations borrow only the diagnostic tools of therapy to dissect terrorists' troubled psyches; there is no rehabilitation program.

Perhaps most significantly, President Bush explicitly portrays the terrorists as victimists. Speaking about Al Qaeda at a ceremony honoring the National Endowment for Democracy, he expounded that the militant network 'thrives like a parasite, on the suffering and frustration of others.' Muslim radicals built 'a culture of victimization, in which someone else is always to blame and violence is always the solution. They exploit resentful and disillusioned young men and women, recruiting them through radical mosques as the pawns of terror' (6 October 2005). In other words, Bush maintains that the Middle East 'blame game' gave rise to the ultimate victimists, who, under the victim mantle, now victimize us.

Like the victimist at the center of controversies over US welfare reform and multiculturalism in the 1990s, our current adversary's criminality is multifold, encompassing his bestial aggression and seething resentment, as well as his unconscionable ingratitude. In this regard, it is telling that a new coinage recently surfaced: Islamic or terrorist 'welfare queens' – a pejorative term previously applied by US conservatives to African-American women receiving government assistance. Already raced and gendered for not properly responding to society's generosity – indeed, for even needing it in the first place – the Muslim 'queen' is ever more menacing. Welfare is the elixir of terrorism, or so the argument goes. Slate blogger Mickey Kaus (2001), for example, points to the fact that Zacarias Moussaoui, the French North African charged with conspiracy in connection with 9/11, reportedly turned radical while receiving welfare benefits in London. Reviewing cases of other individuals with ties to terror networks in Europe, Kaus deciphers the independent variable – all were recipients of state support, at one time or another:

> [T]here's a good argument that 'welfare benefits + ethnic antagonism' is the universal recipe for an underclass with an angry, oppositional culture. The social logic is simple: ... relatively generous welfare benefits enable those in the ethnic ghetto to stay there, stay unemployed, and seethe. Without government subsidies, they would have to overcome the prejudice against them and integrate into the mainstream working culture. Work, in this sense, is anti-terrorist medicine.

The connection between welfare and terrorism resurfaced after the 2005 summer bombing in London, when investigators learned that at least one of the suspects resided in public housing (Steyn 2005).

Finally, the anti-terror campaign invokes another feminized archetype – the wimpy American leftist. Liberals, progressives – in fact anyone who publicly expresses hesitations about the administration's policies – are deemed dangerously soft on terror, accommodating of the enemy, and undermining America's fortitude in a time of war. Bush and his allies attempt to stifle and derail public discussions by alleging that investigations and criticism only facilitate future attacks. As Karl Rove boasted, in contrast to the left's misguided sensitivity, conservatives confronted the enemy with the mental metal and military force to defeat him (Dinan 2005).

The nation as victim

George W. Bush's conception of the offenders – even those who were not verifiably part of the 9/11 attacks, but were soon baptized as 'helpers and enablers' of terror – is inseparable from his construction of America as a victim. The White House elaborates a crude Manichean world whose building blocks come only in two contrasting shades: good and evil, bondage and freedom, us and them. Bush's millennial rhetoric undergirds a paranoid public culture that emerged in the wake of 9/11 and may qualify as another phase in the history of American demonology. Twelve years after the demise of communism, America found renewed certitude as it faced, once again, a monumental foe. As in previous demonological moments, America's enemy is conceived of as ruthless, omnipotent and omnipresent, largely external, but very likely among us as well.

Bush's battle between good and evil reinforces the stark opposition of blameworthiness and blamelessness as these concepts were shaped and reshaped in the US 1990s debates over victimhood. He insists upon the unqualified innocence of the United States, refusing to acknowledge any wrongdoing, negligence or mistake in the events that led to 9/11, as though admitting any failing or flaw would belittle America's moral standing. Conflating causality and blame, the White House was reluctant, and sometimes overtly refused, to study seriously the circumstances of 9/11. Illinois Republican Congressman Ray LaHood (2002) borrowed from the anti-victimist lexicon when he asserted that instituting an investigative body would be little more than 'another one of those blame game commissions that ... is just looking to lay blame on an administration or a director of an agency.'

Only after public pressure for investigation became too strong to resist did the Bush administration relent. Once it was clear that no weapons of mass destruction existed, the administration freely spread blame around and personal pronouns took a plural form. Such obstructionism served transparent political needs. Exposing official ineptitude might call the administration's competence into doubt. Furthermore, the study of the events that led to 9/11 (or a reasoned inquiry into the motives of Al Qaeda leader Osama bin Laden and his men) stood against the vision of the conflict as a millennial struggle between righteous innocence and radical blameworthiness. America could not retain its status as a victim if any causal link between its behavior and the attack could be established. It thus upheld the notion that the only true victim is the thoroughly innocent one.

Numerous commentators point to 9/11 as the date America lost her innocence, but perhaps the inverse is true: the events of September 2001 enabled America to regain her innocence. After all, America had lost her innocence several times before – in the World War II bombing of the US naval fleet at Pearl Harbor by the Japanese; in the 1960s assassinations of President John F. Kennedy, black civil rights leader Martin Luther King, Jr, and Attorney General and presidential candidate Robert F. Kennedy; in the 1970s military loss to a communist-led national liberation movement in Vietnam and the unconstitutional 'dirty tricks' of President Richard Nixon during the Watergate scandal; and more recently in the 1990s domestic bomb massacre engineered by a white supremacist in Oklahoma City and the mass shooting of other students by white teenagers in Columbine, Colorado. At most of these tragic junctures, claiming a lost purity depended upon a highly selective collective memory. A different historical amnesia has afflicted the nation since 9/11. The violation created the possibility of reclaiming virtue and engaging in new transgressions. 'In order to ... sustain the affective structure in which we are ... victimized and ... engaged in a righteous cause rooting out terror,' Judith Butler (2002) suggests, 'we have to start the story with the experience of violence we suffered.' To begin the narrative elsewhere would open the possibility of an explanation for the attack and undermine the nation's claim to a place within the Cult of True Victimhood.

One muscular remedy to the danger posed by at least two feminized archetypes – the victim and the victimizer – was to remasculinize America by restoring patriarchal power. During the 2004 presidential campaign, both US political parties aspired to assume the mantle of masculinity. Republicans peddled the incumbent George W. Bush as the embodiment of strength, virility, and determination. Meanwhile, Democrats vied to convince American voters that their guy was the real man 'reporting for duty.'

The War on Terror also gave license to worship manly virtues and buff male bodies. *Wall Street Journal* columnist Peggy Noonan (2001) waxed erotic: 'It is not only that God is back, but that men are back ... I am speaking of masculine men, men who push things and pull things and haul things and build things, men who charge up the stairs in a hundred pounds of gear and tell everyone else where to go to be safe.' The burly men that feminist journalist Susan Faludi claimed were 'stiffed' and dejected by the new global economy, Noonan thinks 9/11 raised to royalty: 'I have seen the grunts of New York become kings of the City.' How do these newly empowered grunts rule? With chivalry, swoons Noonan. Rugged and silent, like her beloved 'Duke' (actor John Wayne): 'Good men suck it up ... manliness wins wars ...' Social critic Camille Paglia likewise gushes: 'I cannot help noticing how robustly, dreamily masculine the faces of firefighters are.' She continues, 'They are working-class men, stoical, patriotic. They're not on Prozac or question-ing their gender' (Brown 2001). The men are strong, fearless, chivalrous, staunchly heterosexual, and above all they dare not complain.

Refusing victimhood

President George W. Bush's conception of the post-9/11 geo-moral landscape renders him a practitioner of anti-victimist victim politics. America assumes the positions of innocent (feminine) victim as well as her own (masculine) savior. Still, this gendered binary represents only one modality of the post-9/11 victim discourse. For Bush the subject position of victimhood is untenable beyond its feminine register. Even as Washington used the horror of the attack to cast America as a True Victim, it often resorted to another of the anti-victimist models of vener-ated victimhood – the victim who rejects victimhood and refuses to be a victim.

While Bush emphasizes his compassion toward a variety of American sufferers in moments of political necessity – for instance, the Floridians who endured hurricanes in 2004, and, somewhat belatedly, those left homeless after Hurricane Katrina's wrath in 2005 – his approach to the suffering 9/11 inflicted is highly ambiguous. For a variety of reasons, the administration chose to repackage the post-9/11 wars in terms of a global pursuit for freedom rather than simply as a reaction to an attack planned and executed by a few individuals. Exigencies of self-defense did not propel America; she was responding to a higher calling. Necessity generated some of the rhetoric and policy. The war against Iraq was initially peddled as a defensive war to topple a sinister enemy who pos-sessed mighty arms that could devastate the United States. But since no weapons of mass destruction were located, the war was quickly rescripted as a single instance of a historic struggle against tyranny in which the United States found its groove again by rediscovering its ancient mission, its manifest destiny, as a model to the nations of the world.

Regardless of motives, the White House abandoned explicitly identify-ing the events of 9/11 as the sole anchor of its moral cause. The 'war for freedom' has deeper roots in American culture, a long chain of historical myths and icons. It is steeped in a manly heroism that is deeply ambivalent about suffering and sacrifice. Post-9/11 America is juxtaposed not just with a bloodthirsty enemy, but also with the liberalism and moral laxity of Democratic US president Bill Clinton and his wife, now-senator Hillary Rodham Clinton, as well as the 'gay' 1990s. In this tale, the attack corresponds to little more than a turning point in the plot, a moment of reckoning, not a point of origin. Bush's America sees the people who died on 9/11 at the World Trade Center, the Pentagon, and aboard the four planes not as victims but as heroes who – much like the defenders of the Alamo (a small group of men who died fighting Mexican troops in Texas in 1848 trying to wrest that territory for US interests) – 'died for freedom.' He posthumously conscripts or deputizes them to proselytize core American values rather than merely to protect its civilization.

The Bush administration supported efforts to compensate bereaved families generously and in record time. Commentators attribute this more to concern with preserving the US airline industry than with the plight of the victims, however (Belkin 2002). Otherwise, it rarely granted the victims' families the same public standing the victims' rights movement bestows upon relatives of victims of crime. The president appeared more comfortable in the company of law enforcement officers. In his visits to post-9/11 New York, he met and was continually photographed with the 'heroes' – policemen and firemen at the World Trade Center – not grieving families. When some families began to raise nagging questions about 9/11, the White House labored hard to stifle them. Together with its cadre of dependable pundits, it dismissed the families' call for a comprehensive investigation and was thoroughly unsympathetic to their expressed desires to find release, resolve or closure in truth-telling rather than in the killing fields of Iraq and Afghanistan.

As significantly, the Bush administration remains strangely sluggish in commemorating fallen US soldiers or acknowledging their suffering in other ways. In our image-congested culture, injured soldiers and bereaved families have been deleted somehow. For the longest time, the administration refused to release pictures of coffins of American soldiers or military funerals. Only the specter of public outcry forced the president and the secretary of defense to feign greater empathy toward families of American casualties (including the vacuous gesture of signing by hand the secretary of defense's letters of condolences). Practices of commemoration that have become constitutive of the modern state were left to private initiative. When ABC Television anchor Ted Koppel decided to read the names and show the photos of all American fatalities in Iraq during an episode of his widely viewed program *Nightline* in April 2003, his gesture was considered overtly political, unpatriotic and even subversive.

The conservative Sinclair Broadcasting Company accordingly pre-empted the live program on its ABC affiliates, blocking his reading.

The body in pain

It is not the case that the events of September 2001 or the war in Iraq were undocumented. Even as reports and images inundated the public, however, very little of the wounded and dead – American or Iraqi – was seen. Perhaps this lacuna is at the root of the subsequent immense commercial success of actor/director Mel Gibson's film *The Passion of the Christ* (2004). Three thousand men and women perished on 9/11 (and many more died during the subsequent wars), but the only body in torment that was not closeted, which was offered for complete, approving public display in the USA at that time, was that of Jesus. (The film's release roughly paralleled the public distribution of the contested torture photos from Abu Ghraib, the US prison in Baghdad.)

Detailing the last twelve hours of his life, the *Passion* focuses relentlessly on Christ's traumatized body. Richard Dyer (1997) notes in his study of 'whiteness' that Christ represents the essence of the white heterosexual male – the paradox of visibility and invisibility – being in the body but not of it. Gibson's Jesus, by contrast, is strongly embodied in a way that is seemingly alien to the Protestant tradition, rendering the enthusiasm with which evangelical America greeted the film ever more puzzling. Christ reminds us of sacrificial suffering, but Gibson's Jesus is unquestionably a man, not a lamb. Katha Pollitt (2004) describes a major scene in the film as a 'ten minute homoerotic sadistic extravaganza that no human being could have survived, as if the point was to show how tough Christ was.'

Conceived before 2001, the *Passion* nevertheless became emblematic of the post-9/11 atmosphere as well as of the larger campaign to reconfigure the role of victimization in American public life. Gibson registered on celluloid the perfect model of the Cult of True Victimhood. His victim is subjected to pain that is immediate and visible, verifiable yet immeasurable, and he accepts his torture without reservation or complaint, almost existentially (for the meaning of his sacrifice remained entirely outside the subject matter of the film). The *Passion* derives its visual vocabulary from a wide range of sources that have come to dominate our cultural conception of tortured bodies, from images of Nazi concentration camps to Gibson's own history of filmic violence – especially the brutality and martyrology of the historically fictive *Braveheart* (1995).

Gibson's film seems to correspond particularly well with the vernacular efforts to grapple with the violence of the World Trade Center attack and its victims. Post-9/11 iconography thrived in the memorabilia that vendors sold on the streets of New York and in the new public space of the Internet. Much of this rather sentimental folk art employed US national symbols and Christian motifs. Numerous images featured a tearful eagle. Others depicted angels hovering over the inferno of the World Trade Center embracing dying firemen in their wings. Still other illustrations made use of the cluster of mangled steel beams that once supported a building and later towered over the rescue teams, suggesting in their geometrical simplicity the form of the cross. These symbols were blatantly patriotic and partook in the justification of America's belligerence abroad. At the same time, the vernacular crying eagle militated against the official iconography of the aftermath of 9/11 when limited space was granted to any articulation of injury and grief or to open debate over the reasons for and meaning of the attack. Recall that in the maudlin song written by former US Attorney General John Ashcroft and performed by him after 9/11, 'The eagle always soars, like she never soared before.'

The image of Jesus appears to fit uneasily with the more aggressively masculine tropes that flooded the American public sphere after September 11. America's violence abroad not only rejects the Christian imperative to turn the other cheek, it goes far beyond even the cowboy approach of pursuing lowly perpetrators. The US embraced pre-emptive strikes as a supra-principle of its foreign policy. Within anti-victim discourse, however, these contrasting models of manhood – Christ and a sci-fi Terminator-like robotic pre-emptor – cohere, since the latter refuses to be a victim, while the first refuses to be a victimist. Moreover, by finding another anchor for the war on terror, by dislodging the events of 9/11 as the foundation for US policy, America's mission in Iraq assumes an aura of radical altruism. Our troops are not fighting back retributively; they are 'freedom fighters' rescuing tortured men and women from the clutches of a tyrant.

The success of the *Passion* coincided with Bush's repeated invocation of Christ as his mentor or even premier father figure, and participated in making the Bush phenomenology – in substituting one reality for another and conjuring a bigger messianic or millennial 'truth.' Bush's conversion to the cause of world freedom is commensurate with a culture that, regardless of political bent, privileges the fluidity of self-making; a culture that engages in endless play with reality; which embraces and rejects, commodifies and consumes reality, including the reality of victimization. His allegiance to the 'vision thing' (which his father, former president George Herbert Walker Bush, mocked) is so ingrained that key aides deride 'those who believe that solutions emerge from ... judicious study of discernible reality' (Suskind 2004).

Refusing society

In the wake of 9/11, Bush promised to remake America. Carefully avoiding articulating precisely what ills America or specifying the abyss from which it needs to climb, he still repeatedly invokes the grammar of redemption and rejuvenation. Journalist Bob Woodward (2002: 32) reports that Bush claimed to have discerned 'an opportunity' in the horror of 9/11. The opportunity 9/11 afforded Bush to lead the nation reiterates his own experience of conversion, when he reportedly overcame a life of heavy drinking and aimlessness to become a highly driven, self-possessed individual. After 9/11, Bush's personal and political merged. To whom was Bush referring when he declared 'adversity introduced us to ourselves' (14 September 2001)?

The president expresses himself in a redemptive language that both abstracts and anthropomorphizes the nation. What worked for Bush the man will work for Bush's America. Just as individual character and dogged resolve determined his fate, so too will they shape that of the country. 'This country will define our times, not be defined by them,' he instructs us (20 September 2001). This sentiment partakes of the logic of 'American exceptionalism' and the notion that, unlike the rest of the world, the United States resides beyond history. Whereas conservative columnist Charles Krauthammer (2003) posited that 9/11 ended America's 'holiday from history,' Bush determinedly labors to extend the vacation. The model of individual will that anti-victimism nurtures goes far beyond bootstraps ideology to embrace a fantasy of self-invention that exists outside time. As makers of history, we need never be victims, since each of us can choose otherwise, if only we have the right character.

The space between individual self-making and national regeneration is one of the conceptual wrinkles that demands frantic reworking and bridging, especially in a time of national emergency. Even as he propagates fear among the citizenry, Bush promises that the millennial struggle for freedom will be free of sacrifice. While US government officials occasionally remind us that the country is at war, they also emphasize that Americans' only civic duty is to consume. The business of warfare was 'outsourced' to an elite group of professional soldiers equipped with cutting-edge technology (or literally outsourced to civilian companies – as in the case of bodyguards in Iraq). On the home front, Americans should continue to indulge in their rightful prosperity. In fact, perhaps there is not much to worry about since America took the war to the enemy.

Bush does not call even for modest financial sacrifice. There is no need to suspend tax cuts to pay for the debts the war continues to accrue. In this way, Bush's America displays the dangers of what Lauren Berlant (1997) names 'infantile citizenship' – the privatization of the public by which consumerism serves as an alternative to political participation.

The White House conjures a nation devoid of a sense of community, strong social fabric, or collective obligations. Even when Bush appeals to the public as a public, he focuses almost exclusively on individual actions in the private sphere. The president relates to Americans as coreligionists: good Christians, believers in the free market, or worshipers of American 'freedom.' The only social camaraderie permitted is akin to charity work and, in the tradition of 'compassion conservatism,' is left to individual initiative or civil associations rather than to the state. There are no official policies in this regard. It took Hurricane Katrina in September 2005 to lay bare the pernicious effects of ignoring society and neglecting, under the marquee of 'homeland security,' to sustain an infrastructure of government to assist victims. Bush's team may prefer to deal with ideational suffering rather than 'discernible reality,' but when in the fall of 2005 poor people stood on the rooftops of hurricane-ravaged New Orleans pleading for help victimhood could no longer be easily ignored.

In both its domestic and international renditions, anti-victimism has served as an atomizing, individuating discourse – a prime tool of neoliberalism. The post-9/11 version was initially forged a decade earlier to undermine identity politics, multiculturalism, and the welfare state. This approach to victimhood has multiple troubling manifestations, from occluding our collective responsibilities for victims to legitimizing the victimization of others. As we have seen, anti-victimism contributed to waging war by disseminating a counter-epistemology and counter-ethics of suffering, and by deploying Manichean rhetoric, political demonology, and a plethora of gendered archetypes encompassing victims, victimizers, and 'saviors.' While the Bush administration and its defenders charge their critics with 'blaming the victim,' they otherwise recoiled from victimization, averting our gaze and burying it in millennial rhetoric.

References

Belkin, Lisa (2002) 'Just money?', *New York Times Magazine*, 8 December.

Bennett, William (2001/03) *Why We Fight: Moral Clarity and the War on Terrorism*, Washington, DC: Regnery Publishing, Inc.

Berlant, Lauren (1997) *The Queen of America Goes to Washington: Essays on Sex and Citizenship*, Durham, NC: Duke University Press.

Brown, Patricia (2001) 'Heavy lifting required: the return of manly men', *New York Times*, 28 October.

Butler, Judith (2002) 'Explanation and exoneration, or what we can hear', *Grey Room*, 7, Spring.

Cole, Alyson (2006) *The Cult of True Victimhood: From the War on Welfare to the War on Terror*, Palo Alto, CA: Stanford University Press.

Dinan, Stephen (2005) 'GOP defends Rove's 9/11 criticisms of liberals', *Washington Times*, 25 June.

Dyer, Richard (1997) *Whiteness*, New York: Routledge.

Egan, R. Danielle (2002) 'Cowardice', in J. Collins and R. Glover (eds), *Collateral Language: A User's Guide to America's New War*, New York: New York University Press.

Eisenstein, Zillah (2005) 'Imperial democracy/imperial repression and polyversal feminisms', Lecture, Ithaca, NY.

Enloe, Cynthia (2000) *Maneuvers: The International Politics of Militarizing Women's Lives*, Berkeley: University of California Press.

Friedman, Thomas (2002) '9/11 lesson plan', *New York Times*, 4 September.

Gross, Terry (2001) *New Special* (with Billy Collins), National Public Radio, 11 September.

Hawkesworth, Mary (2005) 'Theorizing globalization in a time of war', *Studies in Political Economy*, 75, Spring.

Kaus, Mickey (2001) 'Does welfare cause terrorism?', *Slate*, 17 December, www.slate.msn.com/id/2059799, accessed 11 September 2007.

Krauthammer, Charles (2003) 'Holiday from history', *Washington Post*, 14 February.

LaHood, Ray (2002) Report by Nancy Marshall, *Weekend Edition*, National Public Radio, 15 September.

Noonan, Peggy (2001) 'Welcome back, Duke', *Wall Street Journal*, 12 October.

Pollitt, Katha (2004) 'The protocols of Mel Gibson', *Nation*, 29 March.

Post, Jerrold (1984) 'Notes on a psychodynamic theory of terrorist behavior', *Terrorism*, 7.

Puar, Jasbur and Amit Rai (2002) 'Monster, terrorist, fag: the war on terrorism and the production of docile patriots', *Social Text*, 72, Fall.

Robin, Corey (2001) 'Closet-case studies', *New York Times Magazine*, 16 December.

Steyn, Mark (2005) 'Wake up folks – it's war!', *Spectator*, 30 July.

Suskind, Ron (2004) 'Without a doubt: faith, certainty and the presidency of George W. Bush', *New York Times Magazine*, 17 October.

Woodward, Bob (2002) *Bush at War*, New York: Simon and Schuster.

Young, Iris (2003) 'The logic of masculinist protection: reflections on the current security state', *Signs*, 29, Fall.

9 | Deconstructing the myth of liberation @ riverbendblog.com

NADINE SINNO

The rhetoric surrounding the US invasion and occupation of Iraq has often been articulated in the form of artificial dualisms, employed by a hegemonic American corporate media, which rarely counters the 'official' line of the administration: 'good' versus 'evil,' 'terrorists' versus 'victims,' 'occupation' versus 'liberation,' and so on. In *Language and Politics*, Noam Chomsky mentions the media's complicity in eliciting support for the war through their uncritical dissemination of the government's war propaganda: 'The media uncritically relayed government propaganda about the threat to US security posed by Iraq, its involvement in 9-11 and other terror, etc. Some amplified the message on their own. Others simply relayed it ... Once the war began, it became a shameful exercise of cheering for the home team, appalling much of the world' (2004: 770). The rather dismal situation of the mainstream media – in its distortion of facts, glorification of war, downplaying of atrocities, and support of military 'achievements' – is by no means new or surprising. The media have traditionally played the role of the sender, we (the audience) the receivers. 'Media institutions depend on a silent division, reproduced across social space, between those who make stories and those who consume them' (Couldry and Curran 2003: 42).

Today, however, the dominant, mainstream media are no longer the sole providers of news and information. This era of information technology explosion has witnessed the proliferation of 'alternative producers' of information – who are still located at the margins of the news network, but who are, nonetheless, posing challenges to the mainstream media; prime among them are bloggers who are typing their hearts and minds out on the Web for readers who choose to pursue alternative news outlets.

Riverbend, author of *Baghdad Burning: Girl Blog from Iraq*, a book collection of one year's blog entries, did just that. Frustrated with watching US-based television networks CNN and Fox broadcast inaccurate (or, at best, abridged) information about the war in Iraq, Riverbend, a young Iraqi female living in Baghdad, proclaimed her right to tell her side of the story about the war. This 'Third World' woman carved out a space, a territory, not usually accessible to most marginalized people of her gender, age, or nationality. She appropriated technology, namely the Internet blog, to provide her alternative narrative of what is going on in her immediate environment. She also appropriated English, the language of the dominant discourse, thus making her views accessible to a wide audience of English speakers who otherwise might not have access to her blog. Riverbend's blogs challenge the master narrative fabricated and disseminated by US mainstream media through actively deconstructing the war rhetoric, using sarcasm as a means of ridiculing authority figures and the purported 'achievements' resulting from the regime change, recounting stories of the (otherwise) voiceless underdogs, exposing the underlying colonialist motives and repercussions of the invasion, and promoting global activism and transnational dialogue.

Riverbend's deconstruction of war rhetoric is manifested through her relentless challenging of the different binary oppositions often characteristic of war discourse, as articulated by US government officials and the mainstream media. Among the major concepts that she explores (and explodes) throughout her collection are the terms 'terrorism' and 'terrorist(s).' In some of her posts, Riverbend quotes sections of US president George W. Bush's speeches (which are fraught with references to terrorism) and shows how, more often than not, the military 'raids' that are supposed to target terrorists end up killing innocent people instead. For instance, she posts Bush's following announcement: 'Since the end of major combat, we have conducted raids seizing many caches of enemy weapons and massive amounts of ammunition, and we have captured or killed hundreds of Saddam loyalists and terrorists' (2005: 58). In response to him, she writes:

> Yes, we know all about 'raids' ... The 'loyalists and terrorists' must include Mohammed Al-Kubeisie of Jihad Quarter in Baghdad who was 11. He went outside the second floor balcony of his house to see what the commotion was all about in their garden ... Mohammed was shot on the spot. I remember another little terrorist who was killed four days ago in Baquba ... This terrorist was 10 ... no one knows why or how he was shot by one of the troops while they were raiding his family's house. They found no weapons, they found no Ba'athists, they found no WMD. (Ibid.: 58)

In this example, Riverbend does not theorize about terrorism; rather, she simply relays to us actual incidents that have resulted from the same 'raids' that Bush presents as a means of combating 'terrorism.' Thus, 'terrorist' starts to *signify* and *literally* include 'innocent' or 'victim.' Riverbend's entries include a plethora of references to raids in which the army ended up killing civilians. If such incidents were covered regularly by the media, the term 'terrorism' would start automatically to sound dubious to the average American, not just the Riverbend reader, the cynical academic or the peace activist. Such dubiousness, however, would undermine the necessity of waging wars, because once a war is defined in vague, non-oppositional terms – once categories like 'good' and 'evil,' 'civilian' and 'military,' and even 'war' and 'peace' become blurred, apprehension about war becomes inevitable. As Miriam Cooke comments:

> There are risks attendant on the dismantling of the War Story. Why go to war if victory and defeat are not clear-cut, mutually exclusive concepts? Low-intensity conflict may spill into a non-militarized zone, but people still need to believe in the separation of space into dangerous front – men's space – and danger-free home – women's space. And then who would venture into battle if there is doubt about the goodness and loyalty of troops and allies and the total evil of the enemy? (Cooke 1996: 7)

Not only does Riverbend speak of the ambiguity that characterizes the word 'terrorist,' she also describes the Iraqi domestic sphere's current transformation into a militarized zone such that a whole household of innocent men and women could be branded as 'terrorist' (or a terrorist cell) for merely owning more than the permitted 'single weapon' – at a time when neither the police nor the troops have the resources to ensure the safety of Iraqi civilians.

> Every male in the house is usually armed and sometimes the women too. It's not because we love turning our homes into arsenals, but because the situation was so dangerous (and in some areas still is) that no one wants to take any risks. Imagine this scene: a blue mini-van pulls up ... 10 dirty, long-haired men clamber out with Kalashnikovs, pistols, and grenades and demand all the gold and the kids (for ransom). Now imagine trying to face them all with a single weapon ... (Riverbend 2005: 145)

Even more disturbing is Riverbend's assertion that children who witness the raids on their homes will probably grow up to become real terrorists, as a result of falling victims to the troops' occasional abuse of power. 'The troops were pushing women and children shivering with fear out the door in the middle of the night,' she writes. 'What do you think these children think to themselves? Who do you think is creating the "terrorists?!!"' (ibid.: 145). Riverbend complicates the term 'terrorist' and shows how the abuse of power will inevitably breed more terrorism, how the same forces of 'good' that are there to combat terrorism are planting the seeds of terrorism, as they 'terrorize' civilians. Undeniably,

Riverbend provides an insider's war narrative that opposes the myth of war in its clear-cut categories of 'public' and 'private' and which emphasizes everybody's involvement in the victimization, resistance, and survival process.

In addition to her contestation of the term 'terrorism' (and its derivatives), Riverbend also contests the term 'liberation.' For people who lost loved ones, property, and security, 'liberation' is by no means a signifier of 'freedom.' In her description of the early days of the 'war of liberation,' she writes: 'We've been liberated from our jobs, and our streets and the sanctity of our homes ... some of us have even been liberated from the members of our family and friends' (ibid.: 227). Riverbend's use of the word 'liberation' to mean 'freedom from all that constitutes a stable life' is ironic and poignant because it strips the word of all positive connotations; in doing so, she also invalidates the supposedly benevolent ends of war, as she highlights the destructive effects of that 'liberation.' Riverbend's story of liberation invalidates the master narrative on freeing Iraqis from dictatorship and oppression. 'Liberation,' Riverbend concludes, often suggests terrorism in disguise, rather than the opposite of 'terrorism.' In other words, 'liberation' and 'terrorism' are both 'in the eye of the beholder,' the domineering beholder, rather than fixed terms signifying opposite meanings. She writes, 'We've learned that terrorism ... isn't the act of killing innocent people and frightening others ... no, you see, that's called "liberation." It doesn't matter what you burn or who you kill – if you wear khaki, ride a tank or Apache ... then you're not a terrorist – you're a liberator' (ibid.: 228).

Riverbend's use of the terms 'terrorism' and 'liberation' in a subversive manner (and almost always within quotation marks) reflects her ability to play with language and reveal how it has been manipulated by war advocates. In fact, her subversion of common terms and concepts, even her conscious rejection of terms such as 'liberation,' reflects her deep understanding of the power of language and the hybridity of writing as theorized by Mikhail Bakhtin in *The Dialogic Imagination*:

> Every word used 'with conditions attached,' every word enclosed in intonational quotation marks, is likewise an intentional hybrid – if only because the speaker insulates himself from this word as if from another language, as if from a style, when it sounds to him (for example) too vulgar, or on the contrary too refined, or too pompous, or if it bespeaks a specific tendency, a specific linguistic manner and so forth. (Bakhtin 1981: 76)

In brief, words like 'raids,' 'terrorism,' and 'liberation' are a few examples that represent a myriad of war-rhetoric words that Riverbend deconstructs throughout her narrative. Other words that she ultimately complicates include 'insurgency,' 'resistance,' 'civilization,' and even 'Iraqi National Day' – as she infuses them with meanings and connotations normally associated with their antonyms.

In addition to complicating the terms employed by the pro-war rhetoric, Riverbend sprinkles her text with cut-throat humor that targets US and Iraqi officials, thus making them objects of ridicule and stripping them of their authority, if only temporarily – or symbolically. Among those official figures is Ahmad Al-Chalabi, an Iraqi expatriate convicted of embezzlement charges in Jordan, who was prominent in collaborating with the USA to overthrow Iraqi president Saddam Hussein through his position as a member of the executive council of the 'Iraqi National Congress,' a group created in 1992 to work with the USA. Riverbend's introduction of Al-Chalabi as one of the 'puppets' of the American government is tragic-comic: 'This guy is a real peach ... He was a banker who embezzled millions from the Petra Bank in Jordan. My favorite part of his life story is how he escaped from Jordan in the trunk of a car ... a la modern-day Cleopatra if you will ... He's actually America's gift to the Iraqi people – the crowning glory of the war, chaos and occupation: the looter of all looters' (ibid.: 26). Calling a member of the new government a 'peach' and a 'modern-day Cleopatra' (among other things) would inevitably influence her readers' perceptions whenever they see or hear Al-Chalabi speak in public; the reader simply cannot see him the same way, nor take him seriously. Implicating the Pentagon for sponsoring a suspicious, fraudulent, and 'clownish' man also sheds doubts on the motivations and credibility of US officials, making them, too, objects of ridicule. In *The Dialogic Imagination*, Bakhtin discusses the power of laughter in debunking authority: 'Laughter demolishes fear and piety before an object, before a world, making of it an object of familiar contact and thus clearing the ground for an absolutely free investigation of it' (1981: 23).

In addition to poking fun at major Iraqi authority figures (Riverbend goes through the list of Iraqi Council members, calling each one 'flavor of the month'), she mocks US officials such as Secretary of Defense Donald Rumsfeld and President George W. Bush, thus making them, too, objects of 'free investigation.' It is important to note here that Riverbend's humor is never out of context; rather she contextualizes her humorous responses wisely, often responding to an official's visit to Iraq or to an official's public speech or interview (a 'media moment'). For instance, after reading one of Bush's speeches (for lack of a better option, power being out), regarding the situation in Iraq, Riverbend 'paraphrases' the speech according to her own understanding of Bush's message. Her 'abridged version' of the speech reads:

> Friends, Americans, Countrymen, lend me your ears ... lend me your sons and daughters, lend me your tax dollars ... so we can wage war in the name of American national security ... so I can cover my incompetence in failing to protect you ... so I can add to the Bush and Cheney family coffers at your expense and the expense of Iraqi people. I don't know what I'm doing, but if you spend enough money, you'll want to believe that I do. (Riverbend 2005: 59)

Riverbend's parodic reconstruction of Bush's speech is a counternarrative to Bush's master narrative. Her humor is both a defense (of the self from perpetual sadness) and an offense (against authority); it is in that sense that her blogging is both a private and public act. In addition to the therapeutic effects of laughter, the main purpose of Riverbend's paraphrase remains urging the readers to be critical of the motivations and repercussions of this war. In other words, Riverbend's parody reminds us that '[t]he causes of war must be explored' and that 'surely war is not inevitable; it is only made to seem that way' (Cooke 1996: 13).

The humorous sections of *Baghdad Burning* do not allow us the luxury of overindulging in our 'escape' from the painful reality of war. Riverbend swings her narratives between hilarity and heartbreak, thus eliciting from us feelings and reactions as 'ambivalent' and 'complicated' as the occupation she describes. Among the painful narratives that Riverbend recounts in her blogs are those often downplayed (or untold) stories of helpless families, especially women, that have lost family members to smart bombs or who have suffered abuse at the hands of the military. For instance, after describing the great moments of bonding that often occur in bomb shelters, Riverbend takes us aback with a horrifying story about a woman who left a bomb shelter momentarily (to get a supply of food and water), only to come back and find her eight children dead – after a smart bomb found its way into a basement containing over four hundred women and children:

> The bodies were laid out one beside the other – all the same sizes shrunk with heat and charred beyond recognition. Some were in the fetal position, curled up, as if trying to escape within themselves. Others were stretched out and rigid, like the victims were trying to reach out a hand to save a loved one or reach for safety. Most remained unrecognizable to their families ... (Riverbend 2005: 209)

The mother of eight now permanently lives in the bomb shelter, which has become her home. The children of the neighborhood refer to the shelter as '*maskoon*,' 'haunted.' In response to this posting, Riverbend received emails from readers arguing that the bomb shelter was a 'legitimate target' because American officials assumed it was being used for 'military purposes.' Such responses to the story of the bomb shelter are as revealing in themselves. After all, the rhetoric articulated by people justifying the targeting of a bomb shelter mirrors the mainstream discourse; it indicates that these readers have wholly accepted and internalized the legitimacy of the violence as propagated by authority figures. To use Cooke's words, 'When violence is thus deemed justified and its cause and proponents have become widely credible, the seeds of power have been sown' (1996: 98).

In her reply to those who attempted to justify the attack on the bomb shelter, Riverbend merely calls for the military's adherence to the Geneva Conventions, international law protecting prisoners of war from torture, which states: 'In case of doubt whether an object which is normally dedicated to civilian purposes is being used to make an effective contribution to military action ... it shall be presumed not to be so used' (Riverbend 2005: 212). Riverbend's atypically restrained reaction seems to reflect her refusal to honor the comments justifying the rhetoric of violence or to engage in it any further.

Among the stories that Riverbend also posts on her blog is that of a young woman who was imprisoned with her mother and brothers in Abu Ghraib, the US prison in Baghdad, 'home to thousands of criminals and innocents alike' (ibid.: 234), for allegedly being part of some 'resistance,' even though there was no evidence to that effect, and even though it later became clear that the young woman's neighbor had used his connections (with a translator in the army) to implicate the family owing to a fight he had with one of the brothers. The young woman speaks of being beaten in prison and of witnessing the rape of a male prisoner by one of the guards (ibid.: 234). As the young woman tells her story and that of other prisoners, we once again get the perspective of someone who was, literally, *inside* what later became the most scandalous prison associated with this war. It is later, upon seeing the pictures of torture from Abu Ghraib, that Riverbend understands what the young woman meant when she said, 'I'm one of the lucky ones ... all they did was beat me' (ibid.: 235). Riverbend's conscious attempt at including stories within stories – told by the victims themselves – strikes one as a manifestation of Bakhtin's 'heteroglossia,' as her narrative 'permits a multiplicity of social voices' (1981: 263).

In addition to describing the atrocities of war through recounting stories told by the victims themselves, Riverbend exposes and analyzes the neocolonialist and imperialist motivations that propelled the bombing of Iraq. For instance, on the day in 2003 that the UN headquarters in Baghdad was bombed, Riverbend's blog explained how this could never have happened to the Iraq Oil Ministry, which was being 'guarded 24/7 by [US] tanks and troops ... ever since the fall of Baghdad,' and which will 'continue [to be so] under [US Director of Reconstruction and Humanitarian Assistance] Bremer's watchful eye until every drop of oil is gone' (Riverbend 2005: 9). Riverbend calls on the various invading states, as the 'occupying power,' to use some of their resources to ensure the safety of such humanitarian establishments and of Iraqi civilians who were becoming increasingly subject to random acts of violence.

Added to the human and material losses, she demonstrates, are the crumbling of the economy and the subsequent loss of jobs for the majority of Iraqis. In the face of such devastation, however, the USA continues to exhibit (from the viewpoint of many Iraqis, including Riverbend) its neocolonialist motivations. For instance, the rebuilding of Iraq was outsourced to non-Iraqi companies (such as Halliburton Energy Services, a US-based multinational corporation), thus putting Iraq under immense debt and depriving its people of the opportunity of making badly needed profit, let alone rebuilding their own country. Riverbend's blog thoroughly documents the costly rebuilding of Iraq through foreign companies as opposed to Iraqi nationals. Moreover, in addition to providing us with actual figures regarding the gaps in costs, she argues that there are numerous Iraqi experts who – as a result of the first Gulf War against Iraq by the USA – had gained solid experience in rebuilding their country's bridges and buildings for such 'times of danger,' which makes them more qualified than their Western counterparts, who know very little about the country. She writes:

A few already rich contractors are going to get richer, Iraqi workers are going to be given a pittance, and the unemployed Iraqi public can stand on the sidelines and look at the glamorous buildings being built by foreign companies ... I always say this war is about oil ... But it is about huge corporations that are going to make billions off of reconstructing what was damaged during this war. Can you say Halliburton? (Ibid.: 36–7)

Riverbend concludes that it is only natural for Iraqis to roll their eyes upon hearing the word 'reconstruction'; after all, this reconstruction is going to be costly and designed by the foreign powers. Understandably, many Iraqis, she explains, see the USA as a colonizing power whose primary goals are occupation and the abuse of resources rather than liberation. As the great anti-colonialist politician and poet Aimé Césaire put it, 'Between colonizer and colonized there is room only for forced labor, intimidation, pressure, the police, taxation, theft, rape, compulsory crops, contempt, mistrust, arrogance, self-complacency, swinishness, brainless elites, degraded masses' (1972: 21). Yet the official discourse, Riverbend explains, does not tire of flaunting the rhetoric of reconstruction, as if reconstruction is the USA's gift to the Iraqi people, and as if Iraq did not have a great infrastructure – a civilization really – *before* the invasion. Of the myth of the 'pre-invasion' Iraq, she writes: 'Myth: Iraqis, prior to the occupation, lived in little beige tents set up on the sides of little dirt roads all over Baghdad. The men and boys would ride to school on their camels, donkeys, and goats ... Girls and women sat at home, in black burkas, making bread and taking care of 10–12 children' (Riverbend 2005: 34).

Most importantly, Riverbend laments the post-invasion status of Iraqi women, who actually lost many of their rights as a result of the invasion and the ensuing spread of fundamentalism. She writes that, contrary to popular belief, before the US invasion, Iraqi women 'made up over 50% of the working force. [They] were doctors, lawyers, nurses, teachers, professors, deans, architects, programmers, and more. [They] came and went as [they] pleased. [They] wore what they wanted ...' (ibid.: 22). Now, however, Riverbend, like many other women, is jobless; she also cannot go out 'in pants' and has to wear 'a long skirt and loose shirt,' because '[a] girl wearing jeans risks being attacked, abducted, or insulted by fundamentalists who have been ... liberated!' (ibid.: 17). Worse still, women who try to become politically active or who simply try to hold on to their jobs risk their lives, as was the case for Henna Aziz, an electrical engineer, who was assassinated by a group of fundamentalists in the presence of her husband and children (ibid.: 24) and Akila Al-Hashimi, the council member, who was ambushed and murdered by armed men on her way to work (ibid.: 75).

Once again, Riverbend's account of the *post-invasion* situation of women challenges the dominant discourse's narrative on 'women's liberation,' 'democracy,' and 'regime change,' which many officials had also been claiming as justifiable reasons for waging war. In many ways, Riverbend's account of her and other women's fate under occupation invalidates the liberation narrative normally associated with military presences. In fact, this pseudo-liberation narrative had been a prominent feature of the first Gulf War, whereby US officials politicized the women's liberation movement in the USA to gain support for intervening in the

Gulf. In her article 'Military presences and absences,' Therese Saliba explores the connection between military invasion and Arab women's situation:

> The marketing of the Gulf War to US audiences was consistent with popular culture's marketing of the Arab world to the West through the circulation of stereotyped images of Arabs which alluded to the benevolence of the United States or Western influence in their lives. The specifically *gendered* representations of demonized Arab men and captive or absent Arab women fed a revival of colonialist attitudes, and heralded Geroge Bush's new world order to reassert US dominance in the Middle East. (Saliba 1994: 125)

Riverbend educates many readers who have emailed her questions about the hijab, explaining to them that the veil itself is not oppressive, but that imposing it is oppressive – something that was unheard of during Saddam's secular regime, which kept the fundamentalism at bay. That said, Riverbend doesn't glorify Saddam's era; she simply highlights the fact that women had more rights under his regime and that the war advocates who promised to liberate Iraqi men and women from all forms of oppression did not have the Iraqis' interests in mind. As Saliba writes, 'war, while often justified in the rhetoric of liberation, is rarely intended to liberate anyone – least of all women' (ibid.: 132).

Undeniably, Riverbend's interactive blog serves a goal larger than the immediate broadcasting of stories and reflections from the war zone. While giving her readers access to such a perspective is certainly valuable, Riverbend also makes a conscious effort to promote global political activism. For instance, she posts information from transnational bloggers, professors, soldiers, and writers, and she refers her readers to articles, journals, or books that might be helpful in understanding current events. She also comments on other bloggers' posts, thus allowing herself to become part of an online imagined community of thinkers and writers. Her active engagement with other bloggers proves her commitment to the promotion of dialogue. In her book *Global Obscenities: Patriarchy, Capitalism, and the Lure of Cyberfantasy*, Zillah Eisenstein discusses the advantages of cyberdialogue, especially in its mobilization of anti-war activism. 'Such communication allows for diasporic publics to connect with one another and initiates new alliances with people "outside" one's immediate geographical region. These disparate and dispersed communications can be used to build structures for change and mobilize struggles for peace, equality, and a healthy environment' (1998: 168). It is important to note that Riverbend does not post merely the comments and feedback of readers who approve of her blog and her politics. She also posts information from readers who express opposing views, including those who send her hate mail, fraught with *ad hominem* attacks. For instance, she posts the comments of a reader who tells her she should be grateful that Donald Rumsfeld is in power because he is a compassionate man and because if he, the reader, had been in power at the time, he would have 'vaporized [the Iraqis] ten minutes after the Trade center attacks' (Riverbend 2005: 53). Riverbend acknowledges that there is something positive about receiving such an email – a reminder of 'the diversity of blog readers' who 'take time off of watching Fox News to check out [her] blog' (ibid.: 53).

Riverbend's blog fights may be seen as manifestations of the challenges and intimidations that women especially face online, and they bring to mind current articles on the importance of women's participation in the cyber world despite all intimidation. 'Women can and should learn more about their online environment so they can exert more control over their corner of cyberspace,' writes Stephanie Brail. 'The move of many women to create mailing lists and online services is a positive one. Rather than playing the victim, we can take charge and fight back with the same tools being used against us' (2003: 154). Furthermore, the ease with which Riverbend navigates technology – proudly calling herself a 'Girl Geek,' who can uncover cyber tricks primarily employed by male hackers who try to steal her identity and taint her site – manifests her empowerment, a digital empowerment that many feminists emphasize today. 'Now, what we will need,' writes Karen Coyle, 'is a conspiracy of sisters that begins with the recognition that there is nothing inherently masculine about computers. We must learn to read the computer culture for the myth that it is ... and we start it all with a simple thought that could be the beginning of a revolution: *How hard can it be?*' (1996: 54).

Upon starting her blog, Riverbend wrote: 'So, this is the beginning for me, I guess. I never thought I'd start my own weblog ... All I could think, every time I wanted to start one was "but who will read it?"' (Riverbend 2005: 5). She expressed the same apprehension and humility characteristic of progressive subcultures often located at the margins of society and equipped with limited resources. Little did she know that her collection would ultimately gain a relatively wide readership, let alone be published in a book with blurbs by Susan Sarandon. While *Baghdad Burning* has not really infiltrated the mass media yet, its increasing popularity today – at least among academics, political activists, and journalists – is certainly a step forward in making 'the globe a habitable home,' where individuals from different geographical regions, especially women, can establish connections and mobilize other activists in their struggle for justice (Eisenstein 1998: 168).

References

Bakhtin, Mikhail (1981) *The Dialogic Imagination*, ed. Michael Holquist, Austin: University of Texas Press.

Brail, Stephanie (2003) 'The price of admission: harassment and free speech in the Wild, Wild West', in *Contesting Media Power: Alternative Media in a Networked World*, New York: Rowman & Littlefield.

Césaire, Aimé (1972) *Discourse on Colonialism*, trans. Joan Pinkham, New York: Monthly Review Press.

Chomsky, Noam (2004) *Language and Politics*, ed. C. P. Otero, London: AK Press.

Cooke, Miriam (1996) *Women and the War Story*, London: University of California Press.

Couldry, Nick and James Curran (2003) 'Beyond the hall of mirrors: some theoretical reflections on the global contestation of media power', in *Contesting Media Power: Alternative Media in a Networked World*, New York: Rowman & Littlefield.

Coyle, Karen (1996) 'How hard can it be?', in Lynn Cherny and Elizabeth Weise (eds), *Wired_Women: Gender and New Realities in Cyberspace*, Toronto: Seal Press.

Eisenstein, Zillah (1998) *Global Obscenities: Patriarchy, Capitalism, and the Lure of Cyberfantasy*, New York: New York University Press.

Riverbend (2005) *Baghdad Burning: Girl Blog from Iraq*, New York: Feminist Press.

Saliba, Therese (1994) 'Military presences and absences', in Joanna Kadi (ed.), *Food for Our Grandmothers: Writings by Arab-American and Arab-Canadian Feminists*, Boston, MA: South End Press.

10 | 'Rallying public opinion' and other misuses of feminism

JENNIFER L. FLURI

In this essay, I critique the gendering of military discourses and violent action by the USA in Afghanistan through analysis of documents from the US Congress pre- and post-9/11. The trope of 'saving' Afghan women resonated within Congress and became an effective method for 'rallying public opinion' and congressional support for US confrontation with the Taliban, the Sunni Islamist and tribal Pashtun nationalist movement in Afghanistan, and the subsequent US military action in that country. My critique does not deny the systematic marginalization and abuse of women under the Taliban; rather my analysis traces the misuse and overuse of the 'saving and/or protecting women' trope in Afghanistan to support and legitimize US military violence – without a corresponding congressional-level understanding of the longitudinal and systemic outgrowths of this violence, which is both gendered and particularly significant for many vulnerable populations in Afghanistan.

Women, gender, and violence

Men's and women's experiences of violence during military conflicts are often shaped by gender and intersected by race, ethnicity, socio-economic class, location and/or dislocation (Giles and Hyndman 2004). Multidimensional approaches to research on gender, conflict, and dislocation are required in order to thoroughly examine the complicated and shifting gender identities women and men experience in conflict zones or in flight from these zones (see Hans 2004). Essentialist definitions of masculinity and femininity are a hallmark of military violence, which often evolve into more distinct categories as military conflicts escalate (Yuval-Davis 1997). These gendered stereotypes are both reinforced and, in some cases, altered for the purpose of powerful political actors (Goldstein 1995). For example, the 'saving women' trope extends a legitimate reason for waging violent conflict, while marginalizing women as political and social agents. This solidifies men's roles as both perpetrator and protector in the shaping or implementing of military violence (see Enloe 1993).

Military violence corresponds with combat masculinity, which is defined and enacted both within and outside the military during periods of heightened nationalism (Dowler 2001; Moser and Clark 2001; Tickner 2002). Wartime femininity also serves to reinforce the saving/protecting women trope, because this form of femininity requires the 'protective' force of violent masculinity to secure its fragility and feminine representation of the homeland/motherland.

Here I investigate the policy-driven use of gender essentialism and the manipulation of women's victimization in Afghanistan under the Taliban as a political (and military) strategy to 'save and protect' Afghan women prior to and after the events of 9/11. The public spectacle of Taliban atrocities against women assisted in garnering support from US citizens for military action in Afghanistan and simultaneously displaced political reflexivity regarding US foreign policy in Afghanistan from the 1980s to 9/11 (see Mamdani 2004; Moghadam 1999, 2002). The following excerpts from US congressional documents highlight the testimonies from Afghanistan's leadership, political groups, and members of the humanitarian and aid community prior to (and immediately following) 9/11, who identify disarmament rather than military engagement as a prime method for destabilizing the Taliban and creating stability in Afghanistan.

The reasons for waging war against Afghanistan offered by members of the US House and Senate are, however, strongly built around the hegemonic-masculine war-chatter of revenge and 'justice,' with Afghan women providing the strategic nodal point for the cartographic framing of Afghanistan as a wild land in need of taming, where terrorist camps, abuse of women, and lawlessness abound (see Dalby 2003). The burqa, the full-body garment worn by some women in Afghanistan, as part of this congressional framing, remains the leading visual cue in the USA for identifying a difference between Islamic women's oppression and liberation respectively (Hunt 2002; Young 2003).

Various governments and paramilitary groups have implemented the 'saving women' trope as a reason to legitimize military violence in Afghanistan's recent nearly thirty years of conflict (Kandiyoti 2005). For example, the Soviet Union's 1979 invasion of Afghanistan was riddled with discourses of 'saving' Afghan women from Afghanistan's patriarchal social structures. Afghanistan's mujahedin resistance groups, in response, were 'protecting' women from the military and ideological invasions of the Soviets, and the Taliban's rise to power was also marked by the powerful discourse of saving women from the gang rapes and lawlessness associated with the mujahedin (Rashid 2001). The categorical use of women to garner and morally support the use of violence is consistent in these various cases. This trope, as argued by various feminist scholars, is powerful and does little to assist the lives of women, empower them, recognize their agency, or understand the effects of violence and militarism on their everyday lives (Enloe 2000; Hunt 2002; Young 2003).

In order to critically investigate the manipulation of these gendered-war stereotypes, I examine in the next sections of this chaper the US congressional documents related to the burqa, US military action, and the 'saving women' trope. This is contextualized by interviews from the summer of 2006 with members of RAWA (Revolutionary Association of the Women of Afghanistan), an Afghan women's group that promotes women's rights and secular democracy; with women and men in leadership positions in the parliament, judiciary, and ministries in Kabul, the capital of Afghanistan; and with 'ordinary' citizens living in Kabul. (All names have been replaced with pseudonyms to protect their identities.)

Setting the stage: Afghan women and the US burqa fetish

A US Senate Foreign Relations Committee hearing entitled 'The Taliban: Engagement or Confrontation?' was held on 20 July 2000. I highlight here two of the primary themes within the resulting document of the hearing: 1) the treatment of women under the Taliban; and 2) the 'appropriate' US response to women's issues and terrorist training camps in Afghanistan.

At the hearing, Dr Shorish-Shamley, representing the Women's Alliance for Peace and Human Rights, presented a detailed account of the severity of women's poor health, lack of security, and decline in various social indicators in Afghanistan. Her discussion outlined the gender biases of Taliban rule and the embodied effects of this rule on women. The burqa was not mentioned in her statement as a primary issue for women or as connected to social indicators. She clearly stated several times in her prepared statement that the treatment of Afghan women by the Taliban was neither cultural nor Islamic, and requested US and UN assistance to focus specifically on bringing an end to human rights violations and recognizing democratic elements in Afghanistan.

Her presentation never mentioned the need for US military support, invasion, or bombing as a necessary method for security, rather highlighting the need for diplomacy.

Hamid Karzai (installed as president of Afghanistan in 2004) also spoke at the US Senate meeting regarding the Taliban's political and military position in Afghanistan. Karzai highlighted the problem of international intrusion into Afghanistan and the Taliban regime by separating the Afghan Taliban as 'neither radical nor against Afghan values and culture' from the foreign influences on the Taliban that had created 'militancy and terrorism' in the country. In response to questions from senators regarding US military involvement, Karzai responded accordingly:

> The United States bombed terrorist bases in Afghanistan in 1998. The government of Russia threatened to bomb these bases. Bombings or the threat of bombing will not remove the terrorist bases from Afghanistan. Such actions will only add to the problems and prolong the suffering of our people and, most of all, solidify the presence of terrorist groups. [Later in the document] ... The United States can encourage the UN Security Council to adopt effective measures, to have a cease-fire in Afghanistan and bring about an arms embargo. (Karzai 2000)

Karzai did not focus on women or identify the treatment of women by the Taliban in his presentation before the Senate committee, and the burqa was not mentioned. Karzai's and Dr Shorish-Shamley's presentations, however, both highlighted the need for security through arms control and diplomacy, and both called for an improvement in social indicators through education, training, and healthcare. Conversely, US senators Barbara Boxer, Karl Inderfurth, and Sam Brownback highlighted the burqa as both a primary issue for Afghan women, and as a tool for garnering public support for US involvement in Afghanistan. Boxer's discussions of the burqa highlighted the early politicization of the burqa in the USA as an emblem of Afghan women's oppression under the Taliban.

> And when we got one of these burqas from the Feminist Majority who made it available to us, I had the women in my office and I myself put this on, and it was so claustrophobic that they could barely do it ... Now I want to say that if women choose to wear this burqa for religious reasons that should be their right. But the requirement that women wear the burqa is a clear violation of human rights. (US Senate Foreign Relations Committee 2000)

Sam Brownback said in response to Boxer:

> Thank you, Senator Boxer. And thanks for raising those important issues – women's right [sic] lack thereof within Afghanistan ... *And it's not just cultural; it's criminal.* We should stand up to that at every chance we possibly get. (Ibid.)

Both Boxer and Brownback demonized the burqa and the imposition of it on women as criminal. Also the criminal acts of the Taliban had been clearly denounced as 'cultural' in previous testimonies. The imposed rule of the Taliban and imposition of the burqa on Afghan women (particularly Afghan women without a history of wearing the burqa) were indeed unfair and gender-biased treatment. Here, however, the Taliban were inappropriately identified as part of Afghan culture, despite Shorish-Shamley's and Karzai's notes to the contrary, which further solidified the 'culture' of Afghanistan, rather than the Taliban regime specifically, as problematic (and criminal). Boxer further politicized the situation for Afghan women through the burqa by admonishing Karl Inderfurth, who was US Assistant Secretary of State for South Asian Affairs, claiming that his statement on the Taliban lacked a focus on women.

> Now I have to say, unless I'm missing something, that when a regime clamps down on the majority of its population like it clamps down on women and girls, *and we see from the burqa* the intent is to essentially make these people invisible, give them no recognition as human beings, I have to believe that our country should be very outspoken on this, because *I think it helps us to rally public opinion* against the Taliban, *even more than all the things you're talking about* ... (Ibid.)

Inderfurth's response:

> Well, I would hope that I could allay your concerns and dismay that not more time and attention was paid in this testimony to the tragic situation of women and girls in Afghanistan. I, too, have a burqa, which I have in my office and which I obtained when I was in Kabul several years ago, and I bring it out frequently to demonstrate what that represents. (Ibid.)

Boxer's attempts to place women's issues at the forefront of the congressional agenda are in one respect to be applauded; this should be couched, however, with her politicizations of Afghan women as a means to gain public sympathy and support against the Taliban, by focusing on the burqa as the primary signifier of Afghan 'otherness' in general and women's oppression in particular. Feminist politics should address the agency and actions of Afghan women, listen to their prescriptive ideas for change, and work toward assisting existing women's and feminist organizations. By using women's oppression in Afghanistan as a political tool 'to rally public opinion,' US leaders like Boxer are placing Afghan women in a marginalized position as victims in need of 'saving' from an outside power, rather than addressing and celebrating the agency, resilience, and resistance of Afghan women's and feminist organizations prior to and during the Taliban regime.

These US senators defined the burqa as the primary identifier of women's oppression in Afghanistan; and as Senator Boxer highlights in her statement, the burqa provides a comprehensible symbol of oppression because it is staunchly counter to the US cultural representation of women's independence and liberation. The unveiling and various manifestations of revealing the female body are normative and subsumed into the conceptions of freedom and liberty for women in the United States. The burqa provides an important symbol of oppression for public and political purposes, because of this stark contrast between burqa-clad and uncovered bodies (see Abu Lughod 2002; El Guindi 1999; Barlas 2002).

Boxer – with the support of her male counterparts in the Senate – brought the burqa from the margins of US geographic imagination to the center as the backdrop for Afghanistan and an effective method for mainstreaming citizen support of the USA as the primary 'outsider' needed to 'save and protect' Afghan women from their 'culture.' The primary form of 'saving and protecting' Afghan women quickly turned to the use of military force after the events of 9/11.

Bombs do not distinguish by gender

The impact of military action, and bombing specifically, which were highlighted by the Afghan experts in these congressional documents and by RAWA as counter to the objectives of helping women, children, and men in Afghanistan, were soon ignored in the post-9/11 rush to military action. The following excerpts are from US congressional hearings on Afghanistan held on 31 October 2001, in connection with the International Operations and Human Rights Subcommittee of the US House of Representatives International Relations Committee. I focus on these hearings to address the ways in which war-chatter is gendered and linked to human rights provisions by the hegemonic power of the USA.

Similar to the pre-9/11 Senate committee discussion of women and women's rights in Afghanistan, after the US invasion of Afghanistan, in the post-7 October 2001 US House hearings, human rights issues were both gendered and militarized. In addition to the House representatives, Eleanor Smeal, president of the US mainstream Feminist Majority Foundation, was present as a 'voice' for Afghan women, and stated:

> Women were the first victims of the Taliban, and the public is becoming increasingly aware of this fact. The public has now seen broadcasts on television again and again film footage of women being beaten and executed for violating the Taliban's decrees banning women from

employment, from attending school, from leaving their homes without a close male relative and without wearing the head-to-toe burqa *shroud*. (US Congress 2001)

Smeal referred to the burqa as a *shroud*, and her statement concerning women as the 'first victims' of Taliban atrocities was historically inaccurate. The 'saving women' trope was also used by the Taliban to gain local support in Kandahar province, which led to the Taliban's subsequent rise to power in Afghanistan. One of the most credible and repeated stories for explaining the rise to power of Mullah Omar, a leader of the Taliban, concludes with his ability to save two young girls who were kidnapped and raped by a local warlord. The 'saving' of these young Afghan women has been identified as a key motivator for Afghan men to join the Taliban during the early days of its formation in southern Afghanistan (Rashid 2001).

In her remarks, Smeal, as in many other discussions of the public execution of a burqa-clad woman, Zarmeena, by the Taliban, does not credit RAWA for filming this event. RAWA's film and video documentation of war and violence has and continues to be an integral part of its resistance strategies and platform for political action. On RAWA's website and in its print publications, still and video photography of human rights abuses is carefully intersected with RAWA's political analysis and socio-political solutions to military violence. RAWA's political ideology and the social programs they provide for women, children and men are juxtaposed with the atrocities of the Taliban, Northern Alliance, fundamentalist groups, and international use of forces (such as the US bombing campaigns) in order for RAWA to politically identify the perpetrators of violence and illustrate the organization's socio-political programs (such as healthcare facilities, education programs, and orphanages) as an alternative non-violent tool for socio-political change in Afghanistan. Similar to tearing the burqa from its historical, local, and fluid contexts in Afghanistan, the linking of Taliban atrocities as documented by RAWA with the United States' military solutions, rather than with RAWA's political solutions and/or goals, is another method for the marginalization of women's agency.

RAWA members have all experienced the embodied effects of war and military violence, and these members call for disarmament, diplomacy and security measures, rather than the use of bombs, to eradicate violent groups, such as the Taliban. Violence is never identified by RAWA as an effective method for providing security and improving the lives of Afghan women, children, or men. Conversely, the US House representatives directly linked US bombing and the eradication of the Taliban to US humanitarian aid and assistance in Afghanistan.

At the 7 October hearing, US representatives Cynthia A. McKinney of Georgia and Dana Rohrabacher of California engaged in gendered debate about human rights, the USA, and cluster bombing. McKinney commented:

> The world is watching us ... The people of Afghanistan cannot endure yet another one of our foreign policy failures. We must bring peace and hope to the region. Not yet more suffering and death ... and look what we are doing now ... *our cluster bombs are almost indistinguishable from the food canisters that we are dropping ... how in the world can a 300 billion dollar a year military machine not see to it that the food packets and the bomblets from the cluster bombs they are dropping are not the same color? Is it that they really just don't care?* ... And the world must see that we care. ... We must help put an end to the human rights abuses in Afghanistan.

Rohrabacher replied:

> I think it is wonderful that we are dropping food packages ... The fact that we drop food packages at all says good things about us. The fact that we go out of our way to warn people ... it says something good about us ... I would hope that the cluster bombs kill as many Taliban leaders and Taliban soldiers as they possibly can. There's nothing we could do better for the people of Afghanistan than to kill as many Taliban soldiers who've been repressing them and murdering them as they have been. So let's – if it takes cluster bombs, that's fine. If it takes Samurai swords or pistols, *I don't care what it is, let's get rid of these Taliban, because they're Nazis. They are the Muslim Nazis, and all the good Muslims of the world understand that ... Now we've made a lot about women's rights today and rightfully so. Obviously, the Taliban are to women what the Nazis were to Jews.*

McKinney is the only US representative in the 2001 House hearing to critically address US military action in Afghanistan; her critique falls short, however, and is mired in the staunchly entrenched beliefs that the USA is centrally necessary to stop human rights violations. There is no reflexive understanding or criticism of the use of cluster bombs by other members of the US Congress at this hearing. McKinney reinforces the ideology that the USA should have a major role in preventing human rights abuses – without identifying cluster bombing and its direct role in civilian deaths both immediate and long-term.

Despite McKinney's attempts to critically engage in debate about US militarism, representative Rohrabacher infuses a hyper-masculine language to support the use of cluster bomb 'technology,' subsequently marginalizing McKinney's arguments. Rohrabacher's statements illustrate military action as the keystone of US operations in Afghanistan and incongruently link food aid drops that look like bomblets as a humanitarian rather than a military strategy because we 'warn people' a food package may be a bomb!

I highlight this excerpt from Rohrabacher's testimony to exemplify Gregory's (2004) examination of Afghanistan and US militarism, through the continuous representation of the Afghan 'other,' who is identified in Agamben's terms as the *Homo sacer* (Agamben 1998). The *Homo sacer* is not worthy of being sacrificed for the sake of a divine cause or nation; he/she can be killed with impunity, however, because he/she exists outside the margins of the 'universally held morality' of the United States (see Gregory 2004; Patterson 2005). The Taliban and Afghans who are killed in pursuit of the Taliban and Al Qaeda remain in a continual state of exception. This renders their lives meaningless because they are outside the universal rules of engagement as defined by US hegemony (Gregory 2004). The Foucauldian (1977) and Orwellian posturing by Rohrabacher is further embellished by his gendered war-chatter and its (dis)associated link between the Taliban and the Nazi regime.

In the context of modern US warfare and the use of bombing, there is no gender distinction available. Bombs are not equipped with sensors to kill particular individuals, despite the rhetoric of smart-bomb technology. Aerial forms of military technology provide an efficient and often absolute method of destruction without the technological ability to distinguish between combatants and civilians, women, children, and/or men. The use of 'modern' aerial bomb technology is equally marked by a distinctive increase in civilian casualties. The use of bomb technology distances the citizens of the hegemonic state (namely the USA) from actual experiences of war or corporeal carnage. Similarly the 'saving women' trope justifies the aggressive use of these technologies to both create a sense of US citizen security post-9/11, and further legitimize the use of force as a form of US benevolence and justice rather than aggression and vengeance. As I have argued here, the 'saving women' trope has been integrated into military conflicts in Afghanistan since the late 1970s. The reconstruction and nation-building associated with the period subsequent to US bombing and military engagement is also linked to superiority assumptions of the USA as a hegemonic power both militarily and economically.

I conclude by focusing on reconstruction in Kabul, Afghanistan, in order to illustrate the conflict/post-conflict internationally sponsored and

US consumer-driven conceptions of capitalist modernity and its intersec-
tions with humanitarian assistance. These conceptions of modernity,
and attempts to move Afghanistan from its violent and gender-biased
past into a 'democratic and liberated' future, also require a rejection of
the past when performed in the present, and a respect and recognition
for the past when put into a place of reverence such as a museum, or
something that can be voyeuristically 'experienced' by a tourist. The
burqa as a living performance of criminality, culture, and oppression,
as defined by the US Congress, has no place in the US conception of
the modern Afghanistan.

Security, priority, and (re)construction in Afghanistan

US 'high modernity' is led by consumerism and a formal rejection
of tradition by placing 'traditional practices' into the sphere of rituals
and relics, which both embellish the past and strategically position it in
opposition to the present or the so-called 'progressiveness' of modernity
(Giddens 1994; Taylor 1999). Thus the burqa represents a negative aspect
of tradition, rather than a nostalgic relic that inspires a greater meaning
in modernity through the segregated spaces of museums, and provides
a counter-representation of the present. Traditional practices identified
as rituals and the presentations of relics in museums create 'formulaic
truths': 'Formulaic truth is what renders central aspects of tradition
"untouchable" and confers integrity upon the present in relation to the
past' (Giddens 1994: 104). Thus, in Afghanistan, there are the nostalgic
relics of the past that are included as essential components of modern
preservation, while the burqa represents the negative aspects of Afghan
'tradition' that must be eradicated. Subsequently, the Taliban's destruction of the Buddhist statues in Bamiyan, Afghanistan, further illustrated
the *backwardness* of the Taliban as a representation of contemporary
Afghanistan and the successive need for international intervention.

Paul Bernard's *Wall Street Journal* article juxtaposed Western/US
modernity (and consumerism) with spirituality to illustrate the Taliban's
act as blasphemous to modernity.

> Museums have become our cathedrals, and the big exhibits our pilgrim-
> ages. It is [at] the Louvre, the British Museum, the Metropolitan Museum
> that we satisfy the human need for transcendence. When the Taliban
> blew up the Buddhas, we were not only grieved at the loss of some works
> of art, of a cultural heritage, we felt outraged by a blasphemous act.
> (Bernard 2001: A13)

Bernard's use of the pronoun 'we' (and focus on the 'relics' found in

Western museums) assumes a collective 'Western' understanding of modernity, and cherishes the relics of the past because they help to construct modernity as progressive (see Giddens 1994). In destroying the past, the Taliban were depicted as destroying the modern as well.

Modernity constructed in opposition to tradition is further defined by hegemonic systems of power within the capitalist world economy. Contemporary US modernity constructs a particular superiority, which includes an erasure of individual power through democratic processes and the manipulation of discourse to support the displacement of those outside 'rational modernity,' through the reinvention of inclusiveness veiled by the monotony and uniformity of rampant consumerism, technological and military dominance, and capital accumulation.

Mohanty (1991) argues that the discursively constructed conception of the 'Third World' woman as oppressed and powerless enables the Western construction of the 'First World' woman as liberated, and she suggests 'that the one enables and sustains the other' (ibid.: 74). Similarly, United States policy-makers rhetorically define Afghanistan within the world geopolitical arena as a backward and oppressive society run by religious fanatics in need of militarism as the vehicle for 'progressive, modern, and liberating' politics to emerge. The democratization of Afghanistan is therefore accomplished through the material practices of US capitalist modernity, which is both highly gendered and militarized.

The various attempts to 'save' Afghan women militarily and/or through the market have generally been organized without a thorough understanding of or consideration for the local contextual and family-based controls over women and men in Afghanistan, previous attempts to counter or change which through the central government in Kabul or outside influences have historically failed. Additionally, Kandiyoti (2005) identifies the need for long-term aid focused on social indicators as essential in order to truly improve the lives of women in Afghanistan. In discussions with 'ordinary' men and women in Afghanistan, as well as political and legal officials, in the summer of 2006, a pattern emerged regarding the priorities of international reconstruction projects and the increased role of private sector economic projects in conjunction with rising unemployment for locals in the Afghan population. For example:

> We have the Serena Hotel and it is beautiful. But I wonder is this a priority? The Kabul City Center is also beautiful but what about the hospitals and schools? There are many buildings for schools but they need supplies and more teachers and more resources. You saw the maternity hospital. They do not have a working ultrasound machine or enough

153

beds to service the needs of the patients. (Hameed, interview, summer 2006)

Thus, the systemic violence of war remains in the lack of resources available to most Afghans in Kabul and other provinces, including limited or no access to running water, electricity, food security, and affordable or proper housing. Thus, the cosmopolitan additions to Kabul, such as the five-star Serena Hotel and the Kabul City Center (a high-end mall, café, and hotel), which cater to the international and upper-class communities in Kabul, while social programs and economic opportunities for the un- and undereducated occur more slowly.

In conclusion, I return to my discussions with RAWA members in July 2006, which led back to the Bamiyan Buddhist statues, which exemplify, for RAWA, the way Afghanistan is seen and 'dealt with' by the international community.

Bamiyam is a historical place with many historical things. It is good to rebuild the Buddhas but this is not the priority. The Buddhas should come later. Bamiyam is very poor and clinics and schools are more important. Even though the Buddhas cannot be rebuilt UNESCO is attempting to find ways to preserve the artifact including a proposed light show of how the Buddhas used to look. In this case it is blatant that the first world cares more about historical objects than people's lives. The price of life is becoming cheaper, or at least third world life. Approximately 3,000 people died on 9/11 and there was so much time and money spent, including the push for a huge memorial. Yet there is no memorial for the Hazaras of Bamiyam, only support for inanimate objects. Perhaps this best sums up the international community's attitude towards Afghans. (RAWA members, Kabul, 2006)

Discussions with RAWA and Kabul residents not associated with RAWA, and my own experiences traversing public space in Kabul, confirm that the city is militarized and that there is an evident spatial separation between the international community and the local Afghan population. Most (but not all) international workers live in gated and barbed-wire compounds. US embassy and UN workers are prevented, based on their security requirements, from leaving their compounds or entering an Afghan home. Fear and security are the primary reasons cited by foreign aid and public sector workers for this spatial segregation. For many Afghans, however, international fears are perplexing because of the unbalanced power relations between the international community and the local Afghan population:

Why are they [international workers] afraid of us [laughing]. I mean, they have all the weapons and the cars and technology. What do we have? Our poverty and desire to live. It is funny to me that they are so afraid, behind their walls, that they do not get to see us at all – to know our hospitality and the goodness of our culture. They can bomb and kill us in an instant and what can we do? (Rahman, interview, summer 2006)

The increased militarization of women's, children's, and men's lives in Afghanistan, and the disenfranchisement of the economy within the global capitalist systems, leads me to question our 'First World' concepts of fear, security, and the so-called 'humanity' of US foreign policy and other international aid initiatives. Thus, we *should not* fear the 'oppression and inhumanity' of the Afghans or other Muslim 'others,' which Laura Bush identified as an example of what the 'terrorists want to impose on us.' Rather, we *should* fear the imposition of US congressional and other government discourses that cite humanity and rights, while disseminating these ideals through a 'rational' and efficient destruction of people and landscape to secure *our* enduring power, military superiority, and 'free' market reconstruction.

References

Abu-Lughod, Lila (2002) 'Do Muslim women really need saving? Anthropological reflections on cultural relativism and its others', *American Anthropologist*, 104(3).

Agamben, Giorgio (1998) *Homo Sacer: Sovereign Power and Bare Life*, Palo Alto, CA: Stanford University Press.

Ahmed, Leila (1992) *Women and Gender in Islam*, New Haven, CT: Yale University Press.

Ayotte, Kevin J. and Mary E. Husain (2005) 'Securing Afghan women: neocolonialism, epistemic violence, and the rhetoric of the veil', *NWSA Journal*, 17(3).

Barlas, Asma (2002) *Believing Women in Islam: Unreading Patriarchal Interpretations of the Qur'an*, Austin: University of Texas Press.

Benard, Cheryl (in cooperation with Edith Schlaffer) (2001) *Veiled Courage: Inside the Afghan Women's Resistance*, New York: Broadway Books.

Brown, Janelle (2002) 'A coalition of hope', *Ms*, Spring.

Clark, Kate (2004) 'The struggle for hearts and minds', in A. Donini et al. (eds), *Nation-Building Unraveled? Aid, Peace and Justice in Afghanistan*, Bloomfield, IN: Kumrian Press.

Dalby, S. (2003) 'Calling 911: geopolitics, security and America's new war', *Geopolitics*, 8(3).

Dowler, Lorraine (2001) 'Till death do us part: masculinity, friendship, and nationalism in Belfast, Northern Ireland', *Environment and Planning D: Society and Space*, 19: 53–71.

El Guindi, Fadwa (1999) *Veil: Modesty, Privacy and Resistance*, Oxford: Berg.

Enloe, Cynthia (1993) *The Morning After: Sexual Politics at the End of the Cold War*, Berkeley: University of California Press

— (2000) *Maneuvers: The International Politics of Militarizing Women's Lives*, Berkeley: University of California Press.

Foucault, Michel (1977) *Discipline and Punish: The Birth of the Prison*, New York: Pantheon.

Giddens, Anthony (1994) 'Living in a post-traditional society', in U. Beck, A. Giddens and S. Lash, *Reflexive Modernization: Politics, Tradition and Aesthetics in the Modern Social Order*, Palo Alto, CA: Stanford University Press.

Giles, W. and J. Hyndman (2004) *Sites of Violence: Gender and Conflict Zones*, Berkeley: University of California Press.

Goldstein, Joshua (1995) *How Gender Shapes the War System and Vice Versa*, Cambridge: Cambridge University Press.

Gregory, Derek (2004) *The Colonial Present: Afghanistan, Palestine, Iraq*, London: Blackwell.

Hans, Asha (2004) 'Escaping conflict: Afghan women in transit', in Giles and Hyndman (2004: 232–48), www.hrw.org/campaigns/clusters/myths0307/myths0307web.pdf, accessed 13 March 2007.

Human Rights Watch (2007) *The Myths and Realities about Cluster Munitions*.

Hunt, Krista (2002) 'The strategic co-optation of women's rights', *International Feminist Journal of Politics*, 4(1).

Iacopino, Vincent et al. (1998) *The Taliban's War on Women: A Health and Human Rights Crisis in Afghanistan*, Boston, MA: Physicians for Human Rights.

Kandiyoti, Deniz (ed.) (1991) *Women,* *Islam and the State*, Philadelphia, PA: Temple University Press.

— (2005) *The Politics of Gender and Reconstruction in Afghanistan*, United National Research Institute for Social Development.

Karzai, H. (2000) 'The Taliban: engagement or confrontation?', Prepared statement to a hearing of the Near Eastern and South Asian Affairs Subcommittee of the Senate Foreign Relations Committee, 20 July.

Mamdani, Mahmood (2004) *Good Muslim, Bad Muslim: America, the Cold War, and the Roots of Terror*, New York: Pantheon.

Moghadam, Valentine (1999) 'Revolution, religion, and gender politics: Iran and Afghanistan compared', *Journal of Women's History*, 10(4).

— (2002) 'Violence and terrorism: feminist observations on Islamist movements, state, and the international system', *Comparative Studies of South Asia, Africa and the Middle East*, XXI(1/2).

Mohanty, Chandra Talpade (1991) 'Under Western eyes: feminist scholarship and colonial discourses', in C. T. Mohanty, A. Russo and L. Torres (eds), *Third World Women and the Politics of Feminism*, Bloomington: Indiana University Press.

Moser, C. and Fiona C. Clark (eds) (2001) *Victims, Perpetrators or Actors? Gender, Armed Conflict and Political Violence*, London: Zed Books.

Nagel, Joane (1998) 'Masculinity and nationalism: gender and sexuality in the making of nations', *Ethnic and Racial Studies*, 21(2).

Patterson, Eric (2005) 'Just war in the 21st century: reconceptualizing just war theory after September 11', *International Politics*, 32.

Rashid, Ahmed (2001) *Taliban: Militant Islam, Oil and Fundamentalism in Central Asia*, New Haven, CT: Yale University Press.

Rubin, Barnett R. (2002) *The Fragmentation of Afghanistan: State Formation and Collapse in the International System*, 2nd edn, New Haven, CT: Yale University Press.

Said, Edward (1979) *Orientalism*, New York: Vintage.

Spivak, Gayatri Chakravorty (1987) 'Can the subaltern speak?', in L. Grossberg and C. Nelson (eds), *Marxism and the Interpretation of Culture*, Chicago, IL: University of Chicago Press.

Stowasser, Barbara (1997) 'The hijab: how a curtain became an institution and a cultural symbol', in Asma Afsaruddin (ed.), *Humanism, Culture, and Language in the Near East: Studies in Honor of Georg Krotkoff*, Winona Lake: Esenbrauns.

Taylor, Peter (1999) *Modernities: A Geohistorical Interpretation*, Minneapolis: University of Minnesota Press.

Tickner, J. Ann (2002) 'Feminist perspectives on 9/11', *International Studies Perspectives.*

US Congress (2001) House Committee on International Relations, Subcommittee on International Operations and Human Rights, 'Afghanistan people vs. the Taliban: the struggle for freedom intensifies', hearing before the Subcommittee on International Operations and Human Rights of the Committee on International Relations, House of Representatives, One Hundred Seventh Congress, first session, October 31.

US Senate Foreign Relations Committee (2000) 'The Taliban: engagement or confrontation?', Hearing of the Near Eastern and South Asian Affairs Subcommittee of the Senate Foreign Relations Committee, July 20.

Whitlock, Gillian (2005) 'The skin of the burqa: recent life narratives from Afghanistan', *Biography*, 28(1).

Young, Iris Marion (2003) 'The logic of masculinist protection: reflections on the current security state', *Signs: Journal of Women in Culture and Society*, 29.

Yuval-Davis, Nira (1997) *Gender and Nation*, London: Sage Publications.

'Rallying public opinion'

THREE | **Women's struggles and the wars in Iraq and Afghanistan**

11 | Afghan women: the limits of colonial rescue

SHAHNAZ KHAN

The ongoing Afghan conflict is largely absent from US news and many in the USA believe it to be a war that has been waged and won. The conflict has, however, been front and center in the Canadian media, particularly since 2002, a year that marked the first deployment of Canadian troops in a combat zone since the Korean War (1950–53). Comments promoting the need to uphold 'Western' values of democracy and freedom (Harper 2007) and the need to contribute to the war on terror (CTV News 2005) have helped generate support in Canada for this NATO-led mission. There is a gender dimension to this conflict. Support for military involvement in the region has also been sustained by a continuous recurrence of visual and textual representations of Afghan women which sensational-ize their plight under the Taliban and reiterate that their situation has improved under the current regime. Such comments also suggest that withdrawal of NATO troops will result in women going back to their harsh lives under the Taliban regime. While they do contain some truth, these comments do not present the whole story. They do, however, endorse the neocolonial military intervention in Afghanistan and they fuel a desire to rescue Afghan women – or colonial feminism.

Elsewhere (Khan 2001) I have challenged such colonial feminist views and have argued that liberal feminists in particular have put forward accounts of women's lives which have little connection to the societies in which they live. In particular many feminists have not challenged neo-imperial policies that keep those societies in perpetual subordination. My comments are especially true in the case of Afghanistan, where cold war politics and regional powers have helped keep the country in a state of conflict since the mid-1970s.

My analysis reiterates critiques put forward by Chandra Mohanty (1991), Gayatri Spivak (1999), Uma Narayan (1997) and Lata Mani (1990) about the discursive construction of Third World women in Western accounts. Moreover, Trinh Minh-ha reminds us that such accounts of Third World women's pain and oppression have made them inmates in a private zoo (1989). In this case the zoo is not private; instead it is a public zoo, providing voyeuristic spectacle and affirming splendors and freedoms of a singular Western culture and the misery and oppressive nature of the equally singular Third World/Muslim culture. Within such a zoo, the archetypal image of the veiled woman, even when presented as a speaking subject, remains limited to the immediate sensory experience of what it is like to be confined. The political context and social systems are eliminated.

The bombing of Afghanistan by the United States-led coalition in October 2001 and the Canadian decision to send troops there drew upon decontextualized images of veiled Afghan women to help construct a justification for war. Such images likely endorsed suggestions put forward by the First Ladies of both the United States and Britain, Laura Bush and Cherie Blair, that it was the misogynist Taliban (read terrorists) in Afghanistan who were responsible for the women's plight. The implication was that women in Afghanistan needed rescuing.

The desire to save brown women from brown men, as Spivak has pointed out elsewhere (1988), as a strategy, or excuse if you like, for military involvement in their countries, I argue, is another example of colonial feminism. And is not new. Women in the Third World have heard such rhetoric before. Leila Ahmed has written about the ways in which the liberation of Egyptian women from Egyptian men served as a strategy of British colonial occupation of that country (1992), and Frantz Fanon (1965) spoke about a similar strategy in the context of the French colonization of Algeria. During his recent visit to North America, Afghan president Hamid Karzai's comments also appear to endorse the view of colonial feminists that military interventions have led to Afghan women's liberation. He spoke about the freedoms that women in Afghanistan now enjoy. They no longer have to wear the burqa and they have access to education. His comments seem to suggest that women have indeed been rescued.

While it is true that in 2006 Afghan women have legal rights they did not enjoy under Taliban rule, in this discussion I demonstrate that they are not always able to access these rights. I am also interested in the following questions: How do we historically situate Afghan women's rights? To what extent have timeless tradition and unchanging Islam impacted on Afghan women? Are misogynist Afghan men responsible for the ways in which women live their lives? What are the connections between local conditions and global interests? Particularly how are local gender and social politics influenced by events beyond Afghanistan's borders? How can we better understand women's lives as well as the directions we need to take in order to bring about meaningful change? I begin my analysis with a brief examination of local conditions that influence Afghan women's lives.

Afghanistan: history and geopolitics

Afghan history suggests that women's rights are integrally connected to the politics and fortunes of the diverse groups in power as well as their international supporters. Various regimes in Afghanistan have attempted to implement education and labor market reforms focusing on women. Their efforts have been hampered to a large extent by the country's mountainous terrain, ideal for divisive tribal and ethnic enclaves (Halliday 1979; Weinner and Banuazizi 1994). Women's rights have been unevenly implemented in this context. For instance, in 1920 women were granted the right to vote and had educational facilities available to them. Indeed, Afghan legislation on the status of women was considered among the most 'progressive' in Muslim states and became the model for reforms in Soviet Central Asia in 1926 (Massels 1974). In Afghanistan, however, the reforms had many opponents who successfully agitated for a return to more conservative gender policies and, by the end of the 1920s, many rights had been canceled (Centlivres-Demont 1994; Moghadam 1993).

Women's rights were reinstated in April 1978, when a coup brought an underground Marxist group, the People's Democratic Party of Afghanistan (PDPA), into power. The Soviet Union, along with India, was a major supporter of this regime. The PDPA rule, however, evoked the hostility of the country's neighbors, China, Pakistan, Saudi Arabia and Iran, and was weakened by internal divisions. Nevertheless, the PDPA government committed itself to changing the political and social structure of Afghan society and to bringing under one law the various groups in Afghan society. It proclaimed a series of decrees of which the six articles of Decree #7, focusing on the institution of marriage, were among the most controversial. Moreover, literacy for women was no longer an option but entrenched in law (ibid.).

In the summer of 1978 many Afghans began to flee as refugees to Pakistan. Land reforms and compulsory implementation of the literacy programs among women were some of the reasons that many refugees gave for leaving their country (ibid.). Others pointed to the heavy-handedness of the regime and the fast pace of change imposed against the will of the people, particularly those living in the countryside (Anwar 1988). Resistance to the regime was organized in the camps in Pakistan and soon spread to parts of Afghanistan.

Afghan women had the right to vote in 1920, merely three years after Canadian women were granted the right to vote in 1917 and a full twenty years before Quebec women were allowed to go to the polls in provincial elections. Despite the Western orientalist rhetoric about timeless tradition and unchanging Islam, it appears that violent ideological changes in national politics helped create the conditions of Afghan women's lives. The turbulent Afghan politics had global links as well. I now turn to the international agendas at play in the region.

Cold war politics and its aftermath

The local war in Afghanistan between the PDPA regime and the various resistance groups turned into a more international conflict. The Soviets intervened militarily in 1979 to support the PDPA regime while the resistance received help from the United States, Saudi Arabia and Pakistan. From the late 1970s to the early 1990s, Afghanistan became a cold war battleground for the two superpowers of the time, the Soviet Union and the USA.

Where did the money come from to fund the resistance to the PDPA regime and its Soviet sponsors? Some of it came from Saudi Arabia, and some came from the drug trade linked to the US Central Intelligence Agency (CIA). Faced with funding difficulties, the CIA has encouraged drug trafficking both in South America and Central Asia in order to fund wars (McCoy 2003). Afghanistan is one of the regions where drug trafficking was encouraged and alliances forged with resistance groups. There, where opium was once grown and consumed, with CIA backing its more deadly derivative, heroin, began to be produced both for export and for increasing numbers of local consumers as well.

Now, who are the Taliban and how did they enter this scenario? The Taliban (which translates as *students*) are mainly Pakhtoon – the largest ethnic group in Afghanistan with a considerable number of members who have historically resided on the Pakistani side of the border. These students were politicized in some of the local religious schools, madrasas, many of which received funding from Saudi Arabia. Although initially the Taliban were drawn from camps set up in Pakistan to house Afghan refugees, in time they also came to include other impoverished Pakhtoon children from the Pakistani side of the border as well. The madrasas were encouraged by the CIA to train recruits for the emerging jihad against the Soviets. Such training frequently used CIA manuals.

Soon the Taliban joined the ranks of an international network of Islamist militants gathered and trained by the CIA and Pakistan's Inter Service Intelligence (ISI) to fight the PDPA regime and their Soviet backers. These groups formed the backbone of the resistance of the mujahedin (which translates as *strugglers*) in an important arena in the proxy war between the United States and the Soviet Union. After the fall of the PDPA regime in 1992, the various mujahedin factions turned on each other, vying for supremacy and control. It was in this chaos that the

Taliban emerged as victors. Initially they were seen as a stabilizing force both locally and internationally. Pakistan and the United Arab Emirates recognized the Taliban regime. Although speaking out against human rights violations in Afghanistan, the USA seemed to have granted them informal recognition, for Ronald Reagan hosted Taliban leaders in the White House and called them 'the moral equivalent of America's founding fathers' (Zoya 2006).

Women's rights remained connected to the many upheavals in the country, suggesting that the misogyny of Afghan men may not be the only factor affecting their lives. Indeed, women's rights parallel conditions in the country in which both local and global players had a role.

Valentine Moghadam (1993), who visited Afghanistan in 1989, claims that she saw women in prominent positions in urban areas and in the PDPA government as members of the National Assembly, members of Revolutionary Defense Groups militias, chief surgeons in military hospitals, and construction workers and electrical engineers who often supervised male staff. Ariana Airlines employed female as well as male flight attendants. And the female announcers who read the news were neither veiled nor wore a headscarf. Women were members of trade unions and worked as printers, soldiers, parachutists, and veterinarians.

The situation was very different in the mujahedin resistance movement. The Hizb-e-Islami, led by Gulbeddin Hekmatyar and supported by the United States, Pakistan, and Saudi Arabia, had no public place for women as ideologues or as spokespersons or in any other forum. In effect they were contradictorily situated. On the one hand, they were positioned in the role of the chaste pure woman whose mobility and sexuality are strictly controlled to serve the needs of the community through giving birth to future warriors. On the other hand, even pure women often fell prey to rape and other forms of violence at the hands of the mujahedin (Ganon 1996; Burns 1996; Amnesty International 1994).

In 1996, the Taliban assumed control of Afghanistan. As among the mujahedin there were no women among the Taliban who exercised power. Moreover, Taliban interpretation of Islam appears even more stringent than the mujahedin view. While the mujahedin allowed veiled women on the street, women in areas under Taliban control were initially ordered to stay indoors. All kinds of employment were restricted (Amnesty International 1996). These restrictions were somewhat relaxed in the later years of the regime, and permission was given to a limited number of women to work in healthcare and with international agencies. Widows with no other means of support were also given permission to work (Agence France Presse 2000). Assaults on women, which had been common as the mujahedin struggled for power, declined under Taliban rule. Taliban restrictions, however, created unbearable conditions, particularly for urban women, who were used to more mobility and fewer restrictions under previous regimes.

We know what happened next – the Taliban were accused of hosting Osama bin Laden and the Al Qaeda network, the group allegedly behind the attacks on the USA on September 11 2001. They were ousted from power by the United States-led coalition. Many just went home and found that their villages and their homes had been destroyed by cluster bombs used by the coalition and their families killed and maimed. Many of these men, along with other Pakhtoons, have joined the current insurrection to rid the country of foreign troops.

Current situation

The coalition in Afghanistan, formerly under American command and now led by NATO, is ostensibly in Afghanistan to help build a civil society after years of war and to bring under control those elements which seek to destroy the country. Moreover, Afghan refugees in neighboring countries are to be encouraged to go home. Let us see the extent to which this was happening in 2006, five years after the first bombs fell on Afghan soil.

Military successes were the focus of the Afghan campaign in the early years. Furthermore, 30 percent of the aid promised to Afghanistan was redirected to Iraq, leaving construction and development programs without adequate funds and frequently resulting in huge delays in getting them off the ground.

Much of the development has happened in larger cities such as Kabul, Mazar-e-Sharif and Heart, where new businesses have sprung up which cater to the urban elite, security personnel and employees of foreign NGOs (non-governmental organizations) (Whitting 2005). Kabul in particular has shining shopping malls retailing expensive items and five-star hotels with rooms that begin at US$275 per night (Walsh 2006). Moreover, a considerable amount of development work continues to be contracted to foreign NGOs while locals remain jobless. The benefits of development, it appears, have not reached large numbers of Afghans, for at least 6.5 million out of population of 21 or 25 million are dependent on food aid. At the same time large parts of the country are out of reach of aid workers owing to lawlessness (ibid.).

Afghans also have to deal with the kidnapping of children, who are frequently murdered even after ransom has been paid. They are unable to turn to the authorities because of police corruption or get justice because of judicial corruption (Morarjee 2005). Corruption and voter registration fraud were also rife in the 2006 parliamentary election (Human Rights Watch 2004; Symonds 2004). The Revolutionary Association of Women of Afghanistan (RAWA), a women's right's group, also challenged the election results and suggested that Hamid Karzai had given key government posts to 'Jihadi criminal leaders, former Taliban commanders and some former puppets of the USSR. Those who ought to be prosecuted before anyone else for their crimes against our nation are going to legislate to the people' (Zoya 2006).

It appears that the warlords have an inordinate amount of power in the newly 'liberated' Afghanistan. While the United States allied itself with the warlords to fight the Taliban and Al Qaeda, the Americans also subcontracted the security of much of the country to the warlords, who have actually served to destabilize the country (Zunes 2006). The attacks on Malalai Joya, a member of parliament with the Loya Jirga (a 'grand assembly' meeting of representatives), provide an example. As she spoke out against individuals who continue to commit atrocities under the mantle of government, she was physically assaulted within the Afghan parliament and called a prostitute, an epithet that has serious consequences in Afghanistan. There was a call from at least one person in the parliament that she should be raped, presumably as a way to silence her.

Drug sales are soaring and continue to finance the warlords who have private armies. The soaring drug production accounts for over one-third of the country's income-generating activity and is Afghanistan's largest source of export earning (UNODC and the World Bank 2006). At the same time 92 percent of the global illegal trade in opium originates from Afghanistan (UNODC 2007). Despite a large NATO presence, the country appears to be turning into a narco-state (Huggler 2005). The Senlis Council, a French think tank, suggested a solution. Afghanistan should grow legal opium under a license from the UN, as do India, Turkey and Australia. This would allow it to use opium for manufacturing medicine nationally as well as sell it to the international market. This proposal was rejected by all the powerbrokers – the UN, the USA and the Afghan government. The latter noted that it could not ensure that legal opium would not end up on the black market (Huggler 2005). Would this reticence by any chance be connected to reports suggesting that Afghan cabinet ministers (Harnden 2006), and Karzai's brother, Ahmed Wali Karzai (Gall 2004), are deeply implicated in the drug trade?

The long years of conflict, the American-led invasions, the drug trade and the corruption within the regime coincide with reports suggesting that Afghanistan is the poorest country in Asia (UNDP 2005; ADB 2005). Afghanistan also has the lowest life expectancy in the world – just 44.5 years – as well as insufficient basic healthcare, with a maternal mortality rate among the highest in the world, while education is the worst in the world (Kolhatkar 2005; UNICEF 2006). Twenty percent of Afghan children do not reach their fifth birthday (Whitting 2005), and less than 6 percent of Afghans have access to electricity, most of them on a part-time basis (Walsh 2006). Indeed, the 2004 United Nations National Human Development Report ranked Afghanistan 173 out of 178 countries in terms of human development. To make matters worse, Afghanistan remains among the most heavily landmined regions in the world – landmines kill and maim about a hundred people each month. At the same time demining efforts are hampered by the popular perception that deminers are helping the US-backed government.

What about the Afghan refugees? One of the objectives of the NATO mission is to encourage refugees to go home. Many refugees fear this return because of a lack of security, jobs, affordable shelter, and the continuation of conflict (Zoya 2006). Those who have returned to their own country frequently find they are homeless and live in squatter camps outside Kabul, where they lack adequate shelter and employment opportunities.

The images of shrouded and confined women were a major signifier used to consolidate support for the invasion of Afghanistan. They were to be rescued from the misogynist/terrorist Taliban, timeless tradition, Islam and, of course, from their veils. Colonial feminists used decontextualized accounts of women's lives to help generate support for such rescues. Let us see what this rescue looks like.

The plight of 'rescued' women

Women's rights are enshrined in the current Afghan constitution as equal to those of men. Yet in practice these rights have yet to be fully realized. Policies and practices do not reflect the spirit of the constitution and, some would argue, the rights granted to women in the Qur'an. For example, currently there are no laws that mandate the veil. Yet many, particularly outside the urban areas, continue to veil because it is a part of their dress and they would not go out of their homes without it. Still others wear the burqa because of a lack of security (Kolhatkar 2005; Lamb 2006). Veiling, however, is not the only issue confronting women. Poverty forces many Afghans to sell their female children as brides, some as young as seven or nine years (Kaufman 2003). These married 'women' will no longer be able to go to school, for the Karzai government upheld a law passed in the mid-1970s which forbids married women from attending school. Those not eligible for education will also include the tens of thousands of girls who lost out in the six years when the Taliban held power and who had married without ever attending school at all. But there is more: the Karzai government has attempted to resurrect the infamous Department for the Promotion of Virtue and the Prevention of Vice. This department was set up by the Taliban and was known to enforce bans – against, for example, wearing nail polish, laughing out loud, wearing white shoes and going out without being accompanied by a close male relative (Lamb 2006).

Compounding all this is the jailing of Afghan women for the 'crime' of running away from abusive parents or a violent husband (Sunday Herald 2005). Those unable to free themselves from the conditions of their lives frequently resort to unfortunate choices. Self-immolation is a popular option. Women facing few employment prospects and growing violence are losing hope and burning themselves to death (Esfandiari 2004; Sadid 2006; Salihi 2006). Prostitution is another option – it is one of the few means by which women can earn an income. Here is what thirty-five-year-old Zakia, a sex worker from Kabul, had to say:

> Now I am free to do my work. Under the Taliban, I would never have been able to do this. The only difference now is that I can work as a prostitute, so I guess I am free to do my work. I'm not happy with this job, but I have to do this because I have no choice. (Sisodia 2006)

Although Zakia claims that she could not work in the sex trade in Afghanistan under the Taliban, research conducted by RAWA reveals that as many as 25,000 women worked in the sex trade in 2001. Certainly life has become harder since the invasion of Afghanistan; at the same time Zakia's comments indicate that sex work has become easier. The two trends suggest that there may be many more sex workers in Afghanistan now than before the invasion.

Afghan women face other issues as well. An Amnesty International report (2005) suggests that they are at risk of abduction, rape, forced marriage, and being traded to pay debts or to settle disputes. Another Amnesty International report (2003) suggests that although women have freedom of movement under the law, this is not always so in practice. An official with a local NGO told Amnesty International: 'During the Taliban era if a woman went to the market and showed an inch of flesh, she would have been flogged, now she is raped' (ibid.). Should the woman seek redress through the law she faces extreme discrimination at every level of government. Moreover, the court system is unable and unwilling to protect women from violence or punish the perpetrators. Indeed, Amnesty International (2005) reported physical and sexual abuse of women in police custody. The reality of women's lives challenges their equality as enshrined in the Afghan constitution and Hamid Karzai's rhetoric that women's rights are progressing well in the new Afghan state.

Despite the situation in Afghanistan, it appears that since 2004 the US media have reduced their coverage in Afghanistan (Kolhatkar 2005). In the few instances when Afghanistan is covered, the focus is on 'feel-good' stories with little analysis of the effects of the ongoing US and now NATO presence in Afghanistan. Coverage by the *New York Times* of US Secretary of State Condoleezza Rice's visit to Afghanistan provides an example. Rice was quoted as saying: 'There could be no better story ... than Afghanistan's democratic development' (Brinkley and Gall 2005). There was no analysis of this statement by the authors of the report.

Canadian media do cover the Afghan war. This coverage, however, is largely limited to descriptions of military maneuvers and successes as well as accounts of successful development projects. As in the US media, there is also limited analysis of the negative effects of the war on the everyday lives of Afghans, including the lives of women. The negative stories largely focus on the Canadian and other foreign lives lost in the conflict.

In identifying the difficulties women in Afghanistan continue to face, I also want to point to signs of positive change. For the first time in Afghanistan, there is now a Ministry of Women's Affairs, and a job center opened for women in Kabul in December (Sunday Herald 2005). Four million students, comprising 40 percent of the children in the country, have enrolled in school since the fall of the Taliban (UNDP 2005). In October 2004, over eight million people voted in the presidential election, and the Loya Jirga (although male-dominated) ratified a new constitution. Non-drug-related activities constituted 15 percent of the economy in 2005 and some one thousand schools, clinics, and government buildings were constructed in the same year (Paris 2006). United Nations programs are also attempting to disarm and demobilize militiamen, and reintegrate them into civilian life (UNDP 2005). But after decades of conflict and the almost complete destruction of the country's infrastructure, the road to democracy, security and prosperity for Afghans will be long and hard.

The road ahead

At present the road ahead appears constructed on some 'common-sense' assumptions that Western values and freedoms will guide Afghans to achieving their social and national goals. The major obstacles seen in the way of such lofty goals are Afghan culture, 'timeless' tradition, Islam, and of course the terrorist Taliban. In this view, women's rights appear interconnected to the practice of veiling. There are several problems with these assumptions.

First, to hold up the West as a model for the rest to emulate draws upon orientalist views of the superiority and universalism of modernity claimed by the West. It does not take into account the fact that Islamic cultures contributed to modernity in a fundamental way. The veil in particular is held up as a symbol of the backwardness of Afghan society; the choice to unveil, which was non-existent under the Taliban and is technically available in the present era, is offered as one of the major achievements of the liberation of Afghanistan. The fact that many women continue to veil, both because they want to and because it is safer for them to do so, is frequently forgotten. Such Eurocentrism will not suffice in a highly politicized region. Instead, an over-reliance on this vision, particularly with military backing, will likely generate a more entrenched militant Islam. This is what appears to be happening in the area.

A second problematic assumption suggests that military operations in Afghanistan are part of the larger war on terror, and the US-led coalition is fighting to rid the world of the Taliban terrorists. This is a simplistic reduction that renders all Taliban schooled in madrasas as Al Qaeda terrorists. The two are not the same. Al Qaeda, largely put together through the help of the United States, Pakistan, and Saudi Arabia, comprises men from all parts of the Muslim world. The Taliban are Pukhtoons, the largest ethnic group in Afghanistan, a group with sizable numbers inside Pakistan as well. They are heavily armed with weapons – including anti-aircraft missiles – given to them by the United States to fight the Soviets. These older weapons are supplemented by the new ones they have purchased from the proceeds of the drug trade. The Taliban insurgents include youths who grew up in refugee camps in Pakistan as well as members of other Pukhtoon tribal groups. They fight to free their homeland from foreigners – first Soviet and now NATO troops. Some may identify with the conservative ideology of the Taliban but others many not (Zunes 2006). Treating all Pukhtoons as Taliban terrorists endorses Eurocentric views that 'our' forces are legitimate while those that battle against us are not. Such reductionism does not allow for an understanding of the ground realities and will likely not help bring about a lasting peace.

Many Pukhtoons, particularly in the rural areas, are indeed misogynist, and their vision of society is different from that of most Islamic societies. Customary practices among the Pukhtoons in both Pakistan and Afghanistan, known as Pukhtoonwali, provide a fertile environment for conservative interpretations of Islamic laws (Sardar Ali 2000). While in the past such interpretations were largely restricted to rural areas, with the arming and politicization of the Taliban, many of whom adhere to the Pukhtoonwali code, laws based on these practices spread wherever the Taliban were able to assert control. As Jacinto (2006) points out, the absence of a strong central state with a functioning legal structure renders this ancient patriarchal code the paramount system under which lives in southern Afghanistan have been regulated, particularly in the last thirty years. Thus it appears that 'timeless' Islam is not responsible for the practices that govern Afghan women's lives. Instead, military agendas of regions outside the nation's borders helped sustain an ancient patriarchal code and spread it to the Afghan urban areas where largely it had not existed in recent history.

The war on drugs is also a problematic issue. Unable to find work and unable to grow food to feed their families, many Pukhtoons have found employment with the warlords while others have joined the insurrection. Still others are now involved in the drug trade. If drug production is the main activity for many people, then the war on drugs also becomes a war on the people whose livelihood it has become. Until other types of employment become available to them, it will be extremely difficult and inhumane to prevent Afghans from growing the only crop that allows them to feed their families. Perhaps we need to re-examine the Senlis proposal that Afghans grow opium for medicine, as well as scrutinize more closely the business interests of those opposed to this option.

The Karzai regime has drafted warlords into the government and this has eroded its credibility. NATO forces, which help support the Karzai regime, are seen as supporting a corrupt regime, and they too have become unpopular with many people. One Pakistani politician noted: 'Buy off every farmer, with whatever it takes. That would be cheaper than what we are spending fighting' (Siddiqui 2007: A19). NATO air strikes are also a problem. Using this method of military engagement, fewer NATO troops are killed and such strikes are a popular strategy for the coalition. Such action also results, however, in greater 'collateral damage' – or civilian deaths. Despite Karzai's assurances to the contrary, the rule of law does not exist in Afghanistan and women are not always able to access the rights promised them by law.

Conclusion

I now return to the popular colonial feminist view (Armstrong 2002; Bush 2007) that NATO military action in Afghanistan is in part aimed at liberating women, and that this liberation is under way. This statement, like other stereotypical truths, has some validity. Certainly the NATO presence provides support to those forces that want to bring about social as well as gender equality. The law has changed and in theory women have rights equal to those of men. But in practice these rights have as yet to be realized. At the same time NATO troops help support a corrupt regime with links to the drug trade. Such support risks labeling as Western, and therefore undesirable, those women, including Malalai Joya, who work to realize the equality enshrined in the law. At the same time the corrupt drug lords consider themselves above the law – and the stage is set for chaos, similar to that of the mujahedin times, to emerge. In the past such chaos caused many Afghans to turn to the purist vision of the Taliban for some sort of stability and order. A recent survey suggests that this trend is under way in the rural areas and in some of the smaller urban centers (CTV 2007).

Should the Taliban return to power, perhaps the security situation in the country will improve. Spectacles of draconian punishment, such as execution by stoning, beheadings and amputations, will likely bring down the incidences of violence. But what about human rights, particularly women's rights? Women will likely be confined indoors and only properly authorized trips outside the home will be permitted, during which women will be chaperoned and encased in burqas.

These issues, however, are not debated in the popular Western press. Instead the local insurgency against foreign troops is called a 'Taliban' insurgency, a catch-all phrase linking Taliban (terrorist) and September 11. To what extent the groups battling foreign troops or forces loyal to the Karzai regime are indeed Taliban, or some other groups fighting against what they consider foreign occupation, and their local supporters, is yet to be determined. The Western media highlight the work of foreign progressive forces working for change while the struggles of Afghans to bring about democracy and security are largely sidelined. In the Western media, the forces of evil are rarely drug mafia, corrupt government officials or cabinet ministers. Instead, the forces of evil are always Taliban terrorists. Such links do not allow us to hear the stories of victims of collateral damage in Afghanistan, or of the victims of the various drug mafias operating in the country. The role of NATO in supporting their nefarious activities is largely not investigated. As the Afghan war recedes from the front pages of the US news – indeed, from world news – and with mostly the successes highlighted, the conflict is seen as a just one, pitting the good guys (NATO and the Karzai regime) against the bad guys (the Taliban). The war is on its way to being won and the women rescued.

I have shown that the situation is much more complex and suggest that this simplistic equation will not provide a lasting solution.

There are some indications that some voices in the West are beginning to realize that a broader consensus is needed in Afghanistan. As John Watson, president of Care Canada, reminds us: 'We did not go into Afghanistan to get rid of the Taliban. We went into Afghanistan to get rid of Al Qaeda and I think we've become confused. They are not nice people but, then again, there are not nice people in a lot of places in the world' (Campion Smith 2006).

Moreover, US Senate majority leader Bill Frist expressed the need to assimilate those who 'call themselves the Taliban' into a larger, more representative Afghan government (Krane 2006). Perhaps Frist is responding to suggestions (Yousafzai 2007) that the Taliban insurgency has spread from Taliban strongholds in southern and southeast Afghanistan to eastern, central and western provinces as well. At the same time, the Taliban and Hezb-i-Islami leader Gulbuddin Hekmatyar have refused to engage in dialogue with the Karzai regime until the foreign occupation ends. Karzai has also begun to face challenges from a united front of communists, royalists and mujahedin. Yet people engaged in a dialogue with these groups must – must – give women's issues a central place in nation-building projects. The heroic developmental and political work of RAWA and other groups reminds us that there have been internal challenges to misogyny and violence during the long years of civil war. These challenges can be validated and supported.

Despite colonial feminist claims that women have achieved equality in Afghanistan, this analysis has shown that such equality has yet to be realized in practice. Moreover, during the current occupation questions of women's rights continue to be peripheral to regional and international politics. NATO support for a corrupt regime will not help bring about social and gender justice within Afghanistan. Karzai needs to take to task those forces (local and global) which serve to destabilize the state. At the same time local insurgents, be they Taliban or other groups, need to be brought to the negotiating table. In building a civil society where the rule of law exists and where people who break the law are punished, conditions will be created where all citizens of Afghanistan will be able to pursue their lives in ways that bring them safety, security and happiness. Only then will Afghan women become active citizens in charge of their lives.

References

ADB (Asian Development Bank) (2005) 'Afghanistan and ADB: fact sheet', www.adb.org/Documents/Fact_Sheets/AFG.asp?p=ctryaftg, accessed 31 December 2007.

Agence France Presse (2000) 'Kabul: Taliban sacks all female civil servants', *Globe and Mail*, 14 April.

Ahmed, Leila (1992) *Women and Gender in Islam*, New Haven, CT: Yale University Press.

Al-Jazeera Magazine (2003) 'Osama bin Laden', www.aljazeera.com/me.asp?service_ID=10319, accessed 1 January 2008.

Amnesty International (1994) 'Afghanistan: Amnesty International condemns international community for ignoring conflict in Afghanistan', News service 279/94, AI Index: ASA 11/WU07/94, accessed 15 December 2007.

— (1996) 'Taliban takes hundreds of civilian prisoners', News service 175/96, AI Index: ASA 11/07/96, accessed 2 October 2007.

— (1997) News service 04/97, AI Index: ASA 11/01/97, accessed 8 January 2007.

— (2003) 'Afghanistan: no one listens to us and no one treats us as human beings. Justice denied to women', www.web.amnesty.org/library/index/engasa110232003.

— (2005) 'Afghan women still under attack – systematic failure to protect', web.amnesty.org/library/index/engasa110072005, accessed 15 May 2008.

Anwar, Raja (1988) *The Tragedy of Afghanistan: A First Hand Account*, trans. Khalid Hasan, London: Verso.

Armstrong, Sally (1997) 'Veiled threat', *Homamaker's*, Summer.

— (2002) *Veiled Threat*, Toronto: Penguin.

Barsamian, David (2003) *Eqbal Ahmad, Interviews with David Barmasian*, Lahore: Vanguard Books.

Brinkley, Joel and Carlotta Gall (2005) 'Afghans put off parliamentary elections again, citing logistics', *New York Times*, 17 March.

Burns, John (1996) 'Walled in, shrouded in and angry', *New York Times*, 4 October.

Burns, John F. and Steve LeVine (1996) 'How Afghans' stern rulers took hold', *New York Times*, 31 December.

Bush, Laura (2007) 'Remarks', Pierpont Morgan Library and Museum, New York, 24 September, home.businesswire.com/portal/site/google/index.jsp?ndmViewId=news_view& newsId=20070924006342&newsLang=en.

Campion Smith, Bruce (2006) 'Canada's strategy is failing, MP's warned', *Toronto Star*, 23 November.

Centlivres-Demont, Micheline (1994) 'Afghan women in peace, war and exile', in M. Weiner and A. Banuazizi (eds), *The Politics of Social Transformation in Afghanistan, Iran and Pakistan*, Syracuse, NY: Syracuse University Press.

CNN.com. (2003) 'New York reduces 911 death toll by 40', www.cnn.com/2003/US/Northeast/10/29/wtc.deaths/, accessed 29 October 2007.

Crawford, Neta (2003) 'Just war theory and the US counter terror war', *Perspectives on Politics*, 1(1), March.

CTV (2005) 'Kandahar mission right thing to do: Martin', 30 July.

— (2007) 'Taliban support is rising in Afghanistan – study', www/ctv.ca/servlet/ARticleNews/story/

CtvNews/20070319/taliban_ support070319/20070319?hub+? World, accessed 19 March 2008.

DAWN (2007) 'Nato admits it killed many civilians in Afghanistan', DAWN.com, accessed 4 January 2008.

Esfandiari, Golnaz (2004) 'Self-immolation of women on the rise in western provinces', RFE/RL, www/rawa/org/immolation2.htm, accessed 1 March 2008.

Fanon, Frantz (1965) *A Dying Colonialism*, New York: Grove Press.

Gall, Carlotta (2004) 'Afghan poppy growers reach record level, UN says', *New York Times*, 19 November.

Ganon, Kathy (1996) 'Terror supplants rockets in Kabul as Islamic ban imposed on all', *Toronto Star*, 6 October.

Guardian (2003) 'Marriage spells the end of learning', www.rawa. org/marriage.htm, accessed 29 November 2007.

Halliday, Fred (1979) 'Revolution in Afghanistan', *New Left Review*.

Harnden, Toby (2006) 'Drug trade "reaches to Afghan cabinet"', *Daily Telegraph*, 5 February.

Harper, Stephen (2007) 'Prime minister announces additional funding for aid in Afghanistan', Prime Minister's Office, www.pm.gc.ca/ eng/media.asp?id=1555.

Herold, Marc (2006a) 'Afghanistan an empty space: the perfect neo-colonial state of the 21st century, part one', Department of Economics and Women's Studies, University of New Hampshire, www.cursor. org/stories/emptyspace.html.

— (2006b) 'A day to day chronicle of Afghanistan's guerilla and civil war', pubpages.unh.edu/˜ mwherold/.

Huggler, Justin (2005) 'Opium farmers sell daughters to cover debts to traffickers', *Independent*, 2 October.

Human Rights Watch (2004) 'The rule of the gun: human rights abuses and political repression in the run-up to Afghanistan's presidential election', www. hrw.org/backgrounder/asia/ afghanistan0904/.

IRINnews.org (2006) 'An interview with Barnet Rubin', UN Office for the Coordination of Humanitarian Affairs, www.irinnews.org/ report/asp?ReportID=54054& SElectREgion=Asia, accessed 18 October 2007.

Jacinto, Leela (2006) 'Abandoning the wardrobe and reclaiming religion in the discourse on Afghan women's Islamic rights', *Signs: Journal of Women in Culture and Society*, 32(1), Autumn.

Kaufman, Marc (2003) 'Afghan poor sell daughters as brides', *MSNBC*, 23 February, www/rawsa.org/ brides./htm.

Khan, Shahnaz (2001) 'Between here and there: feminist solidarity and Afghan women', *Genders*, 33, Spring, www.genders.org/g33/ gee_kahn.html.

Kolhatkar, Sonali (2005) 'Forgetting Afghanistan – again', ZNet.com and CounterPunch.com, rawa. org/sonali.html, accessed 28 March 2008.

Krane, Jim (2006) 'Mission in Afghanistan: can't win, says US senator', *Toronto Star*, 3 October.

Lamb, Christina (2006) '"Ministry of vice" fills Afghan women with fear', *Sunday Times*, July, www/timeonline.co.uk/article/ 2089-20891417.00.html.

Lechner, Frank and John Boli (2004) *The Globalization Reader*, Oxford: Blackwall.

McCoy, Alfred (2003) *The Politics of Heroin: CIA Complicity in the Global Drug Trade*, Chicago, IL: Chicago Review Press.

Mani, Lata (1990) 'Multiple mediations: feminist scholarship in the age of multinational reception', *Feminist Review*, 35: 24–41.

Massels, Gregory (1974) *The Surrogate Proletariat: Muslim Women and Revolutionary Strategies in Soviet Central Asia, 1919–1929*, Princeton, NJ: Princeton University Press.

Minh-ha, Trinh (1989) *Woman, Native, Other: Writing Postcoloniality and Feminism*, Bloomington: Indiana University Press.

Moghadam, Valentine (1993) 'Women and social change in Afghanistan', in V. Moghadam (ed.), *Modernizing Women: Gender and Social Change in the Middle East*, Boulder, CO: Lynne Rienner.

Mohanty, Chandra (1991) 'Under Western eyes: feminist scholarship and colonial discourses', in C. Mohanty, A. Russo and L. Torres (eds), *Third World Women and the Politics of Feminism*, Bloomington and Indianapolis: Indiana University Press.

Morarjee, Rachel (2005) 'Afghan city mourns its lost children, looks back to Taliban', AFP, 10 April, www.rawa.org/child-abuse.html.

Narayan, Uma (1997) *Dislocating Cultures: Identities, Traditions and Third World Feminism*, New York: Routledge.

Paris, Roland (2006) 'NATO's choice: go big or go home', *Globe and Mail*, 25 October.

Rashid, Ahmed (2002) *Taliban, Islam, Oil and the New Great Game*, New Haven, CT: Yale University Press, quoted in Tariq Ali, *The Clash of Fundamentalisms: Crusades,*

Jihads, and Modernity, London: Verso.

RAWA (Revolutionary Association of Women of Afghanistan) (2006) '28th April, mourning for people – joy for fundamentalists', www.rawa.org/apr28-06_html, accessed 28 March 2008.

Rozen, Laura (2004) 'War and piece', *International News and Commentary*, 18 January.

Sadid, Lailuma (2006) 'Suicide and option for desperate war-widows', *Indo Asian News Service*, rawa.org/suicide65html, accessed 1 April 2008.

Salihi, Zarghona (2006) 'Women's rights situation in Afghanistan worries AIHRC', *Pajhwork Afghan News*, www.rawa.org/wom/aihrc.html, accessed 6 March 2008.

Sardar Ali, Shaheen (2000) *Gender and Human Rights in Islam: Equal before Allah, Unequal before Man*, The Hague: Kluwer International.

Shogren, E. and D. Frantz (1993) 'Did Afghan policy boomerang for the US?', *Toronto Star*, 4 August.

Siddiqui, Haroon (2006) 'Expert advice on Afghanistan', *Toronto Star*, 14 September.

— (2007) 'Baluchistan an administrative nightmare', *Toronto Star*, 22 February.

Sisodia, Rajeshreer (2006) 'Lifting the veil on the Afghan sex trade', *South China Morning Post*, 9 April, rawa.org/rospio6.htm.

Spivak, Gayatri (1988) 'Can the subaltern speak', in Cary Nelson and Lawrence Grossberg (eds), *Marxism and the Interpretation of Culture*, Urbana: University of Illinois Press.

— (1999) *A Critique of Post Colonial Reason: Toward a History of the Vanishing Present*, Cambridge, MA: Harvard University Press.

Stiglitz, Joseph (2002) *Globalization and Its Discontents*, New York: Norton.

Sunday Herald (2005) 'Afghan women still in chains under Karzai', 23 January, www/rawa/org/jail-women.html.

Symonds, Peter (2004) 'Afghanistan's presidential election: a mockery of democracy', www.WSWS.org, accessed 2 October 2007.

UNDP (United Nations Development Programme) (2005) 'A Country on the Move', December 2005, www.undp.org.af/Publications/KeyDocuments/afg_on_the_move.pdf.

UNESCO (United Nations Educational, Scientific and Cultural Organization) (2006) 'Retraining Afghan media', portal.unesco.org/ci/en/ev.php-URL_ID=21011&URL_DO=DO_TOPIC&URL_SECTION =201.html, accessed 25 January 2008.

UNICEF (United Nations Children's Fund) (2006) 'UNICEF warns of continued threat facing women and children', www.rawa.org/unicef.html, accessed 21 March 2008.

UNODC (United Nations Office on Drugs and Crime) and the World Bank (2006) 'Afghanistan's drug industry: structure, functioning, dynamics, and implications for counter-narcotics policy', 28 November.

— (2007) 'Afghan opium cultivation soars 59 percent in 2006', www.unodc.org/unodc/press_release_2006_09_01.html, accessed 21 March 2008.

Walsh, Declan (2006) 'Gap between rich and poor widens in Afghanistan', *San Francisco Chronicle*, 1 January.

Weinner, Myron and Ali Banuazizi (1994) 'Introduction', in M. Winder and A. Banuazizi (eds), *The Politics of Social Transformation in Afghanistan, Iran, and Pakistan*, Syracuse, NY: Syracuse University Press.

Whitting, Alex (2005) Crisis profile: 'Afghanistan still the "sick man" of Asia', AlertNet, 20 June, www/rawa.org/sickman/html.

Yousafzai, Rahimullah (2007) 'Much ado about nothing', *Newsline*, September.

Zoya (2006) 'Five years later, Afghanistan still in flames', Znet, www/zmag.org/content/showarticle.cfm?ItemID=11169.

Zunes, Stephen (2006) 'Afghantistan five years later', Foreign Policy in Focus, 13 October, www.fpif.org/fpiftxt/3597.

12 | Gendered, racialized, and sexualized torture at Abu Ghraib

ISIS NUSAIR

I examine here the meaning of difference and the construction of the other within the contours of what Mohanty terms the United States' advanced post-colonial capitalist state project at play in Iraq. I use Edward Said's *Orientalism* and Meyda Yegenoglu's *Colonial Fantasies: Towards a Feminist Reading of Orientalism* as frameworks for analyzing how the essentializing and dichotomizing discourse of orientalism has justified, facilitated and shaped the torture at Abu Ghraib, the US prison established in Baghdad after the US invasion in 2003. Orientalism in this analysis is a discursive regime and an effect of a specific formation of power. In order to examine these sites of power, I trace and analyze how military and political institutions, practices and discourses contributed in a complex and systematic way to the creation of an essential oriental other and to the production of gendered, racialized and sexualized domination at Abu Ghraib.

The war on terrorism and the representation of the other

The premises of superiority, exclusion and ethnocentricism that are at the core of orientalism permeate neo-orientalist discourses as well (Sadiki 2004). The binary opposition between the Orient and the Occident is not only a means to set boundaries between the self and the other, but a representation that is interlocked with the will to power over those others (Said 1979). This was illustrated in the public discourse on terrorism offered by President Bush in the aftermath of the 11 September 2001 attacks on the USA – discourse which divided the world into 'good versus evil' and 'us against them,' and reinforced an absolute view of the world without offering a way of understanding the specifically global aspect of the attacks and the economic and political tensions that contributed to them (Hatem 2004). On 16 September 2001, US president George W. Bush made the association between the war on terrorism and the war against Islam, and described it as a 'crusade' that pitted 'us' against 'them,' giving the conflict a clear religious dimension.

The September 11 attacks generated a hypermasculine identity that draws on a religious code of ethics and orientalist constitutive differences between the self and the other (Nayak 2006). The Bush doctrine, as it came to be called, argued that if you 'harbor them, feed them, house them, you are just as guilty and you will be held accountable.' This discourse dispensed with legal niceties and embraced the lawless motif of the US Old West of 'get them dead or alive' and 'smoke them in their caves/ holes' (Hatem 2004). In a press conference on 17 September 2001, Bush explained that the USA was facing a new type of enemy, one that has no borders and with an extensive network. Yet his representation of this enemy did not go beyond describing it as a barbarian whose objectives were incomprehensible.

This construction of the enemy facilitated the conceptual gendered division between the nation and the enemy, and represented the successful reproduction of US intervention as a superior moral mission (Shepherd 2006). In his State of the Union address on 29 January 2002, Bush offered another articulation of this globalized orientalist discourse, its religious grounding, and its use of superior Western values in order to explain the war and some of its outcomes as good versus evil, light versus darkness, civilization versus barbarism, freedom versus oppression, just cause versus outlaw regimes, security versus danger, and peace versus terror. In this same speech, Bush was very specific in his description of the changing US definition of security in a global world where the USA could no longer feel protected by geographic barriers, and where its security had to be assured by action abroad and increased vigilance at home. Variations on this globalized orientalist discourse have since dominated Bush's speeches and the public discussion of the war on terrorism, reflecting strategic concerns as well as realpolitik in the mobilization for the war on terror (Hatem 2004).

Constructing the other at Abu Ghraib

Within the orientalist discourse, differences are hard to overcome, and Islam, Muslims, and Islamic cultures are represented as an inferior 'other' whose irrationality, backwardness and violence reinforce the superiority of the West, which stands for rationality, enlightenment, progress and civilization (Yegenoglu 1998). Within orientalism, the taming and civilizing mission of the barbaric Orient requires the dissemination of rational procedures of Western institutions of law and order and reorganization of oriental cultures along the principles of the modern, progressive and civilized West (Asad, as quoted in ibid.). Orientalism, therefore, offers an analysis of the structure of those varied Western discourses which represent the Orient and Islam as an object for investigation and control (Tetreault 2006; Abu-Lughod 2002). In order to be able to construct the

West and the Orient in different and distant temporalities, the machinery of colonial discourse does not need terms that are manifestly temporal. It can very well achieve its distancing and temporalizing function by using terms such as 'primitive,' 'backward,' and 'traditional.' This in turn distances or pushes the cultural other back in time, implying and inscribing an 'articulation and ordering of cultural difference' (Yegenoglu 1998: 96).

Cultural difference: the Arab mind

The essentializing discourse of orientalism not only constructs the Orient as the place of sensuality, irrationality, corrupt despotism, mystical religiosity, and sexually unstable Arabs, but also makes the orientalist inquiry into the nature of the 'Islamic mind' and 'Arab character' perfectly legitimate (ibid.). In his introduction to Raphael Patai's 2002 revised edition of *The Arab Mind*, retired US army colonel Norvell B. De Atkine states:

> To begin a process of understanding the seemingly irrational hatred that motivated the World Trade Center attackers, one must understand the social and cultural environment in which they lived and the modal personality traits that made them susceptible to engaging in terrorist actions. This book does a great deal to further that understanding. In fact, it is essential reading. At the institution where I teach military officers, *The Arab Mind* forms the basis of my cultural instruction, complemented by my own experiences of some 25 years living in, studying or teaching about the Middle East. (De Atkine 2002: x)

Colonel De Atkine adds that 'much of the American political science writing on the Middle East today is jargon- and agenda-laden, bordering on the indecipherable. A fixation on race, class and gender has had a destructive effect on Middle East scholarship' (xii). According to him, 'some of the best and most useful writing on the Arab world has been by outsiders, mostly Europeans, especially the French and British. Many of the best and illuminating works were written decades ago' (xii).

In a *New Yorker* article on 14 May 2004 entitled 'How a secret Pentagon program came to Abu Ghraib,' Seymour Hersh describes how *The Arab Mind* became the neoconservatives' bible on Arab behavior. He states:

> The notion that Arabs are particularly vulnerable to sexual humiliation became a talking point among pro-war Washington conservatives in the months before the March, 2003, invasion of Iraq. One book that was frequently cited was 'The Arab Mind,' a study of Arab culture and

181

psychology, first published in 1973, by Raphael Patai ... The book includes a twenty-five-page chapter on Arabs and sex, depicting sex as a taboo vested with shame and repression. 'The segregation of the sexes, the veiling of the women ... and all the other minute rules that govern and restrict contact between men and women, have the effect of making sex a prime mental preoccupation in the Arab world,' Patai wrote. Homosexual activity, 'or any indication of homosexual leanings, as with all other expressions of sexuality, is never given any publicity. These are private affairs and remain in private.' The Patai book, an academic told me, was 'the bible of the neo-cons on Arab behavior.' In their discussions, he said, two themes emerged – 'one, that Arabs only understand force and, two that the biggest weakness of Arabs is shame and humiliation.' (Hersh 2004a)

These representations and essentializing notions of Arabs and Muslims reinforced gendered, racialized and sexualized orientalist references and characteristics and sustained a climate of orientalist domination at Abu Ghraib. The Bush administration insisted on presenting the torture at Abu Ghraib as an isolated incident committed by a few bad apples while disregarding the larger continuum of torture and mistreatment of detainees in Afghanistan, Guantanamo Bay, and Iraq (Williams 2006; Dratel and Greenberg 2005; Harbury 2005; Harf and Lombardi 2005; Danner 2004). On 4 May 2004, US secretary of defense Donald H. Rumsfeld described torture at Abu Ghraib as 'an exceptional, isolated' case. In a nationally televised address on 24 May 2004, President George W. Bush spoke of 'disgraceful conduct by a few American troops who dishonored our country and disregarded our values.' US brigadier general Mark Kimmitt, deputy director of coalition operations in Iraq, told CBS television news program *60 Minutes*: 'Frankly, I think all of us are disappointed by the actions of the few.' This focus on the action of the few stands in stark opposition to a Human Rights Watch 2004 analysis that the US administration policies created the climate for Abu Ghraib.

Racial and sexual difference: the Arab body

Militarized and masculine presumptions about the oriental other were at the heart of the acts of sexual domination at Abu Ghraib. These were not singular or pathologized events, but systematic oppressive acts integral to power relations and complex productions and significations of gender, race and sexuality. In *Orientalism*, Said touched upon the issue of Western male fantasies in which the feminine and weak Orient had to undergo the conquest of the powerful and sexually dominant

West. He demonstrated how the Orient was a counter-mirror image of the other, the superior West, and that the depiction of a single cohesive Orient leads to the essentializing and stereotyping of images, whereby the Orient is classified as backward, unchanging, irrational, menacing, and to be dominated sexually.

Discourse is a system of meaning production related to practices of power. Within this context, manifest orientalism refers to various stated views about oriental society, languages, literatures, and history, while latent orientalism refers to an almost unconscious and untouchable act. It is through this latent structure that orientalism achieves its doctrinal character, its everydayness and naturalness, its taken-for-granted authority (Said 1979). Latent orientalism is transmitted from one generation to another partly because of an 'internal consistency about its constitutive will-to-power over the Orient' (Yegenoglu 1998: 23). In addition, it encourages a peculiarly male and sexist conception of the world. A case in point is the US military psychology assessment report on detainee abuse at Abu Ghraib. This report makes clear the connection between latent and manifest orientalist conceptions of the other and the impact it had on soldiers' behavior at Abu Ghraib. The report indicates that 'soldiers were immersed in Islamic culture, a culture with [a] different worship and belief system that they were encountering for the first time.' The report goes on to explain how the 'association by soldiers of Muslims with terrorism could exaggerate difference and lead to fear and to a devaluation of people.' Difference between US soldiers and Iraqi prisoners reached a level where, according to a military dog handler, even dogs 'came not to like Iraqi detainees. They [the dogs] did not like the Iraqi culture, smell, sound, skin-tone, hair-color or anything about them' (AR15 2005).

This binary division and construction of difference is laden with negative cultural, racial and social connotations. It is associated with constructions of power and hierarchy where the oriental is represented as feminine and the feminine as oriental (Yegenoglu 1998). Within this context, the Orient, seen as the embodiment of sensuality, is always understood in feminine terms and accordingly 'its place in Western imagery has been constructed through the simultaneous gesture of racialization and feminization' (ibid.: 73). This is evident in Sherene Razack's (2004) analysis that what took place at Abu Ghraib is part of a larger 'national project of dominating racially inferior peoples,' and that the violence in these photos is colonial violence, a result of a colonial encounter that is an 'encounter that the soldiers understand to be one between conquerors and racially, morally and culturally inferior peoples.' She adds that the three features of the violence enacted by white militaries in peacekeeping operations are also evident at Abu Ghraib – the violence is openly practiced with dozens witnessing it, it is recorded on film and in diaries, and it is sexualized, with both real and simulated rape and sodomy.

Liz Philipose (2007) describes a colonial landscape at Abu Ghraib that is both racialized and gendered. Assata Zerai and Zakia Salime (2006) analyze the intersection between patriarchal authority, racism, militarism, and elitism, and Richter-Montpetit (2007) describes what took place at Abu Ghraib as a constructed heterosexual, racialized and gendered script that is firmly grounded in the colonial desires and practices of the larger social order. It protects heterosexist normativity and the larger system of racialized masculinity that is put in higher gear at moments of unilateral militarization (Eisenstein 2004). Militarization in this context is a transformative process where individuals or a society come to imagine military needs and militaristic presumptions to be not only valuable but also normal (Enloe 2000). Militarization, in turn, reinforces hierarchical modes of orientalist representations, privileges masculinity, and 'others' anyone who is not in the business of empire-building – with the result that there are few if any civilians left at this moment (Eisenstein 2004).

The question of sexuality governs and structures the subject's every relation with the other (Yegenoglu 1998). This orientalist project institutionalizes gendered and racialized violence through the infantalization, demonization, dehumanization and sexual dominance of the other (Nayak 2006). Linda Burnham (2004) calls attention to the sexualization of national conquest at Abu Ghraib and sees sexual domination as part of a militarist hypersexuality. Hypermasculinity, within this context, is the sensationalistic endorsement of elements of masculinity, such as rigid gender roles, vengeful and militarized reactions and obsession with order, power and control (ibid.).

Photos of torture and abuse at Abu Ghraib are evidence of the violent act of unveiling, stripping and penetration, the ultimate act of cultural and sexual domination over an emasculate Iraqi other. Male Iraqi prisoners were represented in the Abu Ghraib photos as the opposite of what a US militarist and hypersexual soldier or policeman, either male or female, is or should be. The prisoners were represented as helpless, obedient, and docile (read feminine) others. They were sexually dominated, degraded, and forced to simulate homosexual acts. Within this homophobic, militarized, racist, and sexist representation, the perpetrators were defining their position as well as the nature of their domination over Iraqi others.

Taking over eighteen hundred pictures of torture of Iraqi prisoners at Abu Ghraib marks not only the difference between 'us' and 'them' in terms of sexuality, religion, belief system and culture, but makes these pictures available for the whole world to see. The act of taking a picture automatically implies distancing the self from its objectified other, and the process of reproducing these orchestrated images marked and re-corded these representations of absolute and essential *difference from* and *domination over* those others.

Orientalizing the veil

Before analyzing the relation between orientalizing the veil and torture at Abu Ghraib, I find it necessary to provide two examples of the posi-tion on the veil held by British colonial powers in Egypt (1882–1922), and French colonial powers in Algeria (1830–1962). This comparative analysis, examined in the case of Egypt by Leila Ahmed and in the case of Algeria by Marnia Lazreg, is important for understanding the connection between the veil and orientalist discourses of colonial and post-colonial domination.

Leila Ahmed, in *Women and Gender in Islam* (1992), argues that even though Islam's 'oppression' of women formed some element of the Euro-pean narrative of Islam from early on, the issue of women emerged as the centerpiece of the Western narrative of Islam only in the nineteenth century, and in particular in the later nineteenth century as Europeans established themselves as colonial powers in Muslim countries. She adds:

> The reorganized narrative, with its focus on women, appears to have
> been a compound created out of a coalescence between the old narrative
> of Islam and which Edward Said's *Orientalism* details and the broad,
> all-purpose narrative of colonial domination regarding the inferiority,
> in relation to the European culture, of all other cultures and societies.
> (ibid.: 150)

Fusion between women and culture and the idea that other men – men in colonized societies or societies beyond the borders of the civilized West – oppressed 'their' women was to be used, in the rhetoric of colonialism, 'to render morally justifiable its project of undermining or eradicating the cultures of colonized people' (ibid.: 151). According to this thesis, Islam was 'innately and immutably oppressive to women ... the veil and segregation epitomized that oppression, and ... these customs were the fundamental reasons for the general and comprehensive backwardness of Islamic societies' (ibid.: 152). Only 'if these practices "intrinsic" to

Islam (and therefore Islam itself) were cast off, could Muslim societies begin to move forward on the path of civilization' (ibid.).

Veiling, to Western eyes the most visible marker of the different-ness and inferiority of Islamic societies, became the symbol of both the oppression of women and the backwardness of Islam, and an open target of colonial attack. This is illustrated in a demonstration that was organized on 16 May 1958 by rebellious French generals in Algiers in order to show their determination to keep Algeria French. The generals wanted to give the government of France evidence that Algerians were in agreement with them, and they had a few thousand native men bussed in from nearby villages, along with a few women who were solemnly unveiled by French women. After this momentous act, 'all together sang the *Marseillaise* and the military *Chant des Africans*' (Lazreg 1994: 135). Lazreg argues that 'rounding up Algerians and bringing them to dem-onstrations of loyalty to France was not in itself an unusual act during the colonial era. But to unveil women at a well-choreographed ceremony added to the event a symbolic dimension' (ibid.). Lazreg suggests that this event did lasting harm to Algerian women and brought to light the politicization of women's bodies and their symbolic appropriation by colonial authorities. Their sexed bodies were suddenly laid bare before a 'crowd of vociferous colonists who, in an orgy of chants and cries for "Long Live French Algeria," claimed victory over all Algerian *women*,' and particularly over the veiled Algerian woman who represented 'Orientalist mystery and hidden beauty, but also an object of possession and aggres-sion due to the frustration stemming from being seen by her but not seeing her' (ibid.: 135–6).

Unveiling and penetrating bodies and minds at Abu Ghraib

In orientalism, femininity is represented as enigmatic, mysterious, and concealing a secret behind its veil which is projected onto the iconography of the Orient (Yegenoglu 1998). The horror and threat of what is assumed to be 'hidden behind the Oriental/feminine veil is revealed in and by these representations and the more the Orientalist subject has tried to know and conquer the zone of darkness and mystery, the more he has realized his distance from the "authentic," "real" knowledge of the Ori-ent and its women' (ibid.: 73). Within this framework, the Orientals are people who are characterized by dissimulation and dissemblance, which is why it is so hard to understand them and penetrate their minds. The Orientals are 'hidden not only behind their words but also behind their silence, for even their lips are a veil; true life is missing, its absence is dissimulated by appearances and masks' (ibid.).

If dissemblance, dissimulation and concealment are what characterize Orientals, if their lips are a veil and this is why it is so hard to understand them, to penetrate their 'Arab minds,' then there is a need to analyze the role that knowledge/language as a nexus of power about the other has played in the 2003 US invasion and occupation of Iraq. Lack of Arabic speakers among US soldiers and administrators has been quoted by many US officials as an obstacle that needs to be overcome. A 2007 report by the Iraq Study Group noted that of the thousand people who worked at the United States embassy in Iraq, only thirty-three spoke Arabic, and only six of them spoke it fluently. This in addition to the wall erected for security reasons around the Green Zone in Baghdad, which is becoming a literal and figurative wall that separates the US embassy and military administration from its Iraqi others.

If the veiled woman/culture remains always different or infinitely dissimulating in orientalist logic, this is *not* because of the complexity of her/ their being-in-the-world, but because they are always absolutely different (Yegenoglu 1998). In addition, they '*should* remain different, because I should remain the *same*' (ibid.: 57). This deep hostility, according to Yegenoglu, is not a question of liking or disliking the Orientals, their women, and their culture, but a force of negation. Even in death, the subjectivity of Iraqis is denied and invoked as different. 'We don't do body counts,' is what General Tommy Franks said in reference to the 2002 US bombing in Afghanistan (Broder 2003). This policy, introduced by the US military in the aftermath of the Vietnam War, re-enacts the force of negation of the other's subjectivity. Iraqis in this formula of negation are the ultimately present and non-existent others. The Iraq Body Count website questions the sole attention to US/UK and Western deaths in Iraq as well as the evasion, obstruction, and racist double standards that the American and British authorities employ to contain and deflect concerns about casualties in Iraq. The website analyzes the meaning and practice of the 'We don't do bad things' approach of these officials, their denial of responsibility, and the ways in which investigations are announced, forgotten and discarded. A case in point is the response of US secretary of defense Donald Rumsfeld to the massive looting that took place in Baghdad immediately after the 2003 US-led invasion and occupation of Iraq. According to Rumsfeld, 'You cannot do everything instantaneously. It's untidy. And freedom's untidy. And free people are free to make mistakes and commit crimes.' I wonder whether such a clumsy explanation would have been offered had those involved been US or European citizens. Is Rumsfeld telling the 'child-like' Iraqis that with time they will get used to the meaning and practice of 'freedom' and 'democracy'? Who could be held accountable within this discourse of negation of subjectivity? Is this why Iraqi agency has been absent from the planning for the aftermath of the 2003 US invasion and occupation of Iraq? Was the assumption among US policy-makers that the 'docile and child-like' Iraqis who could not yet take full control over their lives were waiting with rice and flowers to welcome the US military? Is this why it took more than twenty months for the US military and political administration to publicly recognize that there was serious resistance to their presence in Iraq? (Jansen 2005; Zakaria 2004).

The colonial doctrine of unveiling, 'the fantasy of penetration, the metaphysics of the veil can all be seen as the avoidance of such *responsibility vis-à-vis* the other, denied by the very structure of sovereign subjectivity' (Yegenoglu 1998: 58). The grand narrative of the colonial gaze is a 'deaf topology of the veil, made up of tales of unveiling, fantasies of penetrating her truth, fantasies of domesticating and reforming and thus controlling her' (ibid.). This is indeed a fundamental characteristic of colonial power. A case in point is the articulation by a French general in his study of the lessons of the Dahar insurrection in North Africa in the nineteenth century:

In effect the essential thing is to gather into groups this people, which is everywhere and nowhere; the essential thing is to make them something we can seize hold of. When we have them in our hands, we will then be able to do many things which are quite impossible for us today and which will perhaps allow us to capture their minds after we have captured their bodies. (ibid.: 117)

In this discourse, the people appear to be veiled indeed; they are visible and invisible, everywhere and nowhere. The fundamental question is to 'seize hold of them,' and the capture that the general articulates aims not at repression in a simple sense, but at the *production* of "minds" and of course "bodies"' (ibid.). Within this context, the colonized should be produced as a new body and mind with certain skills, characteristics, and form: she/he needs to be remade. But to understand this remapping and reterritorialization, we need to position the body of the other within a frame of power and domination.

By posing and presupposing that the veil is hiding something, concealing an essence, the subject turns the veil into a mask that needs to be penetrated, a mask behind which the other is suspected of hiding some dangerous secret threatening his unity and stability (ibid.). This was illustrated in the US government-generated Taguba Report on the treatment of Abu Ghraib prisoners in Iraq.[1] The report states that the intentional abuse of detainees by military police personnel at Abu Ghraib included the following acts: punching, slapping, and kicking detainees; jumping on their naked feet; videotaping and photographing naked male and female detainees; forcibly arranging detainees in various sexually explicit positions for photographing; forcing detainees to remove their clothing and keeping them naked for several days at a time; forcing naked male detainees to wear women's underwear; forcing groups of male detainees to masturbate themselves while being photographed and videotaped; arranging male detainees in a pile and then jumping on them; positioning a naked detainee on an MRE (military 'Meals Ready to Eat') box, with a sandbag on his head, and attaching wires to his fingers, toes, and penis to simulate electric torture; writing 'I am a Rapest' (sic) on the leg of a detainee alleged to have forcibly raped a fifteen-year-old fellow detainee, and then photographing him naked; placing a dog chain or strap around a naked detainee's neck and having a female soldier pose for a picture; a male MP (military police) guard having sex with a female detainee; and using military working dogs (without muzzles) to intimidate and frighten detainees, in at least one case biting and severely injuring a detainee.

Torture at Abu Ghraib was first exposed not by a digital photograph but by a letter from the prison. A woman prisoner inside the jail managed to smuggle out a note in December 2003. The contents of the letter were so shocking that Amal Kadham Swadi and other Iraqi women lawyers, who had been trying to gain access to the US jail, found them hard to believe. The note claimed that US guards had been raping women detainees and that several of the women were now pregnant. It added that women had been forced to strip naked in front of men, and it urged the Iraqi resistance to bomb the jail to spare the women further shame.

Swadi, one of seven female lawyers now representing women detainees in Abu Ghraib, began to piece together a picture of systemic abuse and torture perpetrated by US guards against Iraqi women held without charge in various detention centers in Iraq:

> This was not only true of Abu Ghraib, she discovered, but was, as she put it, 'happening all across Iraq.' In November last year, Swadi visited a woman detainee at a US military base at al-Kharkh, a former police compound in Baghdad. 'She was the only woman who would talk about her case. She was crying. She told us she had been raped,' Swadi says. 'Several American soldiers had raped her. She had tried to fight them off and they had hurt her arm. She showed us the stitches.' She told us, 'we have daughters and husbands. For God's sake don't tell anyone about this ...'

During her visit to Abu Ghraib in March 2004, one of the prisoners told Swadi that she had been forced to undress in front of US soldiers. 'The Iraqi translator turned his head in embarrassment,' she said ...

Another lawyer, Amal Alrawi, says '... relatives who gathered outside Abu Ghraib last Friday said it was common knowledge that women had been abused inside the jail.' Hamid Abdul Hussein, 40, who was there hoping to see his brother Jabar freed, said former detainees who had returned to their home town of Mahmudiya reported that several women had been raped. 'We've known this for months,' he said. 'We also heard that some women committed suicide.' (Harding 2004)

The statement from the Taguba Report concerning 'a male MP guard having sex with a female detainee' seems to be as far as US officials are willing to go in admitting that actual rape of Iraqi women took place at Abu Ghraib. Within the logic of orientalist domination, male Iraqi prisoners are still men, although weak and emasculate others. Acknowledging the actual rape of Iraqi women will shatter the civilizing and rescuing nature of the US military mission in Iraq. Although the moral superiority and saving mission of this project have been damaged by the release of the photos of torture and abuse at Abu Ghraib, these pictures could be blamed on a few bad apples and not on the structure and value system of the US military. Within the sexist and hierarchical logic of militarized hypermasculinity, penetration of and dominance over Iraqi male prisoners at Abu Ghraib could still be justified as something to be resolved between men. For after all, and despite women comprising about 15 percent of the US army, waging war is still constructed within the domain of the masculine. Acknowledging the rape of Iraqi female prisoners exposes the undifferentiated power of penetration and control over not only the bodies of Iraqis (both male and female) but over the land and its resources. This exposure, in turn, strips naked and tears apart the moral foundation of the liberation mission as well as the fundamentals of the US masculinized and militarized enterprise currently at play in Iraq.

The violent act of unveiling and ensuring total control over the body and the land of the other can guarantee the presence of a system of surveillance and the creation of docile and obedient subjects. This, in turn, forms the precondition for the intervening and corrective practices of colonial governing mentality. In this act, knowledge as well as vision is part of an interlocking desire for colonial disciplinary modes of control, and of the sadistic desire to physically master the object of the gaze by ripping it apart (Yegenoglu 1998). Within this context, the aggressive, hostile and violent act of unveiling, stripping, penetrating and tearing apart Iraqi bodies at Abu Ghraib, where the body is left nude, exposed and laid bare, is a guarantee for the colonial power that the body and consequently the mind become knowable, observable, visible and thereby able to be manipulated. This gendered, racialized and sexualized violence maintains discipline and secures the boundaries between the private and the public, and between community, nation and state (Nayak 2006). Within this context, they are all bodies to be disciplined.

Abu Ghraib is but one site of territorial control, a target in the mission to deterritorialize and reterritorialize the land of the native according to colonial values and geopolitical interests. Seizing hold of bodies and minds at Abu Ghraib is part of a larger continuum of control that seeks to seize hold of Iraq itself. This act of unveiling signifies the violent transformation of the Orient itself, which is subject now to neoconservative modes of colonial and post-colonial domination. My aim here is not to perpetuate the essentialist binary logic of 'us' and 'them' or East and West, nor to negate the presence of Iraqi subjectivity and agency. On the contrary, I aim to show that resistance to colonial power or the restoration of the colonized as the subject of history cannot be theorized apart from the orientalist discourse. The history of Iraq is redolent of resistance to orientalist colonial modes of domination, and the case is not any different this time around.

Note

1 The Taguba report is one of twelve military investigations and reviews of detainee abuse. Since October 2001 260 soldiers have faced punishment for detainee-related incidents. Nine individuals in the military, all except one below the level of captain, have been sentenced to time behind bars (McKelvey 2007; Hersh 2004b; Strasser 2004).

References

Abu-Lughod, Lila (2002) 'Do Muslim women really need saving?', *American Anthropologist*, 104(3): 783–90.

Ahmed, Leila (1992) *Women and Gender in Islam*, New Haven, CT: Yale University Press.

AR15 (2005) *Investigation – Allegation of Detainee Abuse at Abu Ghraib: Psychological Assessment*, www. aclu.org/torturefoia/released/ t1.pdf, accessed 10 January 2005.

Broder, John (2003) 'Iraqi army toll a mystery because no count is kept', *New York Times*, 2 April, www.iht. com/articles/91667.html, accessed 10 January 2005.

Burnham, Linda (2004) 'Sexual domination in uniform: an American value', www.war-times.org/issues/ WT_gender&abughraib.html, accessed 10 January 2005.

CBS News (2004) 'Abuse of Iraqi POWs by GIs probed', *60 Minutes*, 28 April, www.cbsnews. com/stories/2004/04/27/60II/

main614063.shtml, accessed 10 January 2005.

Danner, Mark (2004) *Torture and Truth: America, Abu Ghraib and the War on Terror*, New York: New York Review Books.

De Atkine, Norvell (2002) 'Foreword', in Raphael Patai, *The Arab Mind*, New York: Hatherleigh Press.

Dratel, Joshua and Karen Greenberg (2005) *The Torture Papers: The Road to Abu Ghraib*, Boston, MA: Cambridge University Press.

Eisenstein, Zilla (2004) 'Sexual humiliation, gender confusion and the horrors of Abu Ghraib', www.zmag.org/content/show article.cfm?SectionID=12&ItemID =5751, accessed 10 January 2005.

Enloe, Cynthia (2000) *Maneuvers: The International Politics of Militarizing Women's Lives*, Berkeley: University of California Press.

Harbury, Jennifer (2005) *Truth, Torture, and the American Way*, Boston, MA: Beacon Press.

Harding, Luke (2004) 'The other prisoners', *Guardian*, 20 May.

Harf, James and Mark Owen Lombardi (eds) (2005) *The Unfolding Legacy of 9/11*, University Press of America, Inc.

Hatem, Mervat (2003/04) 'Discourses on the "War on Terrorism" in the US and its view of the Arab, Muslim, and gendered "Other"', *Arab Studies Journal*, XI(2), XII(1).

Hersh, Seymour (2004a) 'How a secret Pentagon program came to Abu Ghraib', *New Yorker*, 14 May.

— (2004b) *Chain of Command: The Road from 9/11 to Abu Ghraib*, New York: HarperCollins.

Human Rights Watch (2004) *The Road to Abu Ghraib*, www.hrw.org/reports/2004/usa0604/, accessed 10 January 2005.

Jansen, Michael (2005) 'The prodding of international media and the clamor of world opinion', *Jordan Times*, 6 January.

Lazreg, Marnia (1994) *The Eloquence of Silence: Algerian Women in Question*, London: Routledge.

McKelvey, Tara (2007) *Monstering: Inside America's Policy of Secret Interrogations and Torture in the Terror War*, New York: Carroll & Graf.

Mohanty, Chandra Talpade (2004) 'Imperialism, militarism, globalization: mapping feminist struggles', Lecture at the Feminism Contesting Globalization Conference, Dublin, 8 July.

Nayak, Meghana (2006) 'Orientalism and "saving" US state identity after 9/11', *International Feminist Journal of Politics*, 8(1).

Philipose, Liz (2007) 'The politics of pain and the end of empire', *International Feminist Journal of Politics*, 9(1), March.

Razack, Sherene (2004) 'When is prisoner abuse racial violence?', www.selvesandothers.org/article1527.html, accessed 10 January 2005.

Richter-Montpetit, Melanie (2007) 'Empire, desire and violence: a queer transnational feminist reading of the prisoner "abuse" in Abu Ghraib and the question of "gender equality"', *International Feminist Journal of Politics*, 9(1), March.

Roth, Kenneth and Minky Worden (eds) (2005) *Torture*, New York: New Press and Human Rights Watch.

Sadiki, Larbi (2004) *The Search for Arab Democracy: Discourses and Counter-Discourses*, New York: Columbia University Press.

Said, Edward (1979) *Orientalism*, New York: Vintage.

Shepherd, Laura (2006) 'Veiled references: constructions of gender in the Bush administration discourse on the attacks on Afghanistan post-9/11', *International Feminist Journal of Politics*, 8(1).

Strasser, Steven (ed.) (2004) *The Abu Ghraib Investigations*, Public Affairs.

Tetreault, Mary Ann (2006) 'The sexual politics of Abu Ghraib: hegemony, spectacle, and the global war on terror', *National Women's Studies Association Journal*, 19(3): 33–49.

Williams, Kristian (2006) *American Methods: Torture and the Logic of Domination*, Boston, MA: South End Press.

Yegenoglu, Meyda (1998) *Colonial Fantasies: Towards a Feminist Reading of Orientalism*, Cambridge: Cambridge University Press.

Zakaria, Fareed (2004) *This Week*, ABC, 14 November.

Zerai, Assata and Zakia Salime (2006) 'A black feminist analysis of responses to war, racism, and repression', *Critical Sociology*, 32(2/3).

Orientalism and the politics of torture

13 | Whose bodies count? Feminist geopolitics and lessons from Iraq[1]

JENNIFER HYNDMAN

'What tools can be used to stage criticism of the war [in Iraq]?' (Angela Davis 2006)

In her October 2006 address to the Feminism and War conference in Syracuse, New York, Davis spoke of the 'unrepresentability of war' and made a call to persuade publics and governments to stop war, specifically in Iraq. She argued that more feminist ways of representing and understanding war in the public domain were needed. Here I take up her call to engage these challenges in the context of deadly conflict in Iraq, where war is represented and witnessed in countless ways every day. I probe selected representations of war in Iraq – from body counts to stories of struggle and loss – and attempt to trace their impact on how publics and governments 'see' war.

This is the third piece of writing in a loose trilogy in which I have analyzed war over five years, all of which address the question 'What will it take to stop war?' (Hyndman 2003, 2007). I aim, as an individual and part of larger, more collective efforts, to stop violence against civilians and combat people's ambivalence toward that violence, especially in North America. As a feminist and a geographer, I have argued that more accountable 'visions' and 'versions' of war are needed to incite political change. As an analytic to advance this project, I have contributed to 'feminist geopolitics' as a way to produce knowledge of war more accountably and approach politics differently (Hyndman 2004). Using this framework in the first article in my series, I argued that body counts of civilian deaths in Afghanistan would render the pain and death of ordinary Afghan people more evident to North American publics (Hyndman 2003). Tactically, I proffered that 'their' deaths would count to Americans as much as American deaths, if someone were in fact counting Afghan casualties. Clearly, a feminized roster of civilian deaths was not as important as those of US and allied soldiers lost in battle, but eventually publics would realize that more civilians were killed in Afghanistan as 'collateral damage' in the so-called war on terror than were killed on September 11 2001 in the USA. Highlighting this hypocrisy within the very liberal logic that authorized it seemed politically important, but was not enough to stop the violence. Far from it.

The war in Afghanistan was followed by the invasion of Iraq in March 2003. As for so many others, the very idea of this act incensed me and catalyzed my determination to protest both on the street and on the page. It also led me to abandon faith in my argument for civilian body counts. Such comments remain important but insufficient. Instead, in the second article in the trilogy, I argued that political change lay in the power of the narrative as a modality for representing war, that stories of love, loss, and suffering politically link the fates of Iraqis and North Americans (Hyndman 2007). If war could be represented in ways that made the daily life of Iraqis more apparent, ambivalence could be overcome. I still believe in this approach, just as I think that body counts serve a definite political purpose, but neither approach has changed public opinion enough to affect a change in government policy and practice.

This third essay culminates with a different twist: as the number of US soldiers killed in Iraq exceeds the number of US civilians killed during 9/11, a dark irony of 'fatality equivalence' emerges. US publics are no longer willing to watch 'their' soldiers being killed in Iraq. Support for the war has plummeted. In December 2006, more than 60 percent of Americans polled said that the invasion of Iraq was a mistake (Gamel 2006). President Bush's popularity hit a nadir of 29 percent in 2007 (Krugman 2007), at the same time as a $400 billion tally for expenditures on the war in Iraq was released. When in January 2007 the president announced a 'surge' in troop strength by another 20,000 US soldiers, both Iraqi civilian and US military deaths soared, setting daily records for the highest number of civilian deaths since the war began. April, May, and June 2007 were the deadliest months on record for American troops since the invasion of Iraq in 2003 (Urbina 2007). More than two million Iraqis fled the country between the March 2003 invasion and June 2007, and 1.7 million were displaced inside the country (Swarns 2007). Death rates declined somewhat in 2008 and some Iraqis returned home, but the war rages on at the moment of my writing.

In what follows, I outline my earlier arguments in more detail, engaging in what others have called auto-critique (Anderson 1996). In rethinking my analysis, I place more emphasis on *collective* responses to the war, both in the USA and originating inside Iraq from feminist organizations there. From US-based Code Pink to the Organization for Women's Freedom in Iraq, I explore some of the ways in which anti-war groups enable us to witness war. At the end of the day, however, organized opposition in the USA to the war in Iraq grows as the deaths of US soldiers mount: violence repatriated.

Feminist geopolitics

In exploring the politics of body counts, I employ the concept of feminist geopolitics as an analytical framing of militarized violence and death in Iraq. In my two earlier papers, I argued that feminist geopolitics is an approach to international relations that provides more accountable, embodied ways of seeing and understanding the intersection of power and space. I made the case then, and still contend, that it refers to an analytic that is contingent upon context, place, and time, rather than a new theory of geopolitics or a new ordering of space. Specifically, feminist geopolitics attempts to challenge the prevailing scales and epistemologies of knowledge production in relation to international relations. It eschews the state-centrism of dominant geopolitical commentary, the disembodied epistemology of omniscient knowledge production, and the focus on masculinist practices of militarizing states. Feminist geopolitical analyses are more accountable to the safety of civilian bodies, traversing scales from the macro-security of states to the micro-security of people, their homes, and livelihoods. From the disembodied space of neo-realist geopolitics, feminist geopolitics aims to recast war as a field of live human subjects with names, families, and home towns. By representing war through various permutations and incarnations of narrative, I have argued that feminist geopolitics offers more epistemologically embodied 'accounts' of war which more effectively convey the loss and suffering of people affected by it. Affect is a powerful substitute for ambivalence. Feminist geopolitics destabilizes dominant and often disembodied geopolitical discourse. People as much as states are the subjects of geopolitics.

While recognizing that the value of counting bodies in Iraq is not stable over time or across space, common practices of reporting casualties have become so normalized that they at once obscure and reproduce the workings of geopolitical power that frame these numbers and the stories for which they provide fodder. I still advocate more relational ways of representing Iraqi casualties, by linking Iraqis to North Americans in ways that go beyond merely counting deaths and injuries. Counting bodies is important, but it does not *account* for the remarkable destruction of lives and livelihoods occurring in Iraq today. No metric or measure of trauma and violence should dominate or silence people's narratives of suffering and loss.

The two wars: from Afghanistan to Iraq

The 'fatality metrics' of war, the body counts of soldiers and civilians killed in violent conflict, represent a geopolitics of war in themselves. The deaths of militarized soldiers are officially counted, described, and remembered by the armies that send them in to fight and by the families they leave behind; the deaths of civilians are not. Casualties might be thought of as masculinized (soldier) and feminized (civilian) sides of the body count records amassed by both official and unofficial sources. While counting is an important device for remembering, it is also flawed in the way it transforms unnamed dead people into abstract figures that obfuscate the political meanings of the violence, and its social and political consequences.

Counting bodies does not sufficiently account for the remarkable destruction of lives and livelihoods occurring in Iraq. What we see and read is partial in two senses: it is a selective and always incomplete representation of the crisis at hand, and it has been fashioned in particular ways that are at once institutionalized and convey dominant kinds of meaning (Shapiro 1996). 'Vision is always a question of the power to see – and perhaps of the violence implicit in our visualizing practices' (Haraway 1991: 192), so 'an optics is a politics of position.' These partial representations shape our responses, or not, to the geopolitics of war and the suffering at hand. 'Much of routinized misery is invisible; much that is made visible is not ordinary or routine' (Kleinman et al. 1997: xiii). *How* violent conflict and death are represented in the context of war is at least as important as *how much* destruction and death wreaks havoc on a society.

The more difficult question is how to produce 'responsible' relational representations of war that convey meanings of loss, pain, and destruction without further fueling conflict. More importantly, which impressions and understandings of war actually shape public opinion and government actions, so that struggles to end such violence may be successful? In revisiting feminist geopolitics in relation to body counts, I have argued for analyses that contextualize the effects of violence by connecting the lives and deaths of victims counted during war to those of the audience that consumes that information. Accountability, I contend now as then, is predicated on embodied epistemologies and visibility, but fatality metrics fail to embody the pain or suffering of war. Feminist geopolitics is about putting together the quiet, even silenced, narratives of violence and loss that do the work of taking apart dominant geopolitical scripts of 'us' and 'them.' While the deconstruction of such binary scripts is vital, feminist geopolitics aims to recover stories and voices that potentially recast the terms of war on new ground.

197

Public silence about the death or suffering of innocents in war is a form of political appropriation. The death ledgers, if one can call them that, were highly gendered lists of 'us' and 'them,' named and not, Americans and Afghans, soldiers and civilians. In terms of lives lost, the patriotic value placed on them and their geopolitical value have been highly disparate (Hyndman 2007). One obvious critique of the liberal position is that all lives are not equally valued, as the rights discourse would suggest. By forging this chain of equivalence I have argued for an accountability to the very logic and principles that authorized military force in Afghanistan, namely that of the United Nations Charter and its Security Council resolution. Another critique of liberal logic is that it often authorizes violence in the name of national interests that are part and parcel of liberal modernity.

The anti-war argument and its attendant liberal politics are implicit in the work of Iraq Body Count (IBC 2004), a progressive, non-profit initiative to verify reported deaths in Iraq due to the violence of the occupation and keep a record of Iraqi deaths. IBC relies on second-ary sources from reputable media who use mortuary statistics, health ministry numbers, and police reports; it is run by twenty volunteers from the USA and Britain. The Iraq Body Count project aims to promote public understanding of, engagement with and support for the human dimension in wars by providing reliable and up-to-date documentation of civilian casualties resulting from the US-led war in 2003 in the country. The duty of 'recorder' falls particularly heavily on the ordinary citizens of those states whose military forces cause the deaths.

Their website cites General Tommy Franks of the US Central Com-mand, who says, 'We don't do body counts,' and so IBC does. IBC main-tains: 'Civilian casualties are the most unacceptable consequence of all wars. Each civilian death is a tragedy and should never be regarded as the "cost" of achieving our countries' war aims, because it is not we who are paying this price' (ibid.). As with the liberal logic of intervention in Afghanistan, IBC enlists international law and a UN approach to human security to justify its actions. It openly states that its audience is the American and British publics and governments (BBC 2005).

Methods of counting bodies have never meant so much. I digress very briefly to discuss a debate about *how* body counts have been conducted in Iraq. Mortality statistics, methods, and academic activism were widely covered in the media when the British medical journal *The Lancet* first published a pre-US election study in 2004 which suggested that the number of Iraqis who had died since the US invasion was exponentially greater than Iraq Body Count's reports and other tallies. A wide range of 'fatality metrics' was published by various sources; the number of deaths and methods by which they were counted generated great debate. The argument became a strangely disembodied one about who and what was most accurate. Was accuracy the point?

In early October 2006, a second study by the same researchers was also published in *The Lancet.* The second study found that more than 650,000 Iraqis have died since the March 2003 invasion. In a rare moment of academic commentary, President Bush stated that '[t]he methodology is pretty well discredited' (Oziewicz 2006). The point of the study – that civilian deaths may be higher than anyone expected – was lost completely (again) as media polled various experts on the rigor of the methods employed. In 2007, the United Nations finally weighed in on the body count issue with weighty figures based on Iraqi government data related to the issuance of death certificates: each month since the war began, 3,000 Iraqi civilians have been killed, with 34,000 dead in 2006, ten times the number of American deaths (Tavernise 2007a). Yet the violence of these deaths has been obfuscated by the politics of body counts.

I argued then for a more relational accounting that draws on feminist practice, one that protests about the silent, nameless death counts in Iraq *and* the USA. On 5 October 2005, the *New York Times* reported that 1,929 US soldiers had been killed in Iraq, confirming the death of Corporal John Stalvey the day before. This regular report was interesting precisely because of the newspaper's front-page story: that most of the Louisiana victims of Hurricane Katrina had yet to be named weeks after the disaster occurred. 'The lack of information has robbed the death toll ... of a human face' (Dewan 2005: A20). US government interventions in Iraq and Afghanistan, or lack thereof in New Orleans, represent different missions, objectives, and disasters, but a chain of equivalence can be forged in terms of accounting for death: just as the mostly poor people of color killed by Hurricane Katrina deserve to be named and remembered, so too do those in Iraq and Afghanistan, whether they are soldiers or civilians. (By January 2008, almost four thousand US service members were confirmed dead from the war in Iraq, with no exit in sight.)

The multiple sites hosting meticulous records, biographies, photos, and circumstances of death for US and coalition soldiers are not of central concern, except to note here their authors' assiduous efforts to include all possible details and stories of individuals killed. Geopolitically, the question of who is counted is related to the question of 'who counts?' and 'who cares?' The 'fatality metrics' of body counts is clearly lopsided in the context of Iraq: victimhood is commodified and patriotism publicized for soldiers making the ultimate 'sacrifice,' while

Iraqi deaths are framed as 'the price that must be paid' for introducing 'freedom and justice.'

Making a difference?

Between anonymous body counts and (mostly) nameless other casualties, connections between here and there, us and them, are largely absent from the media consumed in the West. The reported murder of Margaret Hassan, director of the international non-governmental aid agency CARE, in Iraq is an important exception. Her death was a *story* because she was 'one of them' *and* 'one of us.' Irish-born with British and Iraqi citizenship, she had lived in Baghdad for thirty years with her Iraqi-born husband. Ms Hassan came out against the US invasion of Iraq; she had served the needs of Iraqis through her aid work for a dozen years before she was kidnapped and murdered. (The killing is especially enigmatic given that both Al Qaeda and many Iraqis had called for her release.) Her story affected many who watched the war and its toll, largely because it was told. Most are not. How can media coverage of violence render its victims protagonists in the tales told about war? When violence or disaster strikes, reporters invariably seek out the number of fatalities among their nationals as news of local interest. This is a parochial strategy perhaps, but one that links tragedy 'over there' to life 'over here.'

Geographer Gearoid Ó Tuathail (aka Gerard Toal) (1996) assesses the journalism of Maggie O'Kane, an Irish journalist whose visceral dispatches from the front lines of the war in Bosnia-Herzegovina represent a kind of feminist geopolitics at work. O'Kane's journalism is politically and personally engaged in its representation of conflict. Her work offers a 'way of seeing that disturbs the enframing of Bosnia in Western geopolitical discourse as a place beyond our universe of moral responsibility' (ibid.: 171). 'I propose the notion of an "anti-geopolitical eye" not as a distinct alternative way of seeing Bosnia that transcends the geopolitical ... [but] an eye that ... persistently transgresses, unravels and exceeds the frameworks of scripting Bosnia in Western geopolitical discourse' (ibid.: 173).

In reportage of the Iraq war, *New York Times* correspondent Sabrina Tavernise (2007a, 2007b) has paid similar attention to finely scaled narratives of war, pain, and loss. In so doing, she creates her own moral proximity:

A painful measure of just how much Iraq has changed in the four years since I started coming here is contained in my cellphone. Many numbers in the address book are for Iraqis who have either fled the country or been killed. One of the first Sunni politicians: gunned down. A Sunni family: moved to Syria ... The moderates are mostly gone. My phone includes at least a dozen entries for middle-class families who have given up and moved away ... I learned how much violence changes people, and how trust is chipped away, leaving society a thin layer of moth-eaten fabric that tears easily. (Tavernise 2007b: 4.1)

Tavernise forges direct, if professional, links between herself and those who have fled or are dead. She also attends to the neighborhood geographies and treatment of dead bodies:

A serious problem is dead bodies [in the Sunni neighborhood of Dawoodi]. They began to appear several times a week last summer on the railroad tracks that run through the neighborhood. But when residents call the police to pick up the bodies, they do not come. The police are Shiite and afraid of the area ... A few weeks ago, a woman's body appeared. It was raining. Yasir [a forty-year-old Sunni whose house is close to the dumping ground] said he covered her with blankets and called the police. A day later the police arrived. They peeked under the waterlogged blanket and drove away. It was another day before they collected the body. They took it at night, turning off their headlights and inching toward the area like thieves. (ibid.: 4.18)

Tavernise recounts her stories at scales finer than the city or state. She notes that most unidentified bodies were found in six neighborhoods of Baghdad, and tells how the Iraqis most tormented by the violence, the poor, are those least able to protect themselves against it:

Um Qasim, a Baghdad clearning lady, has lost three brothers, a sister-in-law, a nephew, a stepson and a son, all in the past three years. Two of her other sons are in jail in the northern city of Mosul ... Under Saddam Hussein, her main worry was how to feed her family. Now it is how to keep them alive. (Tavernise 2007a)

While these excerpts are a poor substitute for the long stories she has published, they forge connections with people's daily struggles in Baghdad and elsewhere. I cannot begin to comment on representational strategies and the storytelling modalities of the Iraqi counterpart journalists who co-produced many of these kinds of reports, as they have to remain anonymous to protect their lives. In a story on the murder of Shiite pilgrims in March 2007, for instance, the article simply states an 'Iraqi employee of the *New York Times* contributed reporting' (Semple 2007).

Thus far I have spoken about individual reporters reporting on the war and notable personalities killed in Iraq. A reader of my second article rightfully noted that I did not include more collective attempts to protest about the war in Iraq. US-based Code Pink was formed in the fall of 2002 as a playful response to the Bush administration's color-coded Homeland Security warning system, but also as a serious protest against war in Iraq. The women who founded Code Pink in the USA have coordinated with anti-war groups, such as the Organization for Women's Freedom in Iraq, to bring Iraqi women to the USA to tell their own stories of violence, survival, and efforts to promote understanding and cooperation across borders. Code Pink has also launched a campaign called 'Walk in Their Shoes' to visualize and embody the pain and suffering of war on the ground for Iraqi civilians. Likewise, the American Friends Service Committee (2006) organized 'Not One More Death,' a campaign triggered by the US soldier body count hitting 3,000. Both of these efforts ground war in everyday contexts amenable to feminist (geo)politics.

During the summer of 2005, Cindy Sheehan – mother of Casey Sheehan, a US soldier killed in Iraq in April 2004 – began camping outside President Bush's ranch in Crawford, Texas, to protest about the war. She attracted a large following of fellow campers during her time in Crawford, repeatedly raising the question of why US soldiers – sons, daughters, husbands, wives, and lovers – should be dying in Iraq. By invoking names, lives, and relationships of loss to them, Sheehan has been hugely successful in persuading Americans across the political spectrum that the war in Iraq is not worth the lives it costs. The deployment of mothers against war is not new; from the mothers of Russian soldiers fighting in Chechnya to those against conflict in Sri Lanka, mothers' fronts have long been used to mobilize public opinion, lobby governments, and incite the withdrawal of troops from combat zones of political contention (Yuval-Davis 2004; Hyndman and de Alwis 2003). Mothers stand in for their dead sons and daughters, ostensibly speaking *for* these bodies as people whose lives are not taken seriously by the state that deploys or destroys them.

A feminist geopolitics in the context of violent conflict frames war as the stories of civilian people as embodied political and social subjects; the security and survival of the state are not the only story. In so doing, feminist geopolitics destabilizes dominant and often disembodied geopolitical representations and the discourse of which they are part.

The end of a trilogy: without closure

'Our' North American deaths appear to matter much more than 'their' deaths in both Iraq and Afghanistan. The stakes are representational and political. 'The world's most powerful military today is led by a cabal of restless nationalists immersed in an anti-intellectual culture of affect and aggressive militarism' (Ó Tuathail 2003: 857). Ó Tuathail outlines William Connelly's argument that human thought is not merely representational but also 'enactive,' that it is made possible by a level constituted through encounters and negotiations with the world: 'The affective tsunami unleashed by the terrorist attacks of 2001 is a broad and deep one that has set down a powerful somatic marker for most Americans' (ibid.: 859). Another tsunami of dead US soldiers appears to be enacting greater wariness of the war in Iraq, a war Americans now believe has little to do with the attacks of 9/11.

When 'our' losses are mourned and broadcast, the deaths are more fully registered and the violence of the war questioned. These named bodies in the context of Iraq are generally not civilians but soldiers. Californian Maria Ruzicka (2005), in her last dispatch from Iraq, wrote that

> Recently, I obtained statistics on civilian casualties from a high-ranking US military officer ... A good place to search for Iraqi civilian death counts is the Iraqi Assistance Center in Baghdad and the General Information Centers set up by the US military across Iraq. Iraqis who have been harmed by Americans have the right to file claims for compensation at these locations ... These statistics demonstrate that the US military *does* track civilian casualties. (Ruzicka 2005; emphasis added)

Ruzicka was a tireless activist who helped push the bill for the US$17.5 million compensation package through the US Congress for Afghan and Iraqi victims of the war (MacKinnon 2005). She and her driver were killed in April 2005, driving to Baghdad airport. Did her body counts have an impact on the war itself? Certainly she paid a high price for her convictions, though she lived long enough to see some compensation for the families of civilians killed in Afghanistan and Iraq. Her efforts to narrate the stories of families as embodied political subjects, even victims, establishes the 'moral proximity' necessary to link 'us' and 'them.' Ruzicka's actions led the USA to 'do something.' Her efforts were an expression of feminist geopolitics to the extent that they destabilized dominant geopolitical discourse by peopling it and by mobilizing the USA, which invaded Iraq in the name of national security, to provide some material security for the injured civilians and the families of those killed in that very invasion. Like Margaret Hassan, who was both 'like us' and 'like them,' Maria Ruzicka attempted to invoke proximity and familiarity. She, like Sabrina Tavernise in a more journalistic mode, did so by documenting the stories and losses of those affected by the war in Iraq to lobby the US government and inform the North American public.

From strategic to ethnographic to something in between, my position on representing war in ways that protest against its waging has shifted more than once. In February 2007, I asked Andrea Buffa of Code Pink what she believed to be the catalyst transforming US public opinion from a pro-war stance to an anti-war position. 'Honestly, I think it's the mounting deaths of US soldiers.' People are fed up seeing so many American military personnel return home in body bags. Membership is increasing among anti-war groups that represent active military personnel and veterans (Urbina 2007). Military Families Speak Out, founded in 2002, has 3,500 members, 500 of whom joined in the first six months of 2007. Iraq Veterans Against War began in 2004; it has 500 members with 100 joining in May and June of 2007 (ibid.). The Appeal for Redress Project, which advises active-duty military members on how to communicate with the US Congress about their opposition to the war, has approximately two thousand members, almost half of whom joined in the first six months of 2007. Driving around upstate New York in July 2007, I met an Iraq Veterans Against War bus twice in one day. Opposition to the war in Iraq by those mandated to fight it is ubiquitous.

The politics of representing and knowing war is constantly changing. In a dark revelation based on superb reporting, the *New York Times* conducted its own domestic 'body count,' enumerating the number of US civilians murdered by US soldiers who have served in Iraq and Afghanistan. In January 2008, the paper reported that at least 121 people had been killed by service members, three-quarters of whom were still in the military at the time the murders were committed. One third of the victims were spouses, girlfriends, children and other family members (Sontag and Alvarez 2008). Violence repatriated.

Here I have illustrated the fact that embodied epistemologies and narratives of people's experience of pain and suffering provide alternate ways to frame war. The question of who is counted and who counts as subjects in this landscape of political violence points to a feminist geopolitics that may be more successful at disrupting the dominant geopolitical script of the 'war on terror' in Iraq and elsewhere. Feminist geopolitics builds on the strengths of critical geopolitics, and in so doing recasts political possibilities by identifying fissures in dominant geopolitical scripts. But it goes farther: it resuscitates the narratives of those affected by violent conflict, and renders visible geopolitics as the fate of people, not simply as struggles between states over oil and weapons of mass destruction (though the war in Iraq is that too). Civilian body counts still matter, just as people's stories of survival and loss serve to embody the numbers when debates on method and sources obfuscate violence. Collective action and coalition politics to protest against the war continue, yet it appears that American deaths still count more than Iraqi ones in 2006, five years after the war began.

Note

1 The author gratefully acknowledges permission from Blackwell to include in this chapter selected sections from a previously published article: J. Hyndman (2007) 'Feminist geopolitics revisited: body counts in Iraq', *The Professional Geographer*, 59(1): 35–46.

References

American Friends Service Committee (2006) 'Not one more death', www.afsc.org/3000, accessed 18 December 2006.

Anderson, Kay (1996) 'Engendering race research: unsettling the self–other dichotomy', in N. Duncan (ed.), *Bodyspace: Destabilising Geographies of Gender and Sexuality*, New York/London: Routledge.

Asad, Talal (1997) 'On torture, or cruel, inhuman, and degrading treatment', in A. Kleinman, V. Das and M. Lock (eds), *Social Suffering*, Berkeley/LA/London: University of California Press.

BBC (2005) *Hard Talk* (with John Sloboda, head of IBC), 6 September, available at www.bbc.co.uk/hardtalk, accessed 13 September 2005.

Code Pink (n.d.) *Walk in Their Shoes*, at www.codepinkalert.org, accessed 18 December 2006.

Dewan, Shaila (2004) 'The perils of imprecision', *The Economist*, 6 November.

— (2005) 'Weeks later, most storm victims still unnamed', *New York Times*, 1 October, p. 20.

Fisk, Robert (2005) 'Secrets of the morgue: Baghdad's body count', *Independent*, 17 August.

Gamel, Kim (2006) 'Suicide bomber kills scores in Baghdad', *Globe and Mail*, 13 December, p. A17.

Gregory, Derek (2004a) 'Editorial: the Angel of Iraq', *Environment and Planning D: Society and Space*, 22.

— (2004b) *The Colonial Present*, Oxford: Blackwell.

Haraway, D. J. (1991) *Simians, Cyborgs, and Women: The Reinvention of Nature*, London: Free Association Books.

Hyndman, Jennifer (2003) 'Beyond either/or: a feminist analysis of September 11th', *ACME: an international e-journal of critical geographies*, 2(1).

— (2004) 'Mind the gap: bridging feminist and political geography through geopolitics', *Political Geography*, 23.

— (2007) 'Feminist geopolitics revisited: the case of Iraq', *Professional Geographer*, 59(1).

Hyndman, Jennifer and M. de Alwis (2003) 'Beyond gender: towards a feminist analysis of humanitarianism and development in Sri Lanka', *Women's Studies Quarterly*, 31.

IBC (Iraq Body Count) (2004) 'Iraq body count', www.iraqbodycount.org, accessed 27 October 2005.

Kleinman, Arthur, Veena Das and Margaret Lock (eds) (1997)

'Introduction', in *Social Suffering*, Berkeley/LA/London: University of California Press.

Krugman, Paul (2007) 'Valor and squalor', *New York Times*, 5 March.

MacKinnon, Mark (2005) 'My friend died helping Iraqi civilians', *Globe and Mail*, April.

Ó Tuathail, Gearoid (1996) 'An anti-geopolitical eye: Maggie O'Kane in Bosnia, 1992–93', *Gender, Place and Culture*, 3(2).

— (2003) '"Just out looking for a fight": American affect and the invasion of Iraq', *Antipode*.

Oziewicz, Estanislao (2006) 'New study estimating number of dead in Iraq hotly contested', *Globe and Mail*, 12 October.

Puar, Jasbir (2004) 'Abu Ghraib: arguing against exceptionalism', *Feminist Studies*, 30(2).

Ruzicka, Marla (2005) 'Aid worker's words – just a week before she was killed', *USA Today*, 19 April, available at aolsvc.news.aol.com/news/article.adp?id=20050417194109990006, accessed 25 August 2005.

Semple, Kirk (2007) 'Eight Iraqi soldiers and three pilgrims are killed on Shiite holy day', *New York Times*, 11 March.

Shapiro, Michael (1996) *Carto-graphies of War: Mapping Cultures of Violence*, Minneapolis: University of Minnesota Press.

Sontag, Deborah and Lizette Alvarez (2008) 'Across America, deadly echoes of foreign battles', *New York Times*, 13 January.

Swarns, Rachel (2007) 'Senators denounce Bush policy limiting refuge for Iraqis', *New York Times*, 17 January.

Tavernise, Sabrina (2007a) 'Iraqi death toll exceeded 34,000 in 2006', *New York Times*, 17 January, online edition.

— (2007b) 'It has unraveled so quickly', *New York Times*, 28 January, Section 4.

Urbina, Ian (2007) 'Even as loved ones fight on, war doubts arise', *New York Times*, 15 July.

Yuval-Davis, N. (2004) 'Gender, the nationalist imagination, war, and peace', in W. Giles and J. Hyndman (eds), *Sites of Violence: Gender and Conflict Zones*, Berkeley/LA: University of California Press.

14 | 'Freedom for women': stories of Baghdad and New York

BERENICE MALKA FISHER

As the US government talks about 'freedom for women' to help justify the invasion and occupation of other countries, feminists well may ask whether the concept of freedom still has meaning for our thinking and activism. Feminism, as a complex and often fragmented movement, has generated overlapping, competing, and often ambiguous notions of individual and collective freedom. In order to discover or rediscover what remains viable in this abstract notion, we need to continue talking to each other about what freedom means to us.

This piece draws together a number of disparate stories about women's struggles toward freedom: freedom from the constraints of tradition, from the suffering caused by war, from the fears and despair that sometimes keep us from freely speaking our political minds. These stories suggest how contradictions and complicities permeate our efforts to live freer lives. They encourage us to look at the conditions that support women's freedom and the consequences of the choices that we make. In the spirit of feminist theory, I use this storytelling approach to raise a series of questions, infused with the drama of lived experience.

First question: does freedom emerge through opportunity plus education?

The setting is Baghdad, 1934, the Tigris Palace Hotel. Beth Ostry, age twenty-six, wears a black silk evening gown. She has a round, high-cheeked face, and a beautifully curved, athletic body. She's dining with an older Iraqi Jewish couple, together with a young Iraqi Jewish lawyer. Beth – later my mother – is the eighth of nine children, born in Russia to a Jewish family that fled violence and poverty to settle in Canada. She has taken a strange route to dining at this elegant hotel, from Yelizavetgrad to Winnipeg to Baghdad.

When Beth finished college in Winnipeg near the start of the Great Depression, she felt lucky to get a job as a bank teller. It seemed natural to stay at home to be of help to her aging parents. There was a boyfriend in the picture – everyone expected them to marry – but Beth was in no hurry. When her parents asked her to come with them on a fiftieth-wedding-anniversary trip to visit relatives in Palestine, she leapt at the chance.

A family album, now fragile with age, tells the story of her travels: my tall grandfather wears his bowler hat, dressed for a tourist outing in London. My tiny grandmother perches on a camel in Egypt. My mother and her parents visit historic sites in Palestine and then pose for pictures with her mother's white-bearded brother and his wife in their garden.

When Beth's parents prepare to go home, she cannot bear to end her adventures. She looks in vain for a job to support herself in Palestine and then, just as she is about to give up hope, meets the directors of an Iraqi school for Jewish children – a branch of the Alliance Israelite Universelle. They offer her a position teaching English. She accepts, and after a harrowing trip across the desert finds herself in Baghdad's Jewish ghetto. The intensity is overwhelming: she feels nearly crushed by the masses of people and animals. Realizing that she will be living in this place for the next year, she panics: 'I was petrified,' she writes in her autobiography, 'why was I here?'

While Beth tries to figure out what she has gotten herself into, the girls in her all-female classes face another kind of future. At thirteen or fourteen, they are headed for arranged marriages. Beth believes this is why they don't want to study. Only a few older girls – some too poor to marry – show any real interest in learning. My mother finds it tragic that their families will not let these older ones continue their schooling. Education has made it possible for her and her siblings to take advantage of the freedom the New World has offered them. For her students, all the doors seem closed.

Baghdad, 2003. In the wake of the US bombing and invasion, violence and chaos disrupt Iraqi grade schools as well as universities. The well-known blogger Riverbend describes what happens in her family. Her cousin's seven- and ten-year-old daughters are excited about starting school in the fall. They look forward to seeing their friends, to buying new pencils and notebooks and backpacks. But this year their parents consider it too dangerous for the girls to pick out their own supplies: a whole contingent of adults – two women and two male relatives – must make the shopping expedition. When the girls are ready to leave for school, their father accompanies them 'with a pistol at his waist.'

As the violence increases, the girls' mother gets increasingly fearful. She decides to tutor them herself. Riverbend strongly suspects that the threat of violence provides a reason for her cousin's wife to keep her daughters where she really wants them to be, at home and close to her. The blogger argues that even with home schooling, the girls will fall behind.

Riverbend is one of the many urban, educated Iraqi women who held professional jobs before this war. From the 1970s to the late '80s, such educational and job opportunities expanded dramatically, although the war between Iraq and Iran fostered a serious conservative backlash. The US occupation has brought a painful reduction in the freedoms remaining for highly educated women. Professionals began losing not only their jobs but their lives. Nevertheless, like my mother, Riverbend sees education as crucial to opening the doors of opportunity – doors now closing on her nieces.

Her blogs do not describe what her cousin's wife is thinking, but I try to imagine her fears: children held in dark places for ransom. Barely adolescent girls raped and left for dead. Girls and boys bombed into bits – heads and hands scattered over Baghdad's streets. The new school notebooks now soaked in blood. I imagine that if I were in Iraq and these were my children, I would be far too afraid for their lives to send them to school.

Union Square, New York City, 2003. We are standing in our Thursday Women in Black vigil, which condemns Israeli occupation of Palestinian land and calls for a just peace. On and off, people shout at us. Most of the shouters are middle-aged Jewish men. This one's typical: he asks whether we're Jewish, and when some of us nod he starts to yell 'Traitors! traitors!' I wince at his aggression and am deeply troubled by his accusation. Although my parents were not ardent Zionists, they thought that diaspora Jews needed a place of last resort in case their countries – and the world – failed them. I found this widespread belief puzzling. It seemed to me based on two related and somewhat contradictory fantasies: that a powerful body like the US government or the diasporic community could guarantee the protection of the Jewish state and/or that Israeli Jews could make themselves safe and secure through military might. These fantasies have given birth to a terrible reality entailing the oppression – at times it seems the intended annihilation – of the Palestinian people. I'm angered and ashamed that Jews are doing this.

Yet I also resonate with a Jewish fear of our own annihilation that underlies the shouters' anger. Some of the political demands that I support – including the call for negotiations and an end to US military support to Israel – may involve unforeseen consequences for both Israelis and Palestinians. Although I believe that the desperate need for peace and social justice in Israel/Palestine justifies taking risks, I can't be sure how great they will be and for whom. In any case, I am not the one taking them. Tendrils of doubt curl around my commitment to non-violence. As the shouters direct their verbal venom at our group, uncertainty and ethical confusion tie my tongue. I stand in the vigil, mute, holding a sign that says as much as I can manage at the moment: 'Jewish Voice for Peace.'

At home, with my books, I wonder whether more intense study will resolve these doubts, whether I ever can reach the level of certainty that so many of my comrades, as well as the shouters, seem to have attained. We are all, at the moment, free to speak our political minds. But education alone has not freed my tongue. My feelings, it appears, are divided.

Second question: do our desires lead us toward greater freedom?

The setting shifts back to Baghdad, 1934. My mother does not give up trying to share the benefits of her own education with the Alliance students. During their daily recess in the schoolyard, the girls run around yelling at each other. Beth would like them to make better use of their playtime. A college basketball player herself, she teaches them the elements of the game. They quickly make it their own. Now, while they run around screaming, they also fight over the ball. I imagine my mother pursing her lips in displeasure: the girls are far too excited by this new addition to their recess repertoire to pay attention to her rules.

Things go better for Beth during her evening at the Tigris Palace Hotel. After their dinner, my mother's party drifts into the main dining room where there is dancing. It's not appropriate for the single man in their group to ask her to dance, but within a few minutes she is introduced to a visiting American, a young Jewish businessman, who is not confined by such cultural limits. Before entering the room, Beth has noticed a number of sheikhs who have come, she believes, to watch Western women dance in their low-cut gowns. To hide her décolleté, she has pinned the collar of her jacket up around her throat. In this oddly adjusted outfit, the American stranger takes her in his arms. His brown mustache brushes lightly over her wavy auburn hair, as his opening words rise over the lively music: 'What the hell are you doing in Baghdad,' he demands in his sharp New York accent, 'and what the hell have you done with your dress?' Five months later they are married.

When my mother tells and retells this story to me as a child, I feel safe and excited, as I do in the movies: my father is Gregory Peck, my mother Ava Gardner. In this dream-like image, my mother is totally different from the skillful homemaker and woman who orders my life – while my father orders hers. I picture her free, glamorous, lusted after by sheikhs and traveling Americans, following her desires wherever they lead.

After the end of the war, my father has begun his foreign traveling again. My mother is alone a lot, with four children.

Baghdad, 1991, then the embargo. Nuha al-Radi is a liberated woman, an artist and writer whose journals appear in the book *Baghdad Diaries*. As the bombs begin to fall on her city, art takes second place: she concentrates on holding her household together, making sure that loved ones are safe, and keeping herself sane. It's bad enough to have to defecate in the garden when the toilet stops working but far worse to endure the US planes flying overhead twenty-four hours a day.

Nuha al-Radi's survival depends in part on her rich sensuality: the color and scent of a flower, the special taste of a dish, the antics of a pet dog all sustain her through the years of deprivation. She also raises her spirits and those of her friends through her finely honed sense of irony. US imperial arrogance provides endless material for her satiric barbs. Her feelings ebb and flow freely, from joy to anxiety, from amusement to dread. When the violence lessens, she returns to her art. Now she makes sculpture out of what is left of her country – stones and the parts of broken cars.

Union Square, 2004. The Women in Black steering committee has organized a special event, and lots of people stop to listen to the speakers. I am particularly moved by one young Israeli activist who is so ardent and full of hope. These days, I am rather short on hope: chronic despair depresses my political passion. It is painful to want peace with justice when you've lost so much faith in their possibility. Some activists talk about continuing to do their work with a broken heart. I've been suffering from heartbreak ever since watching the first plane crash into the World Trade Center and fearing that the US response would plunge the world into decades of war and suffering. Personally, I do not have much in the way of decades left. Nor (as our gray and white heads attest) do most of the women standing in this vigil. Yet our shared desire for peace has not died. As our young speaker finishes her talk, the weight inside me lifts a bit. Turning toward the wrinkled face closest to mine, I say: 'Really beautiful.'

Hopefulness grows when the social soil is rich in nutrients. So does our desire for freedom. But the ground in which our desires are rooted is rocky with contradictions. In Baghdad, my mother is free to pursue her romantic desires because she is protected by British colonialism, the Iraqi Jewish community, and the upward mobility of her immigrant parents, who have given her a ticket home. Nuha al-Radi's desire to please her senses, the desire that helps her survive, can be fulfilled in part because of her class advantages. My own political passion is sustained by the creation of a certain kind of political space, protected (though neither fairly nor well) by a state against whose policies I protest.

211

Desire fuels so many of our actions. But desires in and of themselves cannot guarantee that the ends we seek are good ones. Our hearts mislead us too often. That is one of the many reasons we need lots of information and also friends and comrades to help us reflect on our thinking and judgments.

The third question: is freedom made possible by our connections with others – and which others?

My mother's adventures continue on a train from Palestine to Egypt, 1934. Beth and her sister Ethel shift uneasily on the hard benches of this hot, crowded car. They are taking a roundabout route to New York, where Beth will be married. They are the only Westerners in sight. The others, writes my mother, who calls them 'natives,' glare at them.

Suddenly, a 'large man [appears], dressed in Arab robes, and quietly [sits] next to [them].' She and Ethel, my mother reports, are 'petrified.' The man is tall, with dark skin and a turban. Beth is surprised when he speaks English. He tells them he's an American Jew who is friendly with his Arab neighbors and dresses like them so as not to seem too different. He shares his food and water with my mother and aunt and helps them find their ship when they reach Alexandria.

My mother's mother, Reva, sent her children mixed messages about freedom. 'There's a big, wide world out there,' she told them, 'go out and see what it offers you.' 'But,' she cautioned, 'Gentiles can always turn against you: trust only Jews (though not all of them), and stay connected to your family.' On the train, my mother's sense of freedom is momentarily shaken by a man she quickly assumes to be Arab and not a Jew. She has had a number of positive experiences meeting Arab men, but she has done so under the protection of men who were Jews. She's afraid of men in general, unless they become her protectors.

Ethel's story is different. She sees men as communist comrades, as lovers, and, on and off, as husbands. She has just finished a backbreaking stint on a kibbutz and before that an inspiring visit to the Soviet Union. The Palestine Communist Party has recently embraced the cause of Arab nationalism. It seems rather unlikely that Ethel would be 'petrified' of a man who is Arab. Moreover, given Ethel's feistiness, she certainly would defend both herself and her frightened sister from any male aggression. Beth has drawn Ethel into her 'we,' out of her own fear. My mother doesn't think she can be protected by women. When she marries, she will give up her new-found freedom to a man who she believes will protect her.

Baghdad, 2003. For Riverbend, freedom involves connection to others. Her own remarkable use of the Internet gives new meaning to freedom of speech by connecting her to tens of thousands, perhaps millions, of others – people eager to understand and support (and some of them criticize) her commitment to genuine self-determination for the Iraqi people.

In her blogs, she bristles at the idea of dividing Iraq into religious or ethnic areas. How, she asks, could you divide up Sunni and Shia, Kurds, Turkomen, and Arabs, even Christian, Muslim and Jew, when they can be found in the same regions and even families? Riverbend herself belongs to a tribe, as well as to her extended family. None of this inhibits her freedom, she says. It ensures her safety, especially in times of crisis. These multiple connections also protect Iraqi women from idiosyncratic rulings made by male clerics based on their particular interpretations of Islam. Her own Islam is tolerant, nurturing. Recalling the Gulf War, she says: 'If I did not have something to believe in ... I would have lost my mind.'

Riverbend's strong ties to family and community strengthen her angry responses to the death and suffering women have endured since the US occupation. But she says very little about the political connections Iraqi women have been attempting to forge with each other and across the globe. Her relative silence is not surprising. Years of government control over who 'represents' women, generations of patriarchal oppression within families and tribes, have left a legacy of suspicion toward women who claim to speak for women. The current violence and chaos in Baghdad and many other parts of the country make women's efforts to join together in the cause of their own greater freedom both difficult and dangerous.

Yet Iraqi women continue to work individually and collectively to end the war and institute a more just society. As I open yet another book or go to a film or a conference on the war, I am amazed to find women speaking out under such conditions. I am tempted to see such women as superhuman. In my amazement, I tend to forget that courage, like freedom, is more process than product: an endless struggle, involving connections with others, to realize these intangible and ambiguous human values.

Union Square, 2004 and 2006. It's an ordinary day at the vigil when, suddenly, I feel a strong jolt in my left shoulder, my hands stinging as the sign is torn from them. I catch a glimpse of a man running down the street, and it reminds me of the thin line between safety and danger. The safety of our group depends in important part on our solidarity. We're connected through our shared values and practice. We don't talk much about our political differences.

In recent years, the vigil has grown much smaller. It now includes a number of men, and some of the most committed vigilers come from the Catholic Worker, a peace and justice movement started during the Great Depression. Time has deconstructed our identity politics. But not entirely mine. I tend to rely most on the Jewish women I know best – their backgrounds and the meaning of the vigil to them. I trust the others because of their political affiliations and their evident sincerity.

But the deepest connection I feel is with my Jewish feminist friends in Israel, who continue to strive for peace together with Palestinian women. This is not because I feel closer to these friends than the friends and lover with whom I stand in vigil but because of what the Israeli women represent to me: the self who, with a small twist of fate, might have been me. A self who might have had to deal with the terrible political and moral challenges these women face on a daily basis. In some ways, this connection resembles my relation to those girls, eight or nine years old, whose images appear in photos of Jews being led to concentration camps – the long-nosed, dark-eyed children whose fate could have been mine. To all of them, I feel related through a sort of existential debt. It is strangely similar to the debt alluded to by many of the people who shout at us at the vigil – to their insistence that the Holocaust requires all Jews to support the policies of the Israeli government. The difference is that they, the shouters, believe that such a debt to our people can be paid through military conquest and control, while I think it strengthens our obligation to resist the cycle of violence and injustice.

Back at my desk I try to imagine a world in which these shouters and I could find the sort of accommodation I hope will end the Israeli–Palestinian conflict. Would it be possible to build any degree of trust on the basis of what we have in common? Is the effort to build that trust part of my responsibility as a Jew, a feminist, an advocate for peace? What kind of connection, if any, should I pursue with people who seem to be my political enemies? I know I cannot answer these questions in isolation. My comrades here and in Israel-Palestine, the Iraqi women holding fast to their right to a full and peaceful life, each play a part in my freedom to act as a political being. With all her fears and prejudices, my mother was profoundly opposed to war. With all my fears and inner conflicts, I am her daughter.

Acknowledgments

I am especially indebted to Sherry Gorelick for her generous and incisive political criticisms of several drafts of this piece; to Linda Nathan Marks for her sage editorial advice and her support for my efforts to make more connections between my theater and writing work; and to Lila Braine and Lorraine Cohen for their thoughtful responses.

Main sources

Al-Radi, Nuha (2003) *Baghdad Diaries: A Woman's Chronicle of War and Exile*, New York: Vintage.

Baer, Amy R. (ed.) (2004) *Varieties of Feminist Liberalism*, Lanham MD: Rowman & Littlefield.

Brown, Lucy and David Romano (2006) 'Women in post-Saddam Iraq: one step forward or two steps back?', *NWSA Journal*, 18(3), Fall.

Farouk-Slugett, Marion (1993) 'Liberation or repression? Pan-Arab nationalism and the women's movement in Iraq', in D. Hopwood, H. Ishow and T. Koszinowski (eds), *Iraq: Power and Society*, Reading: Ithaca Press, for St Anthony's College, Oxford.

Fisher, Elizabeth Ostry (1984) 'My family/myself', Unpublished manuscript.

Lasky, Marjorie P. et al. (2006) 'Iraqi women under siege', Code Pink/ Global Exchange, www.codepink4 peace.org.

Mackenzie, Catriona and Natalie Stoljar (eds) (2000) *Relational Autonomy: Feminist Perspectives on Autonomy, Agency, and the Social Self*, Oxford: Oxford University Press.

Malino, Frances (1998) 'The women teachers of the Alliance Israelite Universelle, 1872–1940', in J. R. Baskin, *Jewish Women in Historical Perspective*, 2nd edn, Detroit, MI: Wayne State University.

Nahas, Dunia H. (1976) *The Israeli Communist Party*, London: Portico Publications.

Riverbend (2005) *Baghdad Burning: Girl Blog from Iraq*, foreword by A. Soueif, intro by J. Ridgeway, New York: Feminist Press at the City University of New York.

Svirsky, Gila (2001) 'The impact of Women in Black in Israel', in M. R. Waller and J. Rycenga (eds), *Frontline Feminisms: Women, War, and Resistance*, New York: Routledge.

'Freedom for women'

The war on Iraq

MĨCERE GĨTHAE MŨGO

The land of the Iraqi people is ripped apart
By super power bombs dropping democracy
from war planes
and the barrel of the gun
the mighty play war video games
on millions of innocent lives
Waging *their* war on terror through terrorizing 'the other'
Liberating and civilizing through the terror of the machine gun
We say: No!
        Stop
        No more war!
Iraq is one massive heap of human rubble
A reign of terror now envelops Baghdad
Sadam I has begat Sadam II and
The once beautiful city of Baghdad
is no longer a home but a wilderness
overgrown with bush
as super power bombs drop democracy
to liberate and civilize through terror
We say: No!
        Stop!
        No more war!
Women and little girls scream
and fight back
as their vaginas are ripped apart
by uniformed men from the land of the free
shooting into them the semen of imperial democracy
Abu Ghraib is torn by the screams of tortured captives
Subdued by uniformed women in patriarchal trousers
Holding hounds on leashes to police freedom
We say: No!
        Stop!
        No more war!

FOUR | **Feminists organizing against imperialism and war**

15 | Violence against women: the US war on women

LEILANI DOWELL

As an organizer for the US youth group FIST – Fight Imperialism, Stand Together – I sometimes get the opportunity to meet young women who have faced US military recruiters – in their high schools or colleges, at the bus stops ('They're not allowed on our campus, but they follow us once we leave school,' one young woman told me) – or have faced the notion that joining the military is a way to gain 'discipline' and job training.

While all young people who enlist in the US military face coming home in a body bag or physically or emotionally disabled, women face the added risk of being sexually harassed and assaulted – by their fellow soldiers and officers.

At the beginning of 2006, Colonel Janis Karpinski, the former commander of the US prison at Abu Ghraib in Baghdad, charged that the senior military commander in Iraq had ordered cover-ups of some women soldiers' deaths from dehydration there. Karpinski said that the women were terrified of being sexually assaulted by male soldiers, and as a result didn't drink sufficient fluids in order to avoid using the latrines late at night. Doctors were told not to reveal causes of death publicly nor reveal that it was women soldiers who had died.

One of the most publicized cases of military sexual assault is that of former US army specialist Suzanne Swift, who is now facing a possible court martial for refusing to show up for her second deployment to Iraq. Swift reported three separate incidents of sexual harassment and assault to army officials. Reports say that her case is 'complicated' by the fact that she did not file formal complaints about the first two incidents while they were occurring, even though it is common knowledge that many women do not report cases of assault for fear of reprisals – whether in the military or domestically.

Pentagon spokesperson Roger Kaplan told the *Washington Post*, 'Sexual assault is the most underreported violent crime in America, and that's going to be true in the military as well' (2006). But the truth of the matter is that the hierarchical, patriarchal structure of the military makes it even more difficult to report sexual assault. Often when women in the military do come forward to report assault, they are ridiculed, told to drop the issue, and even face heightened assault. In addition, women who have been assaulted or raped in the military report poor medical treatment, lack of counseling, incomplete criminal investigations, and threats of punishment for reporting the assaults.

In Swift's case, her mother became so concerned about her daughter's situation that she called her congressperson, Democratic congressman Peter A. DeFazio. His office told her that it couldn't help her unless Swift signed a privacy waiver – meaning she would expose her identity while she was still under the command of the sergeant who was harassing her. In another instance, Swift reported sexual harassment by another sergeant to the equal opportunity officer at Fort Lewis. The sergeant was given a letter of admonishment and reassigned to another unit – a mere slap on the wrist. The *Post* says that in the army's news release about her case, officials 'noted how well the complaint process worked' in this incident (ibid.).

In the book *For Love of Country: Confronting Rape and Sexual Harassment in the US Military* (Nelson 2002), Terri Spahr Nelson states that two-thirds of US women soldiers say they have experienced unwanted, uninvited sexual behavior. Research from the Miles Foundation, which specializes in services to victims of violence linked to the US military, shows that 30 percent of female veterans have reported rape or attempted rape while on active duty. A US Department of Defense investigation found that women of color and women who are younger, poorer, and lower in rank are more likely to be assaulted.

The Pentagon says that more than five hundred sexual assaults have been reported involving US forces in Iraq and Afghanistan since the US invasion of those countries.

The *Post* also says the Pentagon has 'stepped up efforts to aid in reporting such incidents.'

Sexism, racism and homophobia are inculcated into the ranks by Pentagon officials and these hatreds permeate military culture. Less than twenty years ago, Marine Corps drill instructors routinely used such chants as 'One, two, three, four, every night we pray for war. Five, six, seven, eight, rape, kill, mutilate' (San Francisco Chronicle 1989). According to a 2004 *Nation* magazine story, the latest army basic training chant is 'What makes the grass grow? Blood, blood, bright red blood!' (16 December 2005). The level of violence against women GIs confirms the reactionary character of the Pentagon military machine.

Attitudes of arrogance, superiority, and power over others are re-inforced while soldiers are conditioned to engage in violent behavior. The Pentagon will never do anything to change what is essentially a rape culture in the military. The Pentagon functions as an instrument of violence against oppressed people, and as such cultivates a culture of violence that targets women, people of color, and lesbian, gay, bi and trans people.

And as the number of women in the US military increases, the Pentagon's violence is more starkly exposed. Young women are joining in growing numbers seeking jobs, skills and the means to support themselves and their children. More than 59,000 female troops have been deployed overseas as part of the wars against Iraq and Afghanistan.

The pattern starts even before women join the ranks. In March 2005, the Indianapolis *Star* reported on the case of a thirty-six-year-old recruiter who had been arrested for sexual assault against six young women, most of them high-school students. This case was the latest of at least six reported cases of sexual assault by recruiters in the two years since the passage of the federal No Child Left Behind Act, which allows military recruiters greater access to students' personal information. Similar charges against recruiters were also filed in Baltimore, California and New York.

In the Indianapolis case, investigators said that the recruiter used official information to target young women who were particularly vulnerable to authority, owing to their ages and backgrounds.

In general, violence against women in the United States is by far the most ignored form of violence. According to the National Organization for Women (NOW), every day four women die in the USA as a result of domestic violence, making the number of women who have been murdered by their partners greater than the number of US soldiers killed in the Vietnam War. Approximately 17 percent of pregnant women report having been battered. RAINN, the Rape, Abuse and Incest National Network, reports that every ninety seconds, someone is sexually assaulted in the United States. And to go back to the military, we should note that the number of reported cases of spousal abuse in the military is three to five times higher than civilian rates.

Of course, the intersection of oppression cannot be ignored. NOW reports that young women, low-income women, and African-American women are disproportionately victims of assault and rape. Domestic violence rates are five times higher among families below poverty levels, and severe spouse abuse is twice as likely to be committed by unemployed men as by those working full time.

We have to be careful when we state these statistics, because we don't want to perpetuate the misconception that working-class people are more violent, and we don't want to somehow imply that the ruling class doesn't commit domestic violence. In fact, I would suggest that the exact opposite is true; that it is the policies of the ruling class – including policies that institutionalize sexism and racism in society; policies that fuel war and aggression and take money away from jobs programs, education programs, healthcare; policies that create poverty – which promote and perpetuate this violence. The racism, sexism and homophobia that result from this violence are tools in the belt of those who oppress us, dividing worker from worker.

In the thoroughly sexist society we live in, women often become the scapegoats. And that violence cannot be seen in a vacuum, unconnected to these other issues of oppression.

In 1994, US women's organizations finally secured passage of the Violence Against Women Act, which provides $1.8 billion to address issues of violence against women; $1.8 billion, compared to the hundreds of billions spent on the war in Iraq.

And this is just to deal with the outright violence against women. Meanwhile, the right to abortion is constantly, increasingly under attack. Healthcare and education in the United States are more and more luxuries for the rich. The last census report stated that 13.2 percent of women live below the poverty line.

We can look to the situation for women in the United States to answer the question of whether or not to believe the US government's claim that it wages war in other countries to liberate women.

Let's take, in contrast, the situation of women in Iraq before US sanctions and invasions. Sara Flounders of *Workers World* newspaper reports:

Iraqi women had been guaranteed sweeping rights [as] part of a revolutionary upsurge that began in 1958 ... Nationalizing the oil meant that there were the resources to carry out mass literacy programs; provide free, quality health care; subsidize day care and housing. The government provided a student stipend that was an immediate incentive for families to keep both male and female children in school.

The rapidly growing economy ensured employment for thousands of young women. Iraqi women were guaranteed by law that if they couldn't find a job in the private sector, the government had to provide them a job in their chosen field or educational level. The government was the largest employer of women ... Thirty-eight percent of doctors in Iraq were women. Women were the majority of university students.

The destruction of the 1991 US war on Iraq and the 12 years of strangling sanctions that followed destroyed the economy that had sustained these social changes ... And within six months of the US occupation, free quality health care, so damaged under the years of sanctions, had been totally destroyed ... Free pre- and post-natal care is now a distant memory. Ninety-five percent of pregnant women are anemic. Their babies are born low weight, premature and sick.

Guaranteed six-month paid maternity leave is gone, along with guaranteed jobs. Subsidized day care, food subsidies and housing subsidies are gone. The massive bombing destroyed schools, hospitals, and health clinics. The ministries and social agencies were totally looted as occupation troops stood by. Lack of safety or money to buy books keeps a growing number of children, especially women, out of school. (Flounders 2004)

On 14 March 2006, a delegation of women, organized by the Women's Fightback Network, an affiliate of the International Action Center (www. iacenter.org) and joined by members from the US anti-war women's group Code Pink, went to the Iraqi embassy in Washington, DC, to demand the release of three Iraqi women and their young children from prison. The three women – thirty-one-year-old Wassan, twenty-five-year-old Zainab Fadhil and twenty-six-year-old Liqa Muhammad – were sentenced to death by hanging for resisting the US occupation of their country. In response to international protest, the women – who were originally tried without a lawyer – were granted an appeals trial. At this writing, however, they and their children were still imprisoned.

As Flounders concludes, 'Violence against women is endemic in the Pentagon military machine – not an accident or an aberration' (ibid.). As the war in Iraq continues day after day, as new wars are threatened against Iran and other countries, as the US military budget grows while the budget for social services dramatically shrinks, we must teach these lessons to the future generations of women fighters – fighters for social justice, not US imperialist wars.

References

Flounders, Sara (2004) *Workers World*, 11 March.

Kaplan, Roger (2006) *Washington Post*, 19 September.

Nelson, Terri (2002) *For Love of Country: Confronting Rape and Sexual Harassment in the US Military*, New York: Haworth Press.

San Francisco Chronicle (1989) 6 January.

Solomon, Alisa (2004) 'War resisters go north', *The Nation*, 16 December.

16 | 'We say code pink': feminist direct action and the 'war on terror'

JUDY ROHRER

'We insist, we enlist' echoes through the US army recruiting center in Tuc-son, Arizona, in July 2005. It is certainly not your typical anti-war chant, and this is part of its power. The slogan is taken up by gray- and purple-haired grandmothers at military recruiting offices around the United States. 'Take us, not our young people,' they plead with perplexed recruiters, while police gingerly handcuff them and lead them away through gauntlets of press cameras. This action is just one in a slew of recent feminist anti-war direct action scenarios cropping up around the USA.

The United States has become synonymous with war – the war in Afghanistan, the war in Iraq, the threatened war on Iran are all part of its global 'war on terror.' Women around the USA and throughout the world are confronted, often accosted, by war and militarism on a daily basis. Many, like the feminist direct action groups the Raging Gran-nies, Women in Black, and Code Pink, are taking action, incorporating feminist principles and analysis in creative and effective ways. By these means, these women do not just protest against the multiple injustices of war and militarism, but through their practice, they strive to model a better world.

I write this essay as an activist who became an academic and now struggles to continue with my activism. I write to other feminist academic-activists to challenge us to more seriously consider and involve ourselves in feminist direct action. I fear, as academics, we too easily critique or dismiss direct action instead of constructively engaging with it. There is a certain academic elitism that dismisses activists as naive, essentialist, and limited in feminist analysis. When, as theoreticians, we become more ensconced in the academy, these views can permeate, and we can become reluctant to participate. We can forget that there is no perfect action, no perfect time or place, no way to control all variables. We can forget that theory needs praxis. I try to remind myself that often, as a mentor once said, 'We act our way into thinking,' and not the other way around. Sometimes direct action is a good vehicle for that process.

In this essay I explore the Raging Grannies, Women in Black and Code Pink for what they can show us about creative contemporary forms of feminist anti-war direct action. There are many other groups engaged in such direct action, and even more groups involved more broadly in social justice direct action. I am focusing on these three groups because they have received the most attention from the media and are thus widely known; they are well organized nationally (and, in some cases, internationally), with strong networking among local groups; and they each have a unique direct action strategy and style.

Primarily using each group's websites and my own experience as resources, I briefly consider organizational histories and purpose; signature style and action; feminist principles and analysis (implicit or explicit); and strategies for dealing with 'peaceful women' essentialism (i.e. the assumption that women are innately peaceful and anti-militarist). I end with a discussion of how we might evaluate the effectiveness of the groups' feminist anti-war direct action. By profiling these groups and addressing the questions of essentialism and effectiveness, I hope to help interrupt academic discourses of dismissal or perpetual critique. I do not mean to posit feminist direct action as a panacea, but rather to suggest that, in all its messiness and contradiction, it can be a useful tool and is at least worth our serious consideration, if not our involvement.

Feminist direct action in the USA

When I speak of 'direct action' I am drawing on my experience as a direct action/civil disobedience trainer, on and off, for the past seventeen years (Central America solidarity, US anti-interventionism, anti-militarism, queer liberation, resistance to the prison industrial complex, etc.), and on the work of many activists in many different struggles. Direct action is a tactic of public disruption and confrontation – sometimes illegal, as in the case of civil disobedience (CD), and sometimes not. Broadly, direct action seeks to draw attention to an issue by interrupting 'business as usual.' Its goals are often multiple and can include: arousing public awareness of an issue (via the media, the Internet, bystanders, and so forth); applying pressure to a target (be it government agency, corporation, university, media outlet, etc.); disabling a target (for example, missile silos, logging equipment, military recruitment offices, factory farms); modeling the world we want to live in; and building community.

Direct action, understood broadly as I have defined it above, has been part of US history since its very beginning as a country. The dumping of tea into Boston harbor by colonists to protest against the British imperial tax is often cited as an early instance. US labor history is built on work slowdowns, pickets, sick-outs, strikes and any number of strategies to build solidarity and apply pressure to management and owners. US social movements of all kinds have used direct action – from the segregation-protesting bus boycott of the black civil rights movement in Montgomery, Alabama; to the American Indian Movement's occupation of Alcatraz Island in the San Francisco bay to reclaim indigenous land; to the Black Panthers chanting and marching for self-determination on the steps of the California state capital; to the marches and boycotts of the United Farm Workers and the Chicano/a movement; to 'die-ins' and the occupation of the National Institute of Health by AIDS activists protesting against US government inaction on drug testing for the HIV virus; to disability activists in their wheelchairs disrupting traffic to protest about inaccessible public transportation. To varying degrees women, and feminist principles, have played a role in many of these actions, often struggling for voice and representation in male-dominated groups or organizations.

Feminist anti-war/anti-militarist direct action in particular has a long, honorable history, and the three groups I focus on draw inspiration and ideas from those who have gone before. Over the years, there have been encampments at military sites; civil disobedience at the Pentagon; hammering on missile silos; confrontations with military recruiters at schools; military trains and convoys stopped by blockades; dramatizations of the impact of a military-centered versus a people-centered national budget and of the environmental costs of militarism as disadvantaged communities end up footing that bill.

Participants often expose the state's wars and inhumanity through strategic use of their own fragile bodies. Their use of irony, humanization, humility, and vulnerability characterize these actions, and differentiate them from more self-righteous, aggressive, masculinist anti-war organizing. Historically, many women anti-war activists and organizations have mobilized women's gendered roles and experience in service of their protest. The three groups I focus on follow suit, although with varying degrees of care not to naturalize their politics in their sex-gender.

Raging Grannies

The Raging Grannies originated in 1987 in Victoria, British Columbia, as part of the anti-nuclear movement, and now includes sixty groups in the USA, Europe and Canada. Their signature action includes floppy straw hats and radicalized versions of traditional and popular songs. They have no central organization but use the Internet, phone, mail and visits to share songs and tactics with each other. The Raging Granny San Francisco Peninsula website states: 'Raging Grannies worldwide rage for peace, social and political justice, and environmental preservation. Our purpose is to create a better world for our children and grandchildren.

We operate with a sense of outrage, a sense of humor, and a commitment to *non-violence*.'

One of the grannies' effective recent scenarios was their gentle occupation of military recruiting offices in 2005. Across the USA, these actions garnered a good deal of attention as the grannies moved in with songbooks and homemade cookies, and insisted that the recruiters enlist them instead of the young people. In many instances the women refused to leave and were arrested. The action in Tucson made it all the way to CNN news.

Since 'grannying' is an inherently gendered activity, there is certainly a gendered positioning that goes with being a Raging Granny. While different chapters are more or less feminist in their organizing and analysis, members all use both their age and their gender effectively, playing on tropes of wizened crones, innocent old ladies, and everyone's favorite granny. In her discussion of the Raging Grannies' philosophy on the organization's International Geocities website, Rose DeShaw of Kingston, New York, writes,

> Grannying is the least understood yet most powerful weapon we have.
> Sometimes, looking back, we can see grannying was the only thing that
> could have met the need ... From the most ancient times, the strong,
> wise, older women were the ones who advised, mediated and fought for
> what was right.

We could read this statement simply as essentialist, but I would like to give it more consideration. DeShaw is talking about some of the activities of 'grannying' that women have engaged in. While we might wish for more cultural and historical specificity, DeShaw situates grannying as a 'powerful weapon' women have at their disposal. This is expressly different than talking about it as something women just do because they are women.

Women in Black

Women in Black (WIB) is an international peace network in the USA and Europe. It is not an organization, but a means of mobilization and a formula for action. According to its website (womeninblack.org), WIB vigils were started in Israel in 1988 with women protesting against Israel's occupation of the West Bank and Gaza. WIB actions often take the form of women wearing black; standing in a public place in silent, non-violent vigil at regular times and intervals; carrying signs (often uniform in appearance); and handing out leaflets. WIB's signature style is black dress and silence.

Having been a part of the San Francisco Bay Area Women in Black, I can testify to the impact of a group of women, dressed in black, standing in silence while the chaos of the city swirls around them. The disjuncture trips people up and makes them stop, and when they stop, even for an instant, you can see the wheels churning in their heads and hearts. In contrast to the Raging Grannies' use of humor, song and theatrics to get attention, WIB actions capture people through their somber, silent determination.

Women in Black are explicitly doing feminist organizing. On their website, they write, 'We have a feminist understanding: that male violence against women in domestic life and in the community, in times of peace and in times of war, are interrelated. Violence is used as a means of controlling women.'

They also directly address 'peaceful women' essentialism:

> Women-only peace activism does not suggest that women, any more than
> men, are 'natural born peace-makers.' But women often inhabit different
> cultures from men, and are disproportionately involved in caring work.
> We know what justice and oppression mean, because we experience
> them as women. Most women have a different experience of war from
> that of most men. All women in war fear rape. Women are the majority
> of refugees. A feminist view sees masculine cultures as specially prone to
> violence, and so feminist women tend to have a particular perspective on
> security and something unique to say about war.

Here WIB activists carefully articulate a feminist politics regarding war that is based in a gendered experience of violence and not some inherent female characteristic.

Code Pink

Code Pink was founded in the USA in November 2002 by a group of veteran women activists who organized a march on the White House to protest about the second pre-emptive US strike on Iraq. Their website (www.codepink4peace.org) states: 'CODE PINK is a women-initiated grassroots peace and social justice movement working to end the war in Iraq, stop new wars, and redirect our resources into healthcare, education and other life-affirming activities.' Their name is a parody of the Bush administration's color-coded advisory system. As one chant goes, 'You say Code Red, we say Code Pink.' They announce a 'Code Pink alert: signifying extreme danger to all the values of nurturing, caring, and compassion that women and loving men have held.'

Their signature style is pink flamboyant dress, in particular pink slips or camisoles, and boas. One progressive journalist quipped they are 'the activist equivalent of Victoria's Secret Catalog meets The Nation Magazine' (Milazzo 2005: 100–04). The pink slip is the uniform for their signature action, the issuing of pink slips (literally) to leaders who they believe need to be fired for supporting war. They encourage 'outrageous acts of dissent,' withdrawing consent, non-violent civil disobedience, and all forms of feisty activism. They seem to be constantly in the news as they tirelessly interrupt congressional hearings, confront policymakers wherever they go, occupy offices, and camp out in front of officials' houses.

Given all the lingerie, one might wonder, is Code Pink really a feminist organization? Their web FAQ page states: 'CODE PINK is a women-led organization that seeks to empower women politically, creating space for women to speak out for justice and peace in their communities, the media and the halls of Congress.' Here they deliberately avoid the new 'F-word' ('feminism'), choosing instead language including 'women-led' and 'empower women' and 'space for women.' This seems to be a strategic move to appeal to as many people as possible while still maintaining feminist principles.

On its website Code Pink, like Women in Black, directly addresses 'peaceful women' essentialism:

> ... Women have been the guardians of life – not because we are better or purer or more innately nurturing than men, but because the men have busied themselves making war. Because of our responsibility to the next generation, because of our own love for our families and communities and this country that we are a part of, we understand the love of a mother in Iraq for her children, and the driving desire of that child for life.

While this statement directly states that women are not 'more innately nurturing than men,' it does imply that men naturally make war. It also implies that women are 'guardians of life' because of our actualized/potential motherhood, which is a cornerstone argument for the notion of naturally peaceful women.

Are they effective?

An oft-heard jaded response to direct action is that, regardless of how many people participate, it does not stop injustice or change public opinion. It is worth considering the multiple elements of feminist direct action against such a critique. What are the goals of the organizers of such actions? Are they immediate, long-range, or both? Is there one or more than one constituency being organized and how is that managed? What do participants identify as their reasons for joining an action and how do they match up with the organizers' goals? How much has to do with conscience? How much has to do with process? How might we think about these actions as acts of cultural transformation? How do the media figure?

All three of the groups discussed here have been successful at achieving many of the purposes of direct action: building public awareness; applying pressure to a target; modeling a better society; building solidarity, and so forth. They have interrupted 'business as usual' in some very different, very creative ways, all of which have built from a feminist foundation. I believe, however, that, much like teaching, the lasting impacts of direct action are not often readily or immediately apparent – ironically, they are not 'direct' – but often best seen through a long historical lens.

Many indigenous peoples have a philosophy of acting with responsibility for seven future generations while remaining on the path of ancestors. This is similar to the Hebrew saying that 'it is not up to you to complete the task, but neither are you free to desist from it.' This does not mean we should not evaluate activism – it is crucial that we keep figuring out what is working and not working. That is best done by assessing each action against its measurable goals, while keeping in mind that long-term impacts are not immediately apparent.

Other critiques of these actions are more gendered. A common one suggests that the actions are not hard-hitting enough, not serious enough, too 'soft' to actually strike back with any consequence against the war machine. It is useful to think about how this criticism emerges from a fully masculinist, militarized society that privileges and rewards violence. In this culture, non-violence gets gendered as feminine, passive, and ineffectual. Yet, as beautifully articulated on a protest sign in Oakland, California, many feminist activists believe 'the use of violence shows a lack of imagination.'

A related critique echoes the age-old attack on feminist organizing by charging divisiveness or separatism. A white gay man recently articulated this position to me, saying he felt excluded by these feminist direct action groups and offended because he thought they suggested that only women want peace. He could not see himself as a feminist. He could not imagine connections between 'his' issue – non-discrimination against gays in the military – and the campaigns of these feminist groups. The linkages between these struggles were not clear to him.

Finally, one other dismissal of feminist direct action is the assumption that first you have fill-in-the-blank revolution and then you deal with feminist goals. Yet we know that any fill-in-the-blank revolution worth its salt is always already feminist.

Conclusion

I think there is an ongoing discussion to be had about how to act as women without reinforcing 'peaceful women' essentialism and, at the same time, challenging or answering these critiques of feminist direct action. The Raging Grannies, Women in Black, and Code Pink demonstrate the deep desire women have to speak and act on how our opposition to war is connected to our gendered experience as mothers, sisters, daughters, partners, grandmothers – as people gendered as 'woman.' We want to talk about how a militarized economy reinforces patriarchy and racism. We want to show how cycles of violence include war – and poverty, battering, lack of educational opportunities, and sexual exploitation. We do not all share the same feminist ideology, nor should we, but with work we can disrupt the spin that may either discount, or assume, our politics because of our gender.

In the end, I am hoping that we might allow ourselves to be inspired by these groups and their actions. Yes, it is messy acting as feminist women dealing with essentialism. Yes, it is often hard to measure effectiveness. Yes, there are many ways in which we make mistakes, in which we disappoint our theories, in which our coalitions do not coalesce. Yes, the minefields of contradiction are many and shifting. Still, I believe that feminist direct action offers one effective avenue for acting our way into thinking, and for contributing to social change along the way – whether dressed in floppy hats, all black, or pink lingerie.

Reference

Milazzo, Linda (2005) 'Code Pink: the 21st century mothers of invention', *Development*, 48(2).

'We say code pink'

17 | Women, gentrification, and Harlem

NELLIE HESTER BAILEY

The Harlem Tenants Council (HTC) is dedicated to the fundamental principle of shelter as a basic human right for every person. The Council was co-founded by me in New York City in 1995, and I serve now as its director. The goal of the Harlem Tenants Council is to counter displacement and homelessness caused by gentrification and illegal actions of landlords against poor and working-class tenants residing in the greater Harlem community of New York City. The organization seeks to arm tenants with education and leadership skills to challenge the preconceived notion that poor and working-class tenants are not able to engage in public policy debates on housing as community stakeholders. The HTC mission is to strengthen the capacities of working-class tenants to empower themselves with a vision of their collective right to become viable stakeholders in the political process that defines the use of space in their community in a manner that will sustain the historic character of neighborhoods, fortify community ties, and support and expand local institutions that are the backbone of cultural identification that connects people, space and time.

The HTC programmatic thrust combines comprehensive organizing, tenant education, public policy advocacy, and direct actions aimed at preventing displacement and homelessness. The organization functions with a bottom-up leadership structure. The seven members of its board of directors are all female and low-income residents residing mainly in Central Harlem, where HTC draws the bulk of its membership, numbering over five hundred.

There is a direct but not obvious connection between my work with the HTC and the issue of women and war. Our constituents are overwhelmingly women, poor and working-class women of color, predominantly women of African descent living on the economic fringes of Harlem, now a target of unprecedented gentrification that has ushered in an overdevelopment of luxury housing and accelerated the disappearance of low-income units.

But this is not just happening in Harlem. An affordable housing crisis has already reached epidemic proportions across the USA because of unemployment, spiraling rents, and the loss of thousands of federally subsidized units, many through foreclosures. From 2004 to the end of 2005, the US Department of Housing and Urban Development (HUD) commenced foreclosure proceedings on 2,156 subsidized units in fourteen buildings in New York City, even as housing advocates argued that an additional seventy-nine buildings were at risk of being unavailable to renters owing to physical neglect. Nationwide, over 120,000 project-based Section 8 housing subsidies have been lost owing to foreclosure over the past ten years, and in the state of New York during the same period of time, 4,000 units in forty-nine buildings disappeared.

While HUD cried broke, in January 2006 the non-partisan Congressional Budget Office reported $323 billion expended by the USA for the 'war on terrorism,' including military action in Iraq and Afghanistan. During that same month the US House of Representatives approved another $68 billion for military operations in the same countries. By the end of 2006 Pentagon spending for the war in Iraq alone hit $6 billion a month and about $200 million a day. A number of economists, including Nobel Prize winner Joseph Stiglitz, put the final figure for the war (covering direct and indirect costs) at a staggering $1 trillion to $2 trillion, which includes $300 billion in future healthcare costs to cover wounded soldiers. In addition, the rising cost of oil and added interest on the national debt will drive up the figure.

The US Census Bureau Housing and Vacancy Survey reports that between 2002 and 2005 the number of New York City apartments available at monthly rents of less than $1,000 dropped by nearly 157,000, while the number of apartments with monthly rents of less than $600 (considered affordable for low-income families) shrank by more than 56,000. And during the same period the number of subsidized housing units in New York City was reduced by 11 percent. But the number of apartments renting for $1,400 a month or above climbed to 63,000, an increase of nearly 25 percent! In 2006, the number of homeless families entering the city's shelter system grew by 22.9 percent.

Since the passage of the welfare reform legislation in 1996, New York City's homeless shelter population has exploded. In less than five years, after a decade of relative stability, the number of homeless families in the city's shelter system grew by 22 percent in 2001 and another 35 percent in 2001. By 2003 there were more than nine thousand families with children in the shelter system on any given night. In September 2005 the Vera Institute of Justice study, Understanding Family Homelessness in New York City: An in-depth study of families, found that the area represented by Community Board 10 in Central Harlem produced the largest number of families in Manhattan entering the city's homeless shelter system.

African-American female heads of household with children under five represent a typical profile of a homeless family from Harlem.

The Vera Institute study concluded among its findings that 'subsidized housing provided the best protection against repeat shelter use' (Smith et al. 2005). The study made several recommendations, including expanding the availability of federally supported housing programs.

As in Harlem, poor and working-class women of color across the country are grappling with the consequences of welfare reform and the loss of a financial safety net for their families, severely affecting their housing options. And for those considered lucky enough to have some semblance of a home, a 2002 study by the Joblessness and Urban Poverty Research Program at the Kennedy School's Malcolm Wiener Center for Social Policy found that 62 percent of former shelter families with no subsidies spend more than 50 percent of their total income on housing while those with subsidies experience far less.

And something more is at stake in the struggle for housing – the task of preserving the integrity and physical character of the historic working-class community of Harlem. This world-renowned mecca of black culture and revolutionary political agitation has captured international attention with its iconic contemporary leadership, notably black nationalist entrepreneur Marcus Garvey, political and civil rights leader Adam Clayton Powell, Jr, Black Muslim and Black Power leader Malcolm X, novelist and activist James Baldwin, and the seldom-mentioned Ella Josephine Baker, former field secretary for the NAACP and later top senior advisor to the Student National Coordinating Committee (SNCC). It was with SNCC that Ella Baker helped to launch the 1961 Freedom Rides and the voter registration campaigns for black sharecroppers throughout the US South.

Baker would be more than chagrined about what is happening today in Harlem and in other former industrialized inner cities that once employed hundreds of thousands of unionized black workers. Outsourcing has nearly wiped out the US manufacturing base, leaving in its wake an underpaid non-unionized service-sector industry that looks to minimize costs with undocumented labor, pitting low-income workers against one another. While workers battle each other in this induced economic rivalry, urban real estate and banking interests proceed with a gentrification that results in the dispersal of historic urban working-class populations.

Gentrification is more than what the English sociologist Ruth Glass described as a new gentry moving into working-class neighborhoods, turning it around so property values go up, while long-term residents are pushed out. In fact, gentrification is about land. It is about who controls the land, how the land is used, who decides how the land is going to be used. It's about who is allowed to stay on the land. It is about the security of people on that land. It is not just a social science process. It is a political process.

There is a theory that is being pushed about how cities grow, that cities are not going to grow through a manufacturing base. And, yes, the loss of industry has gutted cities in terms of a viable and vibrant economic structure. Employment has been lost for blue-collar workers in the cities and we have seen this in New York City. A 2004 study by the Community Service Society, *A Crisis of Black Male Unemployment and Joblessness in New York City*, found barely one half, 51.8 percent, were employed.

The new theory of growth is that it is hospitals and universities and related businesses that will come in, and that will build the new skyscrapers, and provide relief to the lagging economy. The economists in the ruling elite are saying, in fact, that these three sectors are the new growth machines for cities, that these will replace manufacturing.

This is what the oligarchy of New York City is saying. We organizers in New York City refer to this process by its acronym 'FIRE' – finance, insurance, and real estate. We see the attempted devastation by FIRE of Harlem with Columbia University's current plans. Columbia has announced that it will expand over eighteen acres into West Harlem. Columbia will go up the river, 12th Avenue to 125th. They want to bulldoze the entire eighteen acres – to bulldoze it! We're talking about Manhattan! To bulldoze all of those acres – except for two buildings that the school owns, the Studebaker Building and Prentice Hall Building. Both of those buildings have 'historical preservation' status.

The president of Columbia University at this time, Lee Bollinger, came into New York City riding on the wave of his great liberal victory over the Supreme Court on the issue of affirmative action at the University of Michigan. Bollinger came in and Columbia announced its proposed expansion to the community.

What do they intend to build on these eighteen acres? Here is a link to war:

A bio-research facility that will be built five stories below ground, and will operate at a 'safety level' of three. The most dangerous bio-research level is four, but at level three researchers can experiment with anthrax and other biological weapons. The area in Harlem where they propose to build is low land, next to the river. It is also over an earthquake fault line. And what surrounds this proposed expansion site? Public housing.

So this expansion by Columbia is part of the attempt being made through gentrification to depopulate Harlem, to 'develop' it as part of economic 'growth' in the USA, the world's biggest debtor country. Without question, the war in Iraq and military actions across the globe have plunged the USA into deeper debt. Some economists would suggest that the country is teetering on the brink of economic disaster, and that will trigger a global recession. Already long-term interest rates are on the rise and the once bubbling housing market has started to collapse. Meanwhile, the Bush administration continues with tax cuts for the wealthy.

The impact of this run-away war deficit is having a major impact on the quality of the life of the poor and the working class, particularly women, and specifically women of color, as community services and economic supports are slashed. Certainly the war is having a tremendous impact on the working-class population in Harlem, and in particular on the many women of color, African-American women, who head families in my community.

It is impossible to talk about feminism and war without analysis of the very serious economic problems that the USA has. We can not discuss the impact of war as if that is separate and apart from the economy that is driving the war.

There is an adage that when white America has just a cold, black communities catch pneumonia, and in Harlem we have pneumonia. Full-grown, deadly pneumonia. This is what the Harlem Tenants Council is dealing with.

Gentrification is class warfare waged against poor and working-class people of color. This catastrophe is directly linked to US imperialist war, and is happening not only in Harlem but throughout the country.

We at HTC are trying to look as scientifically as possible at what is happening with gentrification. What are the social forces? How do we dissect and understand what is happening so that we can come up with remedies, solutions, and strategies to deal with this problem of removal from the land and depopulation of communities of color in our cities? Who will provide much-needed resources for grassroots non-profit groups such as ours, in terms of research, in terms of supporting our work? So far, many of the folks in academia produce very wordy, very laudable texts, but rarely is there a transfer of the theory into practice in terms of physical relationships with those of us who are on the ground. Are they doing this research as a personal platform for their own careerism? Do they not see the necessity of really building a movement such as they talk about?

When I got the invitation to speak at the Syracuse University 'Feminism and War' conference, I wasn't sure how I would fit in as an activist who has had many 'excursions' to Columbia University, an adversary of my community in its gentrification expansion. My message on women and war, and the connections to my community, is that academic studies are not enough. We must build a principled anti-imperialist movement connecting domestic and international issues.

Here is one example of building a movement. As President Hugo Chávez of Venezuela worked to build Bolivarian socialism in his country, he visited Harlem in 2006, and announced he was doubling the heating oil subsidy that had already given help to millions of people in the USA. The oil from Venezuela is being distributed through grassroots development corporations that build affordable housing. The price of oil, of course, is very, very prohibitive, so this will be an enormous resource for the people of Harlem, particularly the poor and the working class.

The work of the Harlem Tenants Council has three major components – organizing, educating, and agitation. For social and political transformation, agitation is a must. Because if you don't hit the streets, the work means absolutely nothing. We know from our own experience and from these words of Fredrick Douglass: 'If there is no struggle, there is no progress. Those who profess to favor freedom and yet depreciate agitation, are men who want crops without plowing up the ground, they want rain without thunder and lightning. Power concedes nothing without a demand. It never did and it never will.'

If we do not have agitation, we will not have change. We never have and we never will.

References

Levitan, Mark (2004) *A Crisis of Black Male Employment: Unemployment and Joblessness in New York City, 2003*, New York: Community Service Society.

Smith, Nancy, Zaire Dinzey Flores, Jeffrey Lin and John Markovic (2005) *Understanding Family Homelessness in New York City: An In-depth Study of Families' Experiences Before and After Shelter*, September, New York: Vera Institute of Justice.

18 | US economic wars and Latin America

BERTA JOUBERT-CECI

Gone is the time when US war forced women into factory jobs to produce for the war machine, to fill the vacancies left by the men who were in combat. Now, many women join the ranks of the war-makers. The consequences? Only time will tell, when thousands of women come back from battle fronts, imperialist battle fronts that show the horrendous capability of cruelty and savagery that US imperialism has demonstrated – as photos of US military torture at the Abu Ghraib and Guantanamo prisons attest. But we can anticipate. Instances of sexual harassment and rape of women in the US military have been well documented. If women are discriminated against in civilian US society, how could not they be treated with contempt in such a male-dominated and male-oriented structure as the US military?

And the psychological toll of the viciousness of US wars upon military women will certainly be very high at a time when education programs and healthcare services are being slashed not only for civilians but also for veterans. This is where the 'Support Our Troops' cry, particularly from the right wing in this country, shows its hypocrisy. Where is the support when the physically and/or psychologically wounded troops come home? When the women combatants come back, they will bring with them the nightmares, the terrible experience of witnessing or even participating directly in the dirty business of imperialist war, of murdering innocent civilians, women and children included.

What jobs will be waiting for them? If they left children at home, when they come back how will their role as mothers be? Women bear the heaviest load in caregiving. How will that be affected? Will they have children with birth defects as a consequence of exposure to depleted uranium (DU) or other poisons?

There is much to discuss about women and the US military, but there is one fact true in my community – the Puerto Rican community – as well as in the African-American community and other communities of color, and also in poor white communities, in the USA.

One fact stands alone, and that is the fact that the war does not affect all women equally. I live in Philadelphia now, and the white women of the Main Line, a very wealthy part of Philadelphia, are not affected like the women in the Puerto Rican community. In fact, some of the women in the Main Line might even profit from the war if they or their families own or run corporations associated with the defense industries.

Instead, it is the working-class woman of all ages who is the most affected by US war. Those who depend on basic social services that are now being cut so the Pentagon's budget can expand, those who have to work more hours or in two or three jobs to feed their families and make ends meet. Those who have to pay extra for healthcare because the benefits from their jobs are being slashed.

The women whose children are being recruited and whose dreams of a better future for those children are being wiped out by the military are not from the Main Line. The recruiters are going very aggressively into the poor communities with many empty promises of a bright future and educational opportunities. And this is true not only here in the USA, but, for example, in Puerto Rico, my homeland, which is still under US colonialism. The organization Madres Contra la Guerra, Mothers Against the War, in the west part of the island, recently sent an email with an urgent appeal for help to organizations in other parts of the island to get the US military recruiters out of the schools because they were feverishly going after their children, enticing them with promises of money and education.

But I want to put the concept of war into a larger context. Let us consider the purpose of the US war in the Middle East, a war being waged for domination and profits – particularly for profits to benefit US-based oil companies. For that, the Pentagon has used all kinds of deception, weaponry and the most sophisticated equipment. According to the medical journal, *The Lancet*, more than half a million people have been killed in Iraq for profits.

But the USA can wage war in other ways. I particularly want to draw attention to Latin America because it is from that region that so many immigrants have been coming to the USA in recent years. And women immigrants, particularly the undocumented, have the least protection.

The USA is conducting an undeclared war in Latin America. And it is war, only through other means. Even though the USA has military bases and troops in some countries in the region, for example in Colombia, the war has been carried out through economic strangulation, for the same purpose as the war with bombs in the Middle East: for domination and profits for US corporations. It is so important to place the situation in Latin America in this context because the damages and fatalities are mounting.

It is estimated that 1.1 million people cross the southern border of the USA every single year looking for work in the United States. Not because there is no wealth in their countries – in fact, the entire southern hemispheric region is very rich in oil, gas, precious metals, water, and countless natural resources. It is precisely that wealth and resources the USA wants to control. And so the USA has opened a war front called neoliberalism, with the help of the international institutions that facilitate the expansion of capitalism, the World Bank and the International Monetary Fund. Among some of the bombs dropped by the neoliberal war on underdeveloped countries are the forced privatization of national enterprises and services like education and healthcare; the imposition of austerity measures; and the adoption of so-called 'free trade agreements.' All of these assaults result in misery for the population, in fewer services and a much higher cost of living.

Mexico is a prime example of this kind of war. The North American Free Trade Agreement, NAFTA, devastated the country's economic base, particularly that of the small farmers, and threw them into the ranks of the dispossessed. Cheap imported corn, produced with US subsidies, replaced Mexican corn, a staple in the Mexican diet and the livelihood of thousands of families.

This forced a massive migration of Mexican people into the USA. More than half of the total number of undocumented workers in the United States are from Mexico. They are victims of that economic war. Not only did they have to leave behind their homeland and their families, but in the USA they face racism, violence and the most dangerous jobs, which pay only pennies a day.

This migration has been especially hard for women. Many had to leave their children behind with relatives, risking their lives in order to come to the USA so they can send some money back home. And this migration has had a devastating impact on the children left behind. One example, the story of a boy, Enrique, who travels from Honduras to the United States on the rooftop of trains in search of his mother, is documented in an excellent book by reporter Sonia Nazario, *Enrique's Journey* (2006). Nazario states that thousands of children travel this way yearly for the same purpose, searching for their parents. How many US families employ Mexican or other Latin American women as nannies or house helpers? Do they even think that 'their' nanny is also a mother who longs for her children, unable to have them by her side?

Very often immigrant women hold two or three jobs, mostly in the service sector, cleaning private homes or buildings; taking care of the ill; picking fruit or vegetables in fields where they are exposed to pesticides; or working in dangerous food processing plants. The pay is meager and the jobs usually have no benefits, no healthcare, no pension, no paid vacation. The women live only to work, and work only to survive and send remittances back to their families at home.

This is the result of the US war in Latin America. Immigration laws are being debated in the USA, and even though no law has been finally approved, already $2.2 billion has been allocated for a 700-mile apartheid fence along the US–Mexican border. Several of the smaller cities across the country have proposed or passed racist anti-immigration regulations. Weekly workplace raids by ICE (US Immigration and Customs Enforcement), such as those in New Bedford, Massachusetts, seize Latina documented and undocumented women alike, often deporting them immediately, separating them from their infants and young children, who have no other adult caregivers.

Immigrant women workers have been very active in the demonstrations against the proposed racist anti-immigrant law projects. They are part of the army of 'invisible workers' – the undocumented workers. They need solidarity and should be recognized and embraced for who they are, an important sector of the anti-war movement. And consequently, the anti-war movement should include the demands of the immigration struggle.

The US war in Latin America is not lessening. In fact, because the masses in Latin America have been rising up against US attempts to dominate and impose free trade agreements in their countries, the USA is trying to topple progressive governments in the region.

That is the case with the government of Hugo Chávez in Venezuela. The United States has orchestrated and/or supported many destabilization actions and campaigns against democratically elected President Chávez, including the 2002 coup during which he was briefly deposed. But that coup was defeated by the Venezuelan people in one of the most moving and politically significant actions by the masses in Latin America in recent history. In fact, the people's demonstrations were initiated by Venezuelan women, and, according to INAMUJER, the Venezuelan National Institute of Women, Chávez was 'brought back to power by a popular uprising led by women from the poorest areas of Caracas.'

The United States was also behind the criminal sabotage of the Venezuelan oil industry that endangered every facet of the energy services in the country, including, most importantly, emergency services in healthcare, with significant impact on the lives of women. This sabotage was also defeated by the united actions of the Venezuelan people defending their resources and sovereignty.

The attack against Venezuela was preceded by the US war against

Cuba in the form of a cruel blockade for more than forty years. This additional example of US war on Latin America and the Caribbean has also claimed thousands of Cuban lives.

Because of US hostility and aggression toward Cuba, women in the USA are prevented from learning from the wonderful experience of Cuban women and the process of their liberation from patriarchal capitalist oppression. Their advances in education and healthcare, among so many others, could improve the lives of women in the United Sates and their families.

And women in the USA suffer from the effects of the undeclared economic war on Venezuela also because of what they lose – the capacity to experience the advances of women in that country, the empowerment of those who for decades have been excluded, the opportunity to network and create and strengthen ties, and learn about a different way toward the future.

We as women should discuss and debate, but it is crucial that we act. Debate should be a tool that leads to action; otherwise, debate is futile and sterile. Actions speak louder than words, and there is great need for action in the USA, to oppose these declared and undeclared wars in the most militant way, consistently and relentlessly.

References

Burnham, Gilbert, Riyadh Lafta, Shannon Doocy and Les Roberts (2006) 'Mortality after the 2003 invasion of Iraq: a cross-sectional cluster sample survey', www.thelancet.com.

Nazario, Sonia (2006) *Enrique's Journey*, New York: Random House.

19 | Feminist organizing in Israel

MELANIE KAYE/KANTROWITZ

Beginning mostly with the first intifada (the Palestinian uprising of 1987), Israeli women have become active in all aspects of the peace movement, including – just to mention a few groups – Women in Black, Rabbis for Human Rights, Stop The Wall, and Stop House Demolitions. Women build coalitions between Israelis and Palestinians, including women who are both. Some urge economic or academic boycotts, modeling campaigns on the struggle against South African apartheid. Some become involved with the refuseniks (soldiers who refuse to serve in the Occupied Territories) in groups like Yesh Gvul (meaning both 'there's a border' and 'there's a limit'). *Shministim* are high school seniors, including young women, who publicly refuse their legal obligation of registering for the army. The group Four Mothers called on women's 'naturally' pacific nature during the late 1990s invasion of Lebanon, while non-essentialist feminist New Profile suborns draft resistance and challenges a military state. Dirty Laundry, an anti-Occupation queer group, performs in-your-face street politics, and a Marxist website in Russian makes draft counseling available to emigrants from the former USSR.

Israel is the only nation-state that drafts women. Even before the current intifada (the Palestinian uprising of 2000), groups like New Profile estimated that as many as 50 percent of young Israeli women did not serve – some because of orthodox religious practice. (Orthodox women and men are exempt from service on religious grounds.) But also many young women looked at the rampant sexual harassment and abuse intrinsic to institutions like the Israeli army, which are gender-integrated but not women-liberated, and they – or their parents – figured out ways for them not to serve.

According to one report, 'Sexual harassment of women soldiers ... in the IDF [Israel Defense Force] ... is so widespread as to be all but unremarkable ... [S]exual harassment is seen as a problem that women in the IDF need to learn to cope with, rather than as a practice that men need to learn to refrain from' (Sered 2000). An IDF survey in 2003 found that 20 percent of women in the army said they experienced sexual harassment. When the term 'sexual harassment' was broken down into its various components, however, the incidence turned out to be as much as four times higher. For example, 81 percent of the women reported having been exposed to humiliating innuendo, 69 percent had been exposed to unwanted sexual proposals, 52 percent had experienced embarrassing touching.

Still, the current increase in resistance among young Israeli women is a phenomenon, though the IDF has refused to release the relevant data. Some resisters are explicitly feminist, including one dazzling nineteen-year-old, Idan Halili, who requested exemption based on a feminist rejection of militarism. After spending two weeks in military prison because of her refusal to serve, Halili won exemption from conscription; her views, she was told, deemed her 'unsuitable' (Shabi 2006). Despite women's participation in anti-Occupation work, the public face of both the Israeli military leadership and the Israeli peace movement is almost exclusively WASP, as they say in Israel – White Ashkenazi Sons of Pioneers. At the same time, images of male/state power are complicated inside Israel (as in Jewish communities around the world) by the excruciating history of Holocaust, manipulated to arouse shame and fear, and to blur the distinction between a period of European Jewish powerlessness, and a current reality of an extremely powerful Israeli military, complete with nuclear weapons.

The Israeli/Jew is seen one minute as a *sabra* (native of Israel) paratrooper, the next minute as a shtetl victim, a 'sheep to the slaughter' – just like a woman!

Women in Black (WIB) is a notable exception to dominant male images and women's invisibility in the peace movement. WIB is a big tent, including Israeli and Palestinian leftists and liberals. Its major activity, beginning in 1988, has been the organizing of weekly silent vigils; these were inspired by earlier movements of women who, by demonstrating on the streets, created more public space for women to occupy and be heard in – particularly the actions of Black Sash in South Africa and the Madres de la Plaza de Mayo of Argentina. WIB also has roots in international women's peace movement groups such as the Women's International League for Peace and Freedom (WILPF).

WIB vigils quickly spread throughout Israel; at the peak of the intifada there were nearly forty separate vigils in a country the size of the US state of New Jersey. By 2007 the number had declined to nine, which we might read as discouragement or as women recognizing the need for different strategies. Internationally, WIB action has become well known as a generic feminist anti-war statement. At last count, 335 Women in Black vigils are taking place around the world, including 195 in the USA, many of which focus not on the Israeli Occupation but on the US war on Iraq.

Like Women in Black, New Profile (NP) is a feminist site of anti-Israeli-Occupation energy, offering a strong analysis, along with draft resistance counseling that is supportive and pragmatic. The group aids, abets, and tracks draft and military resistance by those who refuse to register, those who present medical or religious reasons for exemption, or who seek status as conscientious objectors. Some refuse to serve only in the Occupied Territories; others only in Lebanon; some manifest their resistance by simply going AWOL. New Profile reports that it is common for commanders to overlook AWOL or undercount it, as a way of protecting the soldiers. Those on the Israeli right dismiss this resistance as marginal, and they do have a point. Most continue to serve, in a country where the army is a central venue for political and social leadership. The act of refusal can severely marginalize the resister. Even so, draft resistance is on the rise.

There are Israeli voices that recognize that even a genuinely egalitarian army would still leave hanging the issue of what an army does. Connections between militarism and masculinity have yet to be widely understood. NP articulates an explicitly feminist analysis that links male supremacy and militarism with the Occupation. NP co-founder Rela Mazali points out:

> Even though a small percent of Israeli men actually become fighters, 'the powerful fighter' image, so central to masculine identity in Jewish Israeli society, totally obscures and marginalizes these statistics. Emotionally, boys are treated as 'fighters,' and the danger implied in the term – usually perceived and represented as a service to society – arouses a sense of deep respect if not awe. (Mazali 2003)

Some – including some feminists – point to masculinism/militarism as an explanation for why some women resisters are being readily discharged: because they are not considered 'the real thing – a combat soldier.' Therefore, their refusal 'does not count,' is not reported in the Israeli media, and is not publicly visible. One draft resister argued recently that women who resist are still seen as supports or prizes. Women in the USA who remember from the anti-Vietnam War movement the expression 'Girls say yes to men who say no' will find a slogan matching in grossness: 'The best men go to prison; the best chicks go to the prisoners' (Werner 2002).

On the other hand, consider the soldier refuseniks in Yesh Gvul, founded during the first intifada. As Israeli soldiers were ordered to shoot rubber bullets at children throwing stones, so that many children were hit in the eye and blinded, Yesh Gvul responded with an unforgettable poster invoking fatherhood, and the common vulnerability of children. A huge black-and-white photo of a crying Palestinian child whose eye was colored over with red crayon more than suggested blood – and the caption in huge Hebrew letters reads: *What did you do in the territories today, Daddy?*

NP calls the work ahead against militarization the 'civil-ization' of Israeli society. First, NP argues, Israelis need to recognize the pervasive deforming power of militarism in Israeli society. Headlines from the NP web page read: 'Female Soldiers Treated Lower than Dirt,' 'Where Defense Spending Really Goes,' 'A New Declaration of Refusal by *"Shministim"* – Students of the 11th and 12th grades of Israeli High Schools Protesting Violence Against Women in the Military,' 'Infantry Petition: We Won't Do Reserve Duty Anymore.'

Israeli feminists voice complaints similar to those in the USA, where the norm of women as mothers, inherently non-violent, excludes the possibility of non-violent men. Some Israeli feminists were disturbed, for example, by media attention lavished on the Four Mothers – whose sons were stationed in Lebanon in the late 1990s – as though their objection to Israel at war was acceptable because of their position as mothers. Presumably other women, without children, or those who encouraged their children to stay out of the army, are considered less worthy.

But scholar Ronit Lentin sees a change. 'If motherhood and women's "natural" peace making role are central themes in much Israeli feminist peace activist discourse,' a different perspective is emerging from many of the young women draft resisters who express not a 'natural female pacifism' or service to males but 'a commitment to individual morality as opposed to state logic' (Lentin 2001).

In a collection of narratives by women resisters instigated by New Profile, Tal Matalon writes that she became a resister because of the violent death of her friends in a suicide bombing at a Haifa restaurant:

> We lit candles and brought flowers and sat and talked. And then Aviv [a male friend] asked me if I'm still going to refuse. And I said yes. Because it was obvious to me that yes … if people die, it should be stopped, right? More people shouldn't die, should they? But Aviv already stopped listening. For good, actually, because he never talked to me again …
> (Matalon 2004)

Her conscience put her outside her former circle of friends. But as sister draft resister Shani Werner explains, after her 'conscience committee' met, Werner phoned home only to learn 'there had been a suicide bombing in Tel Aviv … a young boy chose to commit suicide in order to kill Israelis. If only I could have told him about other Israelis, the ones who refuse to be his occupiers ...' (Werner 2002: 48–50). Her aspiration is to be inside the circle of justice, friendship, and mutual understanding.

I want to leave you with three voices:

First, a ceremony for atonement, co-created by Yesh Gvul and Rabbis for Human Rights. This is an excerpt from 'A Plea for Forgiveness for the Sins of War,' read on 30 September 2006, opposite the prime minister's office in Jerusalem:

> For the sin that we have sinned before You in carrying out a futile war and in committing major violations of the laws of war,
>
> And for the sin that we have sinned before You in killing hundreds and injuring thousands of Palestinian and Lebanese civilians.
>
> For the sin that we have sinned before You in hardening our hearts,
>
> And for the sin that we have sinned before You in abandoning thousands of Israeli civilians to the crimes of Hizbollah and the negligence of the Israeli Government.
>
> For the sin that we have sinned before You in inequality,
>
> And for the sin that we have sinned before You in hindering and humiliating the minorities and the weak amongst us.
>
> For the sin that we have sinned before You in the oppression of others,
>
> And for the sin that we have sinned before You in the justification of a 'war of no choice.'
>
> For the sin that we have sinned before You by our indifference,
>
> And for the sin that we have sinned before You by obedience to orders that serve the military system, the occupational regime and the oppression and weakening of Palestinian, Lebanese and Israeli civilians.
>
> And for all of these, we have no right to beg forgiveness, until we acknowledge the humanity of others and our responsibility to protect them. (Jewish Peace News 2006)

Moving as this *slichot* is, war itself is not challenged – as long as it's restricted to the military. The second voice reaches much deeper, that of Nurit Peled-Elhanan, the mother of Smadar, who was killed at age thirteen by a suicide bomber in Jerusalem in September 1998:

When my little girl was killed, a reporter asked me how I was willing to accept condolences from the other side. I replied without hesitation that I refused it. When representatives of the Netanyahu – then prime minister – government came to offer their condolences I took my leave and would not sit with them. For me, the other side, the enemy, is not the Palestinian people. For me the struggle is not between Palestinians and Israelis, nor between Jews and Arabs. The fight is between those who seek peace and those who seek war. My people are those who seek peace. My sisters are the bereaved mothers, Israeli and Palestinian, who live in Israel and in Gaza and in the refugee camps. My brothers are the fathers who try to defend their children from the cruel occupation, and are, as I was, unsuccessful in doing so. (Peled-Elhanan 2001)

And finally, here is the voice of Areen Bahour, a seventh-grade Palestinian girl living in Ramallah, from her September 2006 school essay:

A Night in Heaven

I woke up that day to the sounds of the singing birds. I opened my eyes and I was not in my room! I walked out of that strange room and found myself in a palace with my family. I asked if I can go walk outside and my parents replied yes without thinking, unlike always.

I went out and walked and walked, all what I saw around me was green fields and green streets, all with trees and different kinds of flowers. It was a clean place with no pollution.

No one stopped me because I am Palestinian. I found out that I was in heaven. Where there is no occupation, no borders, and no walls in your way. It was a place where you don't need any visa to be renewed to stay in. No one was worried. It was a place where everyone was friendly. There were no people sitting in those green streets asking for money. Everyone was living peacefully.

There, where you can't find anyone screaming or crying or annoying others. Everything was organized as if this strange world was controlled by a remote or a computer.

Then, I opened my eyes to the sound that was waking me up. It was my younger sister. I realized it was all a dream. I wished I didn't wake up from this dream for the rest of my life, and remained in that place where I can live in peace, in a smiling world, where everyone cares about you, where there is no racism, and where you feel like a bird flying in a free world.

All what I mentioned was what heaven really looks like in my eyes. (Jewish Peace News 2006)

For feminist peacemakers in the USA, what remains squarely in the line of vision is the role our government plays in supporting the Israeli Occupation.

Our taxes. This seems like the moment to remind us how the huge military aid that goes from the USA to Israel masks its terms: mostly it's money that must be spent purchasing arms from US corporations.

Our foreign policy. From Iraq to lascivious glances at Iran, there is no settling the state of war without reimagining US foreign policy in the region.

Our voices. Everywhere we look on campuses and publishing houses, at tenure decisions and speaking engagements, at the label of terrorist, and the facts of deportation and imprisonment, much more than the free exchange of ideas about Israel and Palestine is at stake.

References

Jewish Peace News (2006) 5 October.

Lentin, Ronit (2001) *Sociological Research Online*, 9(3).

Matalon, Tal (2004) 'My draft resistance', *Bridges*, 10(1), Spring.

Mazali, Rela (2003) 'And what about the girls? What a culture of war genders out of view', *Nashim: A Journal of Jewish Women's Studies and Gender Issues*, 6, Fall.

Peled-Elhanan, Nurit (2001) 'Speech to Women in Black', www.nimn.org/Perspectives/international/000132.php? section.

Sered, Susan (2000) *What Makes Women Sick? Maternity, Modesty, and Militarism in Israeli Society*, Waltham, MA: Brandeis University Press.

Shabi, Rachel (2006) 'The fight to not fight', *Guardian*, 17 April.

Werner, Shani (2002) 'Letter from a woman draft resister', *Women's World*, 31 December.

— (2004) 'My draft resistance – ten stops along the way', *Bridges*, 10(1), Spring.

Four extremely valuable resources for information about the anti-Occupation movements in Israel and internationally:

New Profile, www.newprofile.org/default.asp?language=en.

Jewish Voice for Peace, www.jewish voiceforpeace.org/.

US Campaign to End the Israeli Occupation, www.endtheoccupation.org.

Bridges: A Jewish Feminist Journal, bridgesjournal.org/; see especially 10(1), 'Amid brief: writings by Israeli Jewish women on peace seeking'.

20 | Reflections on feminism, war, and the politics of dissent

LESLIE CAGAN

I was born in the USA in 1947 and grew up in the shadow of the mushroom clouds that rose from the ashes of Hiroshima and Nagasaki. I grew up in an activist family, and came of age in the 1960s – the era of drugs, sex and rock and roll … and political activism. Deeply involved in the movement to end the US war in Vietnam, I served on the steering committee of the National Student Mobilization Against the War in Vietnam. By the time I graduated from college in 1968 I could not imagine doing anything other than full-time activism.

I don't recall the exact date, but some time in 1968 or 1969 a friend invited me to go to a women's consciousness-raising group with her. 'Are you kidding?' I said. 'I'm a strong woman – after all, I'm the chairman of my campus anti-war group.' I could appreciate the fact that other women might need that, but it wasn't for me. I am forever grateful that she kept bugging me. Eventually I went. It didn't take long to realize that this new wave of feminism was on to something, something that would change my life and the lives of millions of women around the world. The next ten or twelve years I spent primarily as an organizer/activist in the US women's movement and the gay/lesbian liberation movement. I came out of this period – in fact, I *came out* early in this period in claiming my identity as a lesbian – but I came *out of* this period a lesbian socialist feminist. And that has been at my core ever since. It has not only helped me navigate the waters of my personal life, it has been the political touchstone and anchor of the organizing work I've done ever since.

What does that mean? What are the insights and lessons that have helped to ground me and my work all these years – the lessons and insights of feminism in particular? Let me touch on a few:

1   Commitment to inclusion: Process, while not an end in itself, is important. Process is about how we solve problems – personal problems, community or workplace problems, national problems and international problems. This is not merely a question of who gets called on to speak at a meeting (although that can be quite important), but in a much larger way it is about a commitment to inclusion. And,

most especially, inclusion of different voices reflecting different experiences, different realities. I see a direct line between my feminism and what has turned into my decades-long commitment to and practice in coalition-building.

2   Autonomy: Different to separatism, autonomy should not be feared or rejected. It can be a space for community-building, as well as the strengthening of individuals. It can be a space for understanding some aspects of oppression and developing both visions of how life could be different and strategies for change. But since autonomy has its limits – just as identity politics has its limits – the real challenge, it seems to me, is to take the strength gathered and the insights learned in those autonomous movements and use them as building blocks of solidarity and connection – connection to other communities.

3   Emotions: These are a part of every human being's daily reality and do not have to be kept out of political life. In fact there are times when 'being emotional' makes the most sense and can be the most powerful thing we can do. There is no reason to deny our joys and our fears – these are often powerful motivating forces. And there is no reason to hide or curtail our anger – and as well we know, there is plenty to be angry about! The challenge here is to integrate our emotional responses with our intellectual abilities and turn all of that into action – into strategic, effective action. That is no small challenge.

4   Our definition of ourselves as women: Is the contribution of women and feminism to the anti-war movement just that women are mothers and caregivers? This aspect of women's contribution is undeniable, but it is not enough. As feminists we have a lot more to offer this movement – indeed, all movements for peace and justice. Have we not struggled for all these years to allow women to be defined outside of mothering and motherhood? Are we not more – much more – than our biological capabilities? I am not suggesting that we ignore or undermine the importance of mothering, as a biological reality and a social construct, but I am also urging us – and this is particularly relevant in connection to the anti-war movement – to not fall into equating woman and mother.

5   The most fundamental insight from feminism: There is a system of oppression that women experience. Call it sexism, call it patriarchy, call it male chauvinism – there is a reality to gender oppression. It is not the only system of oppression, but if we are to fully understand the dynamics of oppression we cannot ignore or leave out gender – just as we cannot ignore or leave out race or class or sexuality. I do not

want to privilege gender oppression over other oppressions. I want a comprehensive analysis of oppression, one that uncovers the ways in which gender and race and class and sexuality are connected to and inform one another.

So what does all of this have to do with war? What do war and feminism have to do with one another?

The connection I see is that war and feminism are actually opposites of each other. The horror and evil of war can partly be understood in seeing just how much it stands in opposition to feminism and feminist principles. All of the values of feminism are contradicted – if not rendered impossible to achieve – by the realities of war and the machinery of war-making.

On the most obvious level, war is violence. It is about the use of weapons that wound and kill people, as well as destroying infrastructure needed to sustain life. War is, at its core, anti-life. But beyond that, it is about the use of violence to control populations, to impose whole structures of control and domination. It is the grandest example of 'might makes right' and brute force used to determine who is in charge. As such it is both reinforcing of the traditional power that men have had over women, and also profoundly anti-democratic.

Military institutions themselves are also anti-democratic and the opposite of structures based on feminist principles. The top-down hierarchy leaves no room for collective processes or the input of individuals. Even with women now serving in the US military, as well as the armed forces of other nations, the military remains a bastion of male power and privilege.

What about the consequences of war, of even more limited military engagement? When families are ripped apart by bombs or occupying armies, who carries the burden of trying to meet the needs of daily life? As primary caretakers in the overwhelming majority of countries, it is women who have to deal with the destruction war brings to healthcare systems, educational institutions, and all of the infrastructure that makes daily life possible. And, of course, who cares for the wounded, be they the much higher percentage of innocent civilians or those who served in the military?

Feminism insists on finding other ways to resolve problems, whether tensions on a personal level or on an international scale. Out of our feminism we have come to appreciate the humanity and dignity of all those we share the planet with. A world committed to feminist values would not be lacking in differences – but it would be a world where war and violence and domination were not the tools for resolving those differences.

I want to put all of these insights from feminisms in the service of fighting militarism and ending war – and one step in that larger effort must be the ending of this horrific US war and occupation in Iraq.

We know – indeed, the whole world knows – that this is a war that never should have happened. The administration of President George W. Bush lied, and Congress bought those lies: there were no weapons of mass destruction; there was no connection between Saddam Hussein and Al Qaeda; Iraq was not a threat to the security of the USA; and we certainly had no interest in or intention of bringing democracy to Iraq.

There have been terrible costs and consequences of this war: the hundreds of thousands of Iraqis killed, the wounded, the displaced, the unemployed, the suffering in Iraq. By mid 2008 over four thousand US service people killed and tens of thousands dealing with wounds that will stay with them their whole lives. And there were the economic costs of this war: over $500 billion had been spent – that's about $10 million each hour of every day! The US public education and healthcare systems are in ruins, to say nothing of the Gulf Coast and New Orleans, where now, years after the catastrophe of Hurricane Katrina, the most basic services are still not restored and lives are still in massive disarray. With each passing week and month, the human and economic costs of this war have only grown larger.

Ths US war on Iraq never should have happened, the human and economic costs are off the charts, and every public opinion poll shows majority opposition to the war. Most Iraqis want the US troops out and most of the people in the USA want the war to end. And yet, at this writing, the war continues. Every day we hear the horrible reports of death and destruction – even as we barely get any real news from the mainstream media. So what's going on? I want to point to two things that are in play.

The first – OIL! That's what this war is all about. It is not that the oil in Iraq will end up in the gas stations of this country (although some of it might), but rather whoever controls the oil, not only in Iraq but also in the region, can control much of the global economy. That's what is really at stake. And that is what we mean when we talk about the empire-building agenda of the war-makers. This is not about military occupation and colonial control in the ways the world has previously known. It is about control of the world's resources by privately owned, international corporations whose economic interests are protected by the world's most deadly and massive armed forces. These are not corporations loyal to a particular nation or limited to the confines of a specific border – they are global in scale. Let us not forget the power of the international institutions like the World Trade Organization or the meaning of NAFTA and other such cross-border trade agreements.

The second factor – the so-called war on terror. We need to tackle this if we are going to end the war in Iraq, and if we are going to make any headway in stopping other wars from happening.

Since 9/11 – which was a terrible, terrible day – the Bush administration, the neoconservatives, the Republican Party, and most of the leadership of the Democratic Party have invoked the so-called war on terror as the justification for every despicable crime they have committed. During his term George W. Bush continually asserted that US troops could not leave Iraq because they were on the front lines in the war on terror, saying we must stop the terrorists there if we don't want to fight them here.

Do we really believe that these people – those who carry out the gravest acts of state terrorism – are at all interested in fighting terrorism? Of course not. If they wanted to stop terrorism they could start with a massive, worldwide effort to eradicate poverty. There would be respect for international law and the sovereignty of all nations. There would be a commitment to human rights, as well as to political, economic and social justice. But that is not their agenda! (Let me add here – I do not condone terrorism, be it by individuals, by organizations or nation-states!)

9/11 gave them the opening they wanted. It gave them the opportunity to launch their war on terror and drag the world into a state of permanent warfare. They have declared that at any moment, for any reason, in any nation and with any weapon they want – including nuclear weapons – the USA can and will attack. And this is not only about how the USA relates to the rest of the world. It is also about what goes on inside this nation. It is the same people, the same forces, which have been carrying out a brutal assault on women, on poor people, on people of color, on workers, on everyone. Let me be a little more precise: on anyone whose demand for their basic rights might in any way undercut their corporate profits and control.

Does this boil down to a basic economic question? Not quite. I believe the economic issues at play are tremendous and a motor force that is driving all of this. But – and here I go back to one of the lessons from feminism – the economic realities do not function in a vacuum or in isolation from other systems of control and domination. Indeed, if we are going to build a movement, a force, big enough, strong enough, smart enough, creative enough, to turn this world around, then our work must have, at its core, a class, race, gender analysis.

The US anti-war movement has a number of major challenges: how do we stay focused on ending the war in Iraq and at the same time work to prevent new wars and relate to other important issues such as the struggle of the Palestinian people to end the Israeli occupation; how do we build lasting multiracial alliances and organizations and fight against racism; how do we move the massive anti-war sentiment into anti-war action, and effective action?

First, we need to be clear, and remain clear, about our demand. The war must end, it must end now, our troops need to be brought home now, all of our troops need to be brought home now!

Second, we need to expand the pressure on the US Congress. It is not that I have any great faith in the institution – it has, after all, been the greatest enabler in history! But if it was forced to it, it could actually end the war. It could cut off the funding, and without the money it ends.

Third, we need to do whatever we can to stop the flow of people into the US military. We need to actively work against the recruitment of young people and against the deployment of National Guard units to Iraq. We need to support resisters inside the military – not a lot of people right now but each one needs to be supported because s/he is doing the right thing and because it might help to encourage others to refuse to serve in Iraq.

Fourth, we need to take our anti-war activities into every arena of life. Everyone, no matter where one lives or goes to school or works, can be an anti-war activist. The point is not to drop the other work and organizing we're doing but instead to incorporate anti-war efforts into all of that.

Fifth, we need to creatively, non-violently, interrupt the normalcy of everyday life in the USA. We need to be bold in our actions and not concede any space. We need to make every location a space for opposition to the war to be heard and seen. Partly this means continuing public protests locally and nationally, big and small. This also means taking more action that might lead to arrest – action that is designed to disrupt the smooth running of the war machine as well as action that captures public attention because it is different and unexpected.

Some have questioned the value of massive mobilizations. After all, in a period of five years my coalition, United for Peace and Justice, either alone or with others groups, organized no fewer than eight anti-war demonstrations with at least 100,000 people, and two demonstrations with 500,000. And yet the war continued. But there are other important aspects to such mobilizations. The energy that participants walk away with often translates into revitalized activism. The process of building such actions necessitates coalition work and gives us new opportunities to work together, and in so doing we build more trust and capacity. And the mobilizations contribute to a real democratic process in terms of an open exchange of ideas in public spaces.

March 19 2008 marked the fifth anniversary of the US invasion of Iraq. The toll of this war and occupation continued to mount throughout 2007, despite it being the year of President Bush's surge. We were told his decision to send more troops into battle was working. No one knows for sure, but estimates are that at least one million Iraqis have died as a direct result of the US action in their nation. There are now an estimated 4.5 million displaced people, out of an Iraqi population of about 23 million. Half are refugees in neighboring nations, none prepared or equipped to handle the sudden and large influx of people with great needs. Others are still in Iraq but forced to move from their homes. All of this is just the tip of the humanitarian crisis unleashed by this war that never should have happened.

During 2008 we are seeing a dramatic escalation of the tensions between the USA and Iran, with threats of war periodically coming from the Bush administration. It seems that they are once again claiming weapons of mass destruction – a nuclear weapons program – and threats to our security and world peace as their rationale for threatening war – against Iran. Strange as it might be, they seem to expect people to believe them. There were some developments that pulled this dynamic away from the brink of complete disaster, but the danger of the Bush administration deciding to initiate another war remains real as I write these comments. We must be vigilant – we must not let this happen. As horrific as the war and occupation have been in Iraq, a military confrontation with Iran will be even worse.

All of this has occurred as the presidential election cycle moved into full swing. This presented the anti-war movement with some of its greatest challenges yet. Instead of being sucked into the specifics of election campaigning, our peace and justice movement needs to define and assert a relationship to the process that allows us to amplify our demands, expand our base and build our strength as a force for real change. Can we use the election cycle instead of being used by it?

It seems that neither the US Congress nor the Bush administration will take steps toward ending the war and occupation in Iraq during 2008. This Congress – elected in November 2006 with a clear, nationwide mandate to end the war – has not been able to take action. There have been intense and important debates, there have been a growing number of our elected representatives voting against continued funding of the war, but they have not yet found a way to use their real power to make sure this war ends. That is, the power of the purse, the power to cut the funding for the war.

It is all of this that leads us to view 2008 as so critical. This is the year we must build the pressure to end the war in such a crescendo that the new president and the new Congress will know they must take immediate and comprehensive action to end the war once and for all. If not, if that does not happen, then we are likely looking at a decades-long presence of US troops in Iraq, perhaps even longer. This will have implications for that nation and for the region as a whole. It will mean the establishment of a permanent US military force in one of the most oil-rich regions of the world.

There is cause to be hopeful that we can rise to the challenges. The first step is helping others understand how important this year – and our work during this year – really is. The second step is developing the plans to take on these challenges. And the third step is strengthening the alliances between the anti-war movement and other progressive social change movements. All of that is beginning to unfold, but there are still no certainties on the outcome.

Our other challenge is to continue to build the peace and justice movement so that we are stronger than we've have ever been. That means rolling up our sleeves and doing the hard work of direct organizing – knocking on doors, canvassing in places where people gather, massive phone-calling operations and much more. It means bringing new people into our organizations and groups. It means building new coalitions in our communities, and strengthening the ties and connections we already have. It means turning our intellectual understanding of how issues are connected into programmatic reality.

We must now, as we have never done before, envision the force it will take to end this war and bring all the troops home from Iraq, as well as prevent a new war in Iran or anywhere else. We can end this war, we must end it.

Finally, we must find ways to 'keep hope alive,' as civil rights leader the Reverend Jesse Jackson says. When hopelessness sets in, when people believe or feel there is nothing they can do, no way they can win – that's when people give up and stop struggling. As difficult and awful as these times are, we need to keep inspiring and encouraging one another. Now, in a way that perhaps we have never really understood before, we must anchor our work in a commitment to solidarity and unity with the peoples of the world. For that, after all, is where our future lies.

21 | Feminism and war: stopping militarizers, critiquing power

CYNTHIA ENLOE

Why think together about *'feminism* and war'? Why not be satisfied just with using the frame of 'gender and war'? I'm sure the hard-working, hard-thinking editors of this book didn't make the title choice casually. They knew what they were doing. But do the rest of us?

Consciously choosing to ask feminist questions about wars goes well beyond exploring masculinities and femininities, i.e. gender. Asking feminist questions goes beyond even thinking about women and war. Using a feminist curiosity does call on us to engage in both of these explorations – and neither is easy – but it pushes us to go farther, to investigate *power*.

A feminist enquiry into anything entails, *first*, being curious about the creations of meanings for masculinities and femininities; *second*, taking seriously the conditions, ideas and actions of diverse women, but also; *third*, always tracking down what sorts of power are at work, in whose hands, and with what consequences. True, being a feminist investigator takes stamina.

It really is difficult for war-preparing and war-waging governments to militarize women in their roles as mothers. And it is, after all, not chiefly generals who try to militarize mothers and motherhood. It is civilians who are the principal militarizers. But the good news is militarizing mothers is quite hard work; it takes a lot of effort, ongoing effort. And often the militarizers fail.

I remember being in Aberdeen, Scotland, back in the late 1970s. At this point I was not yet thinking feminist thoughts. I was interested in race and ethnicity – especially as experienced by and manipulated by men. In the 1970s, I was trying to track governments around the world – the American, but also the Canadian, the British, Iraqi, Israeli, Filipino, Brazilian, Belgian, and Soviet – as each tried to wield ideas about ethnicity and race in order to create and sustain their own state militaries. So I was up in Aberdeen, Scotland, seeking to understand how Scottish identity was used to recruit young Scottish men into the British military. One day still sticks in my memory. I spent this day with a hapless British military recruiter as he spent hours trying to persuade one Scottish mother to let her only son join one of the Highland regiments. This was a time when the offshore oil boom was beginning in Scotland. A lot of young Scottish men saw their futures as successful, manly Scottish men furthered not by serving in the historic Scottish regiments of the British army but by working for a multinational corporation on a North Sea oil rig.

Back then I wasn't smart enough to give a lot of thought to this young Scottish man's mother; I didn't even ask to interview her to find out why she was so wary of her son joining the regiment. The army recruiter devoted an entire day just trying to persuade this one woman that she'd be practicing good mothering if she permitted her son to join the regiment. I think eventually she held out. The British state had failed. A less than fully militarized mothering had prevailed.

Nowadays, the US Defense Department's recruiting command officials refer to mothers as among the group they call the 'influencers.' Among the 'influencers' they include high-school athletic coaches, high-school guidance counselors, clergy, mothers and fathers. These are the people who recruitment strategists believe have the greatest sway over the perceptions and aspirations of teenagers, especially teenage young men. American recruiters targeting 'influencers' are focused overwhelmingly on those who can shape the aspirations and dreams of young men.

Persuading young women to think positively about enlisting in the military matters to these recruiting strategists, but they see young women chiefly as 'fillers.' Women are recruited today mainly to fill up 15 percent of the US active duty ranks and 24 percent of the National Guard ranks (less of the marines, more of the air force), because currently in the USA it is young women who are more likely than young men to complete high school, and today's US soldiering requires the skills that come with completing a secondary education. Still, it is young men that recruiters must enlist to make up 85 percent of their quotas. So it is the 'influencers' in these young men's lives about whom the recruiters must think.

Coaches, mothers, fathers, pastors and guidance counselors, take note: you are on the Pentagon's collective mind.

Recruiting strategists believe that influencing a woman who is a mother is not the same as influencing a man who is a father. That is, they believe they have to play on notions of a father's expectations of a son's desired masculinity, which are likely to be different from a mother's expectation of a son's masculinity if a recruiter is to persuade each to encourage, or at least allow, their son to enlist. The US Defense Department today probably hires and contracts more social scientists than any other American public institution. This military reliance on – and co-optation of – social science researchers began during World War II when officials were anxious about keeping the civilian public's support of a drawn-out war and about sustaining morale among the country's own soldiers. Today sociologists, anthropologists, and psychologists all play parts in persuading American mothers that what is good for their mothering is to persuade their teenage sons – or at least agree to their sons' wishes – to join the military.

If militarizing mothers were just a 'walk in the park,' it would not take all this strategizing, all this research, all this persuasion, all this co-optation of social scientists.

The good news is that it does take that much effort. The US Defense Department is today one of the largest clients of American civilian advertising agencies. Because advertising agencies see winning Pentagon recruiting contracts as so profitable, one way to chart militarization in the United States today is to read *Advertising Age* or the advertising business sections of local city newspapers. It has been the end of the male military 'draft' – what most people in the world refer to as conscription – in Canada, the United States, Britain, Japan, Australia, South Africa, Belgium and the Netherlands which has helped to militarize civilian advertising agencies. Military recruiting officials need the skills of civilian ad executives to reach potential recruits and their 'influencers.' The advertisements that these agencies are producing and their selection of sites for these ads are sophisticated; they draw on the last eighty years of research into the art of mass persuasion.

Perhaps you have seen one recent US television ad aimed specifically at mothers of sons. We first see a middle-aged African-American woman – now these are actors, of course – sitting in her kitchen. It's the afternoon. She is working at the kitchen table doing her bills. The ad agency and the Pentagon recruiting command have chosen to place this television ad in an afternoon programming slot, between the reruns of *Law and Order* and *Judging Amy*. This is not an ad designed for *Monday Night Football* viewers. It is a feminized advertising strategy. Actually, I saw this ad while having a late lunch at my favorite downmarket café, and it was mainly retired guys at the bar who were watching it. So, the Defense Department hasn't quite got their gender television profiling correct yet. But, returning to the ad itself: as the African-American woman is working at her kitchen table, in walks a very attractive-looking, late teenage African-American fellow, who quite clearly is the woman's son. He says, 'Mom, I think I've figured it out. I think I'm going to join the army.' Now this is an ad from 2006. It's year three of the US military's war in Iraq. The camera moves to a close-up of the mother's face. She just raises her eyebrows, obviously quite skeptical. Her son responds, 'No, Mom, look, we've been trying to figure out how I can go to college. I think ... I think this will do it.' She is shown remaining unconvinced. So then the actor playing her teenage son delivers his scripted punchline, caring son to caring mother: 'But, Mom, it's about time I became a man.'

That Defense Department ad was based on women's presumed maternal anxieties about sons' education and sons' manliness in the early twenty-first century. It should prompt us to devote serious thought – research, writing, teaching, activism – to the ways in which any society mixes the chemistry of maternal care, anxieties about masculinity, the costs of gaining higher education and political manipulation in the lives of individual women.

Power wielded to construct – and inculcate – particular meanings of masculinity and femininity is integral not just to waging war itself, but to making pre-war preparations for the waging of war. Power is, furthermore, wielded to determine which ideas about masculinities and which ideas about femininities will dominate the narratives of that war long after that war is over. That is, a feminist curiosity prompts us to pay close attention to the power at work in *pre*-war years and *wartime* years and *post*-war years. And post-war power-wielding and contests over constructions of masculinities and femininities allegedly driving the past war can go on for generations. Not just our anticipations of war can be militarized in our lives as women and as men, but so too can our memories and our retold stories. And lots of people with power have a stake in shaping our anticipations, our memories and our stories. Just listen to the intensity of current debates among Japanese over World War II practices of sexual slavery sixty years ago. Or think of the mixed messages young American women today are sending to their friends by donning 'Rosie the Riveter' T-shirts: messages about US women gaining strength by answering the government's call to sign up to be wartime industrial workers helping to wage that same war. Even better, think about both of these memory contests – about Japan's 'comfort women' and about 'Rosie the Riveter' – going on simultaneously today, six decades after that war.

Using our feminist analytical skills we can reveal how power is used to construct certain kinds of ideas about manliness and certain ideas about motherhood, to privilege certain ideas about the 'good wife,' and particular ideas about the 'dutiful daughter,' the 'faithful girlfriend,' and the 'liberated woman.' That power-wielding is most effective when the women and men in any militarized society think that these ideas are free floating, out there in the shared culture, not crafted, not inculcated. But war wagers who don't gain control over the popular notions of these standards of masculinity and femininity prior to the launch of a military action will find it harder both to legitimize and to wage a war – and to keep alive positive memories of past wars. Any revelation of conscious intent can put a dent in accepted patriarchal militarized ideas.

It takes feminist digging to bring the workings of power in the militarization of masculinities and femininities up into the light where we can all examine the alternatives. Only by bringing the power wielded to militarize gendered meanings up to the surface can we make militarizing processes at work in our society visible – and thereby open to challenge.

Even though we here in the USA – and in Afghanistan and in Iraq – are immersed in these current wars, even now we should be thinking about the politics of post-war eras. Post-war can be a time that's still defined by war. We can learn from women who are doing the very hard post-war feminist organizing in Sierra Leone, Rwanda, the Congo, Liberia, Serbia, East Timor, Liberia, Nepal, Cambodia, Vietnam and Northern Ireland. Feminists in each of these countries today are working to reconstruct social institutions and rituals and shared stories in ways that do not re-create militarized ideas about – and practices of – the heroic veteran, the sacrificing mother, the loyal girlfriend. To leave these unchallenged, to fail in creating demilitarized alternatives, is to be complicit in planting the seeds for the next war. Women activist thinkers in Rwanda, Nepal and Liberia can be our tutors.

We need to find ways to listen to those grassroots organizers who right now are using feminist ideas to make sure that post-war is not as militarized and patriarchal as pre-war. It requires, these activist women tell us, stamina, imagination, compassion, gritty realism, acute attentiveness at multiple levels of one's society and internationally as well – and, of course, lots of listening. These smart thinkers keep their eyes on doctors treating (or ignoring) post-traumatic stress disease (PTSD); judges deciding on domestic violence cases; social workers seeing women and girls who have survived wartime rape; television producers choosing what dramas and news stories to feature; police recruiters; political parties' electoral strategists; school textbook adopters; legislators drafting inheritance laws; officials tempted to award job training only to demobilized military and insurgent veterans. Every one of them, if not monitored and challenged, can turn into post-war remilitarizers of masculinity and femininity.

Today we can look outside the USA to learn how to think more clearly about this potentially militarizing chemistry in women's lives – pre-war, during a war and in the tenuous post-war peace. Americans are absolutely not the smartest people in the world today when it comes to feminist exploring – and acting upon explorations of – the militarizations of masculinities and femininities. In Turkey, South Korea, Serbia, Italy, Spain, Colombia, Cyprus, Rwanda, Sweden, Australia, Sri Lanka, Israel, India, Nepal and Japan there are women's groups informed by feminist thinking whose members can be our tutors. Some of these groups do their thinking and activism without much outside notice or support. Other groups are loosely connected through such international feminist networks as Women Living Under Muslim Law, Women's International League for Peace and Freedom (WILPF), Women Waging Peace, Women Living in Conflict Zones Network (WICZNET) and Women in Black. Some US women belong to each of these networks, but none of them is US-dominated. The American women associated with each are the learners.

We here in the USA can join a lively international feminist conversation about how militarizers make the militarization of loyalty, liberation, sacrifice and care so appealing to diverse women. We as Americans, even if we have developed a conscious feminist curiosity, remain the underdeveloped ones in today's world. Yet, precisely because we are members of a society that has become so profoundly militarized in part by the successful wieldings of certain masculinities and certain femininities, perhaps today our ears are wider open than they've ever been before. Maybe now we can hear, we can learn more intently and intensely than we ever have.

What so many thoughtful, energetic feminists in other countries have shown us is that militarizers have to work very, very hard to militarize us as mothers, as workers, as activists, as teachers, as students, as consumers, as friends, partners, and girlfriends. Militarization cannot be launched or sustained without women's contributions and women's complicity. That means we, as women, have a lot to withhold. That's a hopeful feminist revelation.

Prosaic poem

MĨCERE GĨTHAE MŨGO

In commemoration of those moments when we make prosaic statements that end up sounding poetic and then we are reminded that ordinary human dialogue is often punctuated with poetry.

Refrain: One day!

One day, we shall rescue our lives from precarious peripheral hanging on and assume the center of historical action. We shall explore every avenue that runs through our lives and create live-roads that know no dead ends, extending them to the limits of human destination. We shall put an angry fullstop to the negation of our human rights.

One day!

One day, we shall undertake a second journey along the bushy path of denied human development, chasing away the wild beasts that prowl the route of our narrow survival lest they make a complete jungle of our already bestialized lives. We shall then cultivate a huge global garden and plant it with the seed of true humanity.

One day!

One day, we shall emerge from the wings and occupy the center stage in full visibility, refusing to be observers and understudies who wait behind the curtain of living drama. We shall liberate the word and become its utterers, no longer cheer crowds or ululators who spur on and applaud the molestors of our affirmative speech.

One day!

One day, we shall explode the negative silences and paralyzing terror imposed upon us by the tyranny of dominating cultures and their languages of conquest. We shall discover the authentic voices of our self-naming and renaming, reclaiming our role as composers, speaking for ourselves, because we too have tongues, you know!

One day!

One day, we shall make a bonfire of currently dismantling and maladjusting economic structural adjustment programs, then engage in the restructuring process, producing coherence around our scattered daily existence till it is full to bursting. We shall stop at nothing short of holding the sun to a standstill until the job is complete.

One day!

One day, we shall move the sun of our existence so that it truly rises from the east of our lives, reaching its noon at the center of our needs. We shall then release it to set in the west of our perverted and dominated history, never to rise again until it learns to shine upon the masses of global being, not on islands of pirated living.

One day!

One day, we shall exterminate the short distance between the kitchen and bedroom of our lives, storm out of the suffocating space between the factory and the overseer of our exploited creative labor, paving a path that leads to the buried mines of our suppressed human potential. We shall walk it if it stretches unto eternity.

One day!

One day, we shall celebrate this earth as our home, standing tall and short, boasting of the abundance and multifariousness of our fulfilled human visions. We shall not look to the sky waiting for unfulfilled prophecies. We shall upturn the very rocks of our enforced stony existence, converting them into fluvial banks of life sustenance.

One day!

Action: end US wars now!

We encourage readers to adapt and use the following call for ongoing organizing. This petition was put forward by an ad hoc committee at the close of the 'Feminism and War' conference and was signed by a majority of conference participants. Reprinted by *Ms* magazine in its winter 2007 issue, the call ultimately also circulated worldwide on the Internet.

The pretext of 'the rights of women' has been and is being used by the current US administration to justify its wars of aggression.

We, participants at the 2006 Feminism and War conference at Syracuse University, condemn the neocolonial, racist, and imperialist wars launched by the US.

We join with world-wide anti-war movements in calling for an end to these wars that are, in fact, worsening the conditions of life for women in the invaded and occupied countries – and in the US.

We are in solidarity with all who are suffering from the consequences of US and US-funded military aggression. We pledge our renewed commitment to end these wars, and we seek the commitment of all those in agreement to actively mobilize against them.

Reference

McFadden, Patricia (2007) 'War through a feminist lens: an African scholar reflects on a US gathering to confront militarism', *Ms*, Winter, pp. 14–15.

Afterword

LINDA CARTY

'They killed a wounded man. It's hard to believe. They killed a man who was completely helpless – like he was some sort of diseased animal. I had read the articles and heard the stories of this happening before – wounded civilians being thrown on the side of the road or shot in cold blood – but to see it happening on television is something else – it makes me crazy with anger.

And what will happen now? A criminal investigation against a single Marine who did the shooting? Just like what happened with the Abu Ghraib atrocities? A couple of people will be blamed and the whole thing will be buried under the rubble of idiotic military psychologists, defense analysts, Pentagon officials and spokespeople and it will be forgotten. In the end, all anyone will remember is that a single Marine shot and killed a single Iraqi 'insurgent' and it won't matter anymore.

It's typical American technique – every single atrocity is lost and covered up by blaming a specific person and getting it over with. What people don't understand is that the whole military is infested with these psychopaths. In the last year we've seen murderers, torturers and xeno-phobes running around in tanks with guns. I don't care what does it: I don't care if it's the tension, the fear, the 'enemy' ... it's murder. We are occupied by murderers. We're under the same pressure, as Iraqis, except that we weren't trained for the situation, and yet we're all expected to be benevolent and understanding and, above all, grateful.'

(Riverbend, *Baghdad Burning II: More Girl Blog from Iraq*, Feminist Press, 2006)

Riverbend, the female Baghdad blogger above, probably speaks for most women in her country who continue to express to anyone who will listen how much they blame the USA for the devastation to the environment and the deterioration in their quality of life since the US invasion of Iraq. As they have endured displacement, a cramped existence in refugee camps in foreign lands, the rape and abuse of their sisters, mothers, and daughters, the slaughter of their loved ones on a daily basis because and at the hands of the US occupiers, and have had to watch helplessly as even their children suffer nervous breakdowns, these women ask how the

Carty

USA can claim to be the most democratic country in the world while it subjects an entire people to a life of imprisonment in their own country through militarization.

Feminists in the USA, as is clear in *Feminism and war: confronting US imperialism*, see this militarization within the USA as well. Both Davis and Eisenstein in this collection offer chilling analyses of the militarization of US-gendered ruling relations and overall culture. As the Bush administration uses 'national security' rhetoric to instill fear of the 'other' in its citizenry, and to breed hatred of cultures they do not understand, we witness the vanishing of many hard-won rights and the privatization and commodification of what in any humane society are guaranteed as rights. Healthcare, education, basic shelter, and affordable childcare are all privileges in the USA, a country that spends more on its military than any other country in the world; indeed, more than all of NATO or the European Union. While the US vice-president, Dick Cheney, who suffers long-standing heart problems, rushes to the hospital every time his heart skips a beat and gets the best and most costly medical attention, many children die in the USA daily from poor heart health and lesser ailments owing to lack of proper and affordable healthcare. In fact, when it comes to children in the USA, the expanding militarized culture has transformed urban schools into more or less militarized fortresses that serve as little more than holding tanks for the youth. In this culture it is not difficult to understand why so many of the same youths end up in prison later on. They are the poor and they are mostly people of color. A disproportionate number of them are in the US military and a disproportionate number of them are in prison. This is no accident.

As the anti-imperialist essays in *Feminism and war: confronting US imperialism* force us to ask: what lessons about democracy and freedom can the United States teach the Iraqi or Afghan people when it is actually practicing direct colonialism on them? Has it examined the questions of democracy and freedom within its own borders? After all, the United States is a country where de facto apartheid still exists; a country that showed the world what it thinks of its citizens of African descent on whose backs the USA was built by leaving them in peril after Hurricane Katrina; a country that builds more prisons than schools because, rather than address poverty and its social implications, it chooses to incarcerate the poor and mentally disturbed. We must ask: how can a US administration claim to be bringing liberation to Iraqi women when in fact those women have lost rights, privileges and freedom as a direct result of the US invasion?

This collection advances the debate about feminism and US wars in this era of globalization and US global hegemony otherwise known as neoliberal capitalism. In that environment, war has become an industry that is utilized for enormous capital accumulation, and the US state and its leading corporations are at the forefront of this military-industrial complex for profit-making. The result is that we see the vast majority of peoples of the global South valiantly resisting US imperialism. If there is a single mobilizing force among peoples of the global South today, from Palestine to South Africa, it is a hatred of the United States' establishment and its foreign policy agenda.

While some of the authors in this collection advocate a world without war, and, indeed, the feminist, anti-imperialist analyses here provide something of a map out of the US state's warmongering mindset, we must never lose sight of the cohesion across peoples of the global South that has resulted from the racist and sexist imperial policies and practices that the USA uses to run its war machine in and on poor countries and people around the globe. It is perhaps time to look to those spaces for lessons on what to do. McFadden makes a cogent argument here about the need for feminists anywhere, particularly in the USA, to examine how our perception of war is determined first by our location, and by how it enters our lives, whether as our everyday lived experience or that of privileged beings for whom it may have little more than a peripheral or distant impact. US feminists are complicit in the US imperial war arsenal build-up because, after all, our tax dollars help to purchase the lethal weapons that are used to maintain military occupation, and to inflict violence on women and children.

Feminist theorizing must directly engage and challenge US racialized and xenophobic neoliberal capitalism and its failures. A transnational understanding of this mode of production as creating the same kind of harm in the USA as it does abroad, and having a devastating impact on the same groups of people within the US nation-state as well as outside its borders, will consciously lead to truly transnational feminist solidarity. In other words, the transnational is here too; it is not only out there somewhere. Feminists in the USA need to understand that Palestinian, Iraqi, Afghani, Rwandan, Salvadorean, Congolese, Pakistani, Sudanese, Vietnamese, Mexican, or African-American women are all our sisters and we must map the path forward together. To accomplish this task, we must interrogate our own spaces of privilege, whether in the academy, in state institutions, or in the private sector, which allow us to engage in the most eloquent transnational feminist analyses while leaving our praxis untouched. Bringing a comprehensive theory of human rights and feminist activism together as cogent praxis will help us to appreciate how imperial occupation in Iraq, for example, has actually exacerbated cultural practices of sexism and misogyny. We must understand and advocate a comprehensive vision of human rights that includes all women and that does not ignore the US administration's war crimes against black and brown women and children around the world. In this regard, we must persistently challenge the US state as it appropriates liberal feminist language seeking universal women's rights.

Feminism and war: confronting US imperialism offers a good beginning toward this end.

About the contributors

Nellie Hester Bailey, a co-founder and executive director of the Harlem Tenants Council (HTC), and a leader in the Troops Out Now Coalition (TONC), organizes alliances focusing on international solidarity and the domestic impact of militarization and police brutality.

Anuradha Kristina Bhagwati is a writer, yogi, and vegan living in Brooklyn, New York. She is a graduate of Yale and Harvard. A former marine captain, she is currently working on a novel.

Leslie Cagan has been a peace and justice organizer for more than forty years. She is the National Coordinator of United for Peace and Justice, the nation's largest grassroots anti-war coalition with 1,400 member groups.

Linda Carty teaches in the Department of African American Studies at Syracuse University.

Berta Joubert-Ceci, active in many struggles in the global South, including removal of the US navy from Vieques in her native land of Puerto Rico, is a leader in the International Action Center and the National Women's Fightback Network.

Huibin Amelia Chew is a member of INCITE! Women of Color Against Violence, and on the staff at the Chinese Progressive Association in Boston. She has an AB in Social Studies and Women's Studies from Harvard University.

Alyson M. Cole is Associate Professor of Political Science at Queens College and the Graduate Center, City University of New York. She is the author of *The Cult of True Victimhood: From the War on Welfare to the War on Terror* (2006).

Angela Y. Davis is Professor of History of Consciousness, and Feminist Studies, at the University of California Santa Cruz, and the author of eight books, most recently *Abolition Democracy: Beyond Empire, Prisons & Torture* (2005) and *Are Prisons Obsolete?* (2003).

LeiLani Dowell, a queer hapa (Hawaiian and black) woman, is a national coordinator of the socialist youth group FIST (Fight Imperialism, Stand Together), and a managing editor of *Workers World* newspaper.

Zillah Eisenstein is a Professor of Politics at Ithaca College. Her recent books include *Sexual Decoys* (2007), *Against Empire* (2005), *Global Obscenities* (1998), and *Hatreds* (1996).

Cynthia Enloe is Research Professor at Clark University. Her most recent book is *Globalization and Militarism: Feminists Make the Link* (2007). Her current work is on women in the Iraq war.

Berenice Malka Fisher, retired New York University professor and author of *No Angel in the Classroom: Teaching through Feminist Discourse* (2001), is currently writing about communication in peace and justice movements.

Jennifer L. Fluri is Assistant Professor of Geography and Women's and Gender Studies at Dartmouth College. Her research interests include analyses of gender, leadership, geopolitics, and international economic development in Afghanistan.

Jennifer Hyndman is Professor of Geography at Syracuse University. She is the author of *Managing Displacement: The Politics of Humanitarianism* (2000) and co-editor of *Sites of Violence: Gender and Conflict Zones* (2004).

Melanie Kaye/Kantrowitz is an activist, writer, scholar, and teacher. Her latest book is *The Colors of Jews: Racial Politics and Radical Diasporism* (2007). She teaches Secular Jewish Studies at Queens College/CUNY. Visit her website at www.diasporism.net.

Shahnaz Khan is Associate Professor of Women's Studies and Global Studies at Wilfrid Laurier University. She is the author of *Aversion and Desire: Negotiating Muslim Female Identity* (2002), and *Zina, Transnational Feminism, and the Moral Regulation of Pakistani Women* (2006).

Patricia McFadden held the Endowed Cosby Chair in Social Sciences at the Women's Research and Resource Center at Spelman College from 2005 to 2007. She is the author of two books and over thirty articles.

Chandra Talpade Mohanty is Professor of Women's Studies and Dean's Professor of the Humanities at Syracuse University. Her most recent book is *Feminism without Borders: Decolonizing Theory, Practicing Solidarity* (2003).

Mĩcere Gĩthae Mũgo, poet and playwright, is Meredith Professor for Teaching Excellence and current Chair, Department of African American Studies, Syracuse University. An activist and black feminist, Mĩcere envisions socialist transformation globally.

Isis Nusair is Assistant Professor of Women's Studies and International Studies at Denison University. Her current research focuses on gendered analysis of coping mechanisms and networks of support among Iraqi women refugees in Jordan.

Eli PaintedCrow is a twenty-two-year retired army veteran who served in Iraq in 2004. A Native American from the Yaqui nation, grandmother of eight, a mother of two sons, her most recent projects are SWAN (Service Women's Action Network) and 'Turtle Women Rising,' a global movement for peace.

Elizabeth Philipose, Associate Professor, Department of Women's Studies, California State University Long Beach, researches the political culture of international laws of war and, currently, spiritualized feminisms in an era of torture consciousness.

Minnie Bruce Pratt is a Professor of Women's and Gender Studies at Syracuse University; a co-author of *Yours in Struggle: Three Feminist Perspectives on Anti-Semitism and Racism* (1984); and an organizer with the National Women's Fightback Network.

Jasbir Puar is an Associate Professor of Women's and Gender Studies at Rutgers University. She is the author, most recently, of *Terrorist Assemblages: Homonationalism in Queer Times* (2007).

Robin L. Riley is Assistant Professor of Women's Studies at Syracuse University. She is co-editor with Naeem Inayatullah of *Interrogating Imperialism: Conversations on Gender, Race, and War* (2006).

Judy Rohrer is an Affiliated Research Scholar in the Women's Studies Program at the University of California, Santa Barbara. She continually seeks ways to connect the academy and progressive activism.

Setsu Shigematsu is an Assistant Professor in the Department of Media and Cultural Studies at the University of California, Riverside. Her work interrogates the relationships between feminisms, imperialisms, militarism, liberation movements, and violence.

Nadine Sinno is a PhD candidate in Comparative Literature at the University of Arkansas, Fayetteville. She holds an MA in English Literature and an MFA in Literary Translation. Her English translation of Nazik Saba Yared's novel *Canceled Memories* is forthcoming from Syracuse University Press.

Contributors

Index

Index

279